Creative Knowledge Environments

Creative Knowledge Environments

The Influences on Creativity in Research and Innovation

Edited by

Sven Hemlin

Associate Professor of Psychology, Centre for Research Ethics (CRE), Göteborg University, Sweden

Carl Martin Allwood

Professor of Psychology, Department of Psychology, Lund University, Sweden

Ben R. Martin

Director of SPRU – Science and Technology Policy Research and Professor of Science and Technology Policy Studies, University of Sussex, UK

Edward Elgar

Cheltenham, UK • Northampton, MA, USA

Published by
Edward Elgar Publishing Limited
Glensanda House
Montpellier Parade
Cheltenham
Glos GL50 1UA
UK

Edward Elgar Publishing, Inc.
136 West Street
Suite 202
Northampton
Massachusetts 01060
USA

A catalogue record for this book
is available from the British Library

Library of Congress Cataloguing in Publication Data

Creative knowledge environments : the influences on creativity in research and
  innovation / edited by Sven Hemlin, Carl Martin Allwood, Ben R. Martin.
    p. cm.
  Includes index.
  1. Creative ability in science. 2. Creative ability in technology. I. Hemlin, Sven,
1948– II. Allwood, Carl Martin. III. Martin, Ben R.

  Q172.5.C74C73 2004
  500—dc22

                                                                    2004047068

ISBN 1 84376 518 7

Printed and bound in Great Britain by MPG Books Ltd, Bodmin, Cornwall

Contents

v

Figures

Tables

Contributors

Carl Martin Allwood, Department of Psychology, Lund University, Sweden.

Jean-Paul Beltramo, Institut de Recherche sur l'Economie de l'Education, CNRS and Université de Bourgogne, Dijon, France.

Lars Bengtsson, Department of Business Administration, School of Economics and Management, Lund University, Sweden.

Isabel Bortagaray, School of Public Policy, Georgia Institute of Technology, USA

Magnus Gulbrandsen, Norwegian Institute for Studies in Research and Higher Education (NIFU), Oslo, Norway.

Sture Hägglund, Department of Computer and Information Science, Linköping University, Sweden.

Sven Hemlin, Centre for Research Ethics (CRE), Göteborg University, Sweden.

Robert Kaiser, Technical University Munich, Chair of Political Science, Germany.

Jan-Inge Lind, Department of Business Administration, School of Economics and Management, Lund University, Sweden.

Ben R. Martin, Science and Technology Policy Research (SPRU), University of Sussex, UK.

Geoff Mason, National Institute of Economic and Social Research, London, UK.

Mika Nieminen, Group for Science, Technology & Innovation Studies (TASTI), Research Institute for Social Sciences, Tampere University, Finland.

Jean-Jacques Paul, Institut de Recherche sur l'Economie de l'Education, CNRS and Université de Bourgogne, Dijon, France.

Lillemor Wallgren, Department of Computer and Information Science, Linköping University, Sweden.

Preface

The aim of this book is to improve our understanding of creative knowledge environments. The various chapters analyse creative and innovative activities as carried out by individuals, groups and organizations. The book's focus is on identifying and understanding the factors relating to the working environment that are conducive to human creativity and innovation.

The editing of this book has been a collaborative effort between two psychologists with a background in cognitive psychology and a science policy researcher. Reflecting this, the book includes chapters covering a broad range of literature, including psychology, sociology and a number of cross-disciplinary fields such as science, technology and innovation policy studies. Despite our rather different disciplinary backgrounds, we share a strong interest in gaining a better understanding of the circumstances that bring about creative research and innovations. The first and the last chapters of the book integrate the findings from the studies reported in the book and from other literature on the subject to address two main questions: what is a creative knowledge environment, and how can creative knowledge environments best be stimulated?

The book is likely to be of interest to students and scholars in a number of research fields as well as to science and innovation policy decision makers concerned with research, teaching and policy measures for the development of creative knowledge environments. As we move towards what some have described as a 'knowledge society', in which knowledge and innovation are playing an ever more important role, the issues considered here are clearly of great topical importance.

The seven chapters forming the central part of this book illustrate various approaches to the analysis of creative knowledge environments. These chapters were selected from a number of working papers presented at the Fourth International 'Triple Helix' Conference held in Copenhagen on 19–20 November 2002. At that conference, we organized five sessions on the theme of 'Creative Knowledge Environments'. We are grateful to all the participants in these sessions for their part in the stimulating discussions and in particular to the contributors to this volume.

The editing of this book and the writing of the first and last chapters were completed when one of us (SH) was supported by a research grant from the Swedish Agency for Innovation Systems (VINNOVA) and was working at the

Centre for Research Ethics at Göteborg University, Sweden; he is indebted to both of these. The second editor (CMA) has during the same period been salaried by the Department of Psychology, Lund University, Sweden; he is grateful for this. Over the same period, another of the editors (BM) was working on research projects at SPRU (Science and Technology Policy Research) funded by various sponsors, in particular the Economic and Social Research Council (ESRC) and the European Commission; he is grateful to these organizations for their support.

This book is dedicated to two individuals who in their different ways have had an immense influence on the editors. One is Donald Campbell who, with his broad mind, covered in depth many research areas relevant to this book in an exciting and integrative way. Among these research areas are philosophy of science, theory of science, sociology of knowledge and research methodology. The other person is Keith Pavitt who, over a period of 40 years, was one of the outstanding pioneers in the field of science and innovation studies, looking in particular at the factors that account for success and failure in relation to science, technology and innovation. During much of this time he was, for one of us (BM), a close friend, esteemed colleague and truly inspirational mentor.

Sven Hemlin
Carl Martin Allwood
Ben R. Martin

1. What is a creative knowledge environment?

Sven Hemlin, Carl Martin Allwood and Ben R. Martin

INTRODUCTION

The starting point for this book is the assumption that creativity is to a great extent influenced by the environment in which people work to produce creative products. This assumption is consistent with the conclusion of Amabile and colleagues who stated:

> Managers at all levels who wish to foster creativity and innovation within their organisations can do so not only by paying attention to what sort of individuals they hire – to the kind of personal characteristics and skills that early creativity research emphasised – but also by paying attention to the *environments* they create for these potentially creative individuals. (Amabile *et al.*, 1996, p.1180; emphasis added).

To adopt this starting point is not, of course, to deny that certain individuals are potentially much more creative than others, depending on the personal characteristics that they possess. Nevertheless the extent to which that creative potential is expressed in practice depends to a considerable extent on the environment in which the individual works. Furthermore people constitute an important part of the environment for others, since most creative work involves interaction or even collaboration with other people.

The focus of this book is creative knowledge environments, by which we mean the environments in which new knowledge is produced by people, especially in their work settings. In order to delimit clearly the scope of the book, we define creative knowledge environments as follows. Creative knowledge environments (CKEs) are those environments, contexts and surroundings the characteristics of which are such that they exert a positive influence on human beings engaged in creative work aiming to produce new knowledge or innovations, whether they work individually or in teams, within a single organization or in collaboration with others.

This definition contains a number of important features. First, one can consider CKEs as the creative environments for people on a number of different scales or sizes. The smallest is perhaps the environment surrounding one individual or a small team or work group, where, for instance, the personal interactions and even whether the room in which they work is painted a stimulating colour may influence their creativity. At the other extreme in terms of size of environment is the global level at which a research institution or a knowledge-intensive firm and its employees operate. At a lower level, a nation will have specific institutional arrangements, laws, economies and regulations, but also other research institutions and firms, both competitors and collaborators, that may hinder or promote creative activities. One could perhaps describe creative environments as a number of nested layers of environmental factors surrounding the unit in which creative activities are undertaken.

A second and related aspect of the definition is that the creative unit as the object of study can be as small as one person, for instance a single researcher trying to solve a problem in his or her laboratory, or as large as a multinational firm navigating in 'market space' to find creative solutions in its search for innovations; or, to take another example, the research situation in an entire country. In between, there are various other possible levels of creative units, such as a university department seeking innovative ways of doing world-class research.

A final point deriving from the above definition of CKEs is that it highlights an essential task for research on CKEs: the need to identify, classify and gain a better understanding of the causal and other relationships linking factors that exert a positive (or negative) influence on those engaged in creative work aimed at producing new knowledge or innovations.

As noted above, CKEs can be analysed on a number of different scales. Although these lie on a continuum, they can conveniently be grouped into three main categories: the macro, meso and micro levels. In what follows, we use the term 'macro level' to include the global, national and interorganizational levels. The 'meso level' comprises research institutions and business companies, while the 'micro level' is made up of research groups or work teams and individuals. At all three levels, we can identify environmental factors that support or hinder creativity and innovation as well as successful performance in general. The levels are dependent on one another in the sense that the conditions at each level of analysis (macro, meso and micro) are affected by events at the other levels. This means that a work team in a company is influenced not only by its immediate environment, such as the management and leadership of the work team, but also by the culture and goals of the whole company and of the sector and country in which it is operating.

In addition there is some merit in distinguishing three basic aspects of CKEs. The first of these is the *physical* environment in which creative activities are carried out. This would include the premises in which the workplace is located, the equipment and other facilities available to staff and the resources available in the surrounding region. Secondly, there is the *social* environment, which may be characterized by such factors as the degree of openness or closedness to new ideas or innovation, and the relations or tensions between colleagues. Thirdly, there is the *cognitive* environment in which individuals and teams draw upon various bodies of knowledge and skills and are perhaps encouraged to adopt a certain cognitive work style (for example, adopting an experimental or 'trial and error' approach). The distinction between social and cognitive environments may be difficult to make in practice, since they are obviously closely related (the cognitive environment tends to be shaped by social processes, while the social environment is often affected by cognitive factors such as understanding and skills), but it is nonetheless analytically valuable.

Why write a book on the theme of creative knowledge environments? One general reason is that all human behaviour is linked, directly or indirectly, to its environment, and this includes creative behaviour and activities. Even apparently personal characteristics or traits are, according to psychologists, heavily influenced by environmental factors. In line with the view expressed by leading psychologists such as Amabile, we believe that environments play a crucial role in relation to creative activities. Consequently there is a need to know more about what types of environment, or what characteristics of them, are effective in stimulating creativity.

A second important reason is that creative behaviour is a vital ingredient for the inventions and innovations that are increasingly important in our world as it becomes more knowledge-dependent. If the factors conducive for creativity in the work environment are better understood, we will be in a stronger position to design environments that promote creativity and to formulate policies to encourage this. In the innovation literature we find that the proponents of the concept of 'systems of innovation' (such as Carlsson, 1997; Edqvist, 1997; Freeman, 1987; Lundvall, 1992; Nelson, 1993) and of the 'Triple Helix' interaction between universities, government and industry (for example Etzkowitz and Leydesdorff, 1997; Leydesdorff and Etzkowitz, 1996, 1998) are seeking to explain how new knowledge and innovations are created. However these conceptual frameworks lack an essential element: what are the characteristics of the environments in which creative knowledge-producing activities are carried out?

In this introductory section, we have attempted to define what we mean by CKEs and identified the main concepts underpinning the notion of creative knowledge environments. We have described how the study of CKEs involves analysing the environmental factors conducive (or antithetical) to creative work and innovations. We have also argued that a book on creative knowledge environments is needed because we do not fully understand what a creative knowledge environment is or how it operates in relation to the generation of new knowledge and innovations. However, so far, we have not said much about 'creativity' or the other components of creative knowledge environments: 'knowledge' and 'environment'. That is the theme of the following section.

BASIC CONCEPTS AND COMPONENTS OF CREATIVE KNOWLEDGE ENVIRONMENTS

We now analyse in more detail the three basic concepts of the notion of a creative knowledge environment; that is, the concepts of 'creativity', 'knowledge' and 'environment'.

Creativity

Creativity is studied within several fields, including psychology, education, administration, history (and in particular the history of science), sociology and political science. In most of these disciplines it is a relatively small and specialized area, although in some, such as psychology, it is growing in importance. In the field of management studies there has long been an interest in creativity because of its links to innovation, and a number of studies have been concerned with precisely the issue of the relationship between creativity and innovation. For instance, there is a journal dealing specifically with this topic, entitled *Creativity and Innovation Management,* while in psychology there is the *Creativity Research Journal* and also the *Journal of Creative Behavior*. However, let us begin by looking first at the notion of creativity. What is 'creativity'?

   In general terms, creativity can be defined as the generation of a product that is not only novel and imaginative but also useful and of good quality (see, for example, Mumford and Gustafson, 1988; Stoycheva and Lubart, 2001; Unsworth and Parker, 2003). Simply defining a novel or imaginative product as creative would take away much of the commonly supposed positive value of creativity and reduce the desirability of CKEs, since low-quality or not very useful products are unlikely to be highly valued, however novel and imaginative they may be. For these reasons, in this book we will define a creative product as one that is not only novel and imaginative but also judged to be useful and of good quality.

   It is also important to distinguish between a creative product and a creative process. On occasions one may be interested more in the features of the process leading to a knowledge product and the extent to which these are more or less creative, but more commonly the focus is on the creative features of the product (see Allwood and Selart, 2001). It is worth noting that there is no necessary connection between a creative production process and a creative product. Although a creative process may lead to novel results, the product may still not be seen as creative if it fails to meet the criterion of being of good quality. In spite of this, it is clear that the nature and characteristics of production processes (be they more or less creative) and the factors influencing them are relevant to any investigation of CKEs.

The identification of a product or process as creative is, per se, a difficult and intriguing problem. Such a judgment is clearly dependent on the prior knowledge and understanding brought into play and the assessment of creativity may thus vary between different contexts and across different historical periods. In addition, in the context of CKEs, it is important to note that the evaluation of a product as creative is (as noted by many of the authors reviewed below) usually a matter of social negotiation and thus at least partly influenced by rhetorical and other communication skills.

Knowledge

The aim of those working in CKEs is to produce knowledge. However, the concept of knowledge is much disputed and CKEs are likely to differ with respect to the form of knowledge involved. In addition, depending on the concept of knowledge that is adopted, the knowledge product may be seen as more or less creative (in the sense of our definition of creativity above which also takes into account the quality aspect). Although quite compatible with (at least Western) common sense, the classical definition in analytical philosophy of knowledge as empirically or theoretically justified, objective truth has long been criticized as philosophically naïve. The truth component in this definition is perhaps the most problematic part, especially when 'truth' is defined in terms of a correspondence between an assertion and reality (that is, a 'correspondence-theoretical' definition of truth).

One consequence of this critique is that the distinction between knowledge and understanding (understanding here being defined as just a conception of something, without any claim concerning the truth status or otherwise of that conception) comes into question and may even be discarded (for example, Woolgar, 1988). While giving up the distinction between knowledge and understanding means that the question of truth (at least in the 'correspondence-theoretical' sense) can be set on one side, we are then left with the situation in which research conclusions are to be seen as merely more or less fruitful 'stories' or 'narratives'. Such approaches to truth can be viewed as essentially pragmatic in that they are usually claimed to be useful or convincing or in some way beneficial. Pragmatically oriented conceptions of truth tend to be more common in, for example, science studies, education studies, management studies and parts of the health sciences in contrast to the natural and life sciences. In our analysis of CKEs, we need to recognize the existence of different conceptions of knowledge, ranging from 'correspondence-theoretical' (and 'coherence-theoretical') concepts related to truth to more pragmatically oriented conceptions (see Hemlin and Wenneberg, 2003).

Apart from the issue of truth, knowledge can also be considered from the perspective of how it is established. Here communication processes are central. As is well known from science and technology studies, knowledge is socially negotiated (or 'socially constructed'): it becomes established as knowledge in a process involving social communication. In considering CKEs, we therefore need to examine different aspects of such communication processes in order to better understand how a knowledge product comes to be evaluated as creative. For example, in many research contexts the truth (or at least truth-likeness) of a knowledge claim may be seen as an indication of its quality and hence its creativity, but in others a more pragmatic criterion of quality may be adopted.

When generating knowledge in any of the various types of CKEs discussed in this book, it is important to convince others of the truth or pragmatic utility of the new knowledge product. In some areas of more 'classical' science, the longer such a conviction persists, the better. However, in the context of many CKEs, for a knowledge product to be considered successful, it may not need to convince forever. Consequently the rhetorical aspects of knowledge production (see, for example, Gross and Keith, 1997) are of importance in seeking a better understanding of the features of CKEs. One example of this in an industrial CKE context would be the ability of a manager to convince the company board of the usefulness or relevance of a specific type of knowledge product (cf. Kanter, 1996).

Environment

In the above discussion, we have conceived of the term 'environment' in a holistic manner, interpreting it to include the totality of the components listed in Table 1.1 below, including the various physical, social and cognitive aspects of these. However, as has been pointed out by Weick (1995) and Ford (1996), there is also a subjective experiential side to environments that is important for CKEs. An individual's perception of the reality he or she encounters is what to a large extent will guide his or her thinking and acting. As a result there is not only the environment to consider in research on CKEs but also, and equally importantly, the various interpretations that are made of the environment by individuals and groups. In general a more detailed analysis of CKEs should include a number of components including a description of the tasks, the general work situation, the individuals in the CKE, workgroups, the organization and the extraorganizational environment. These components are shown in Table 1.1, along with some of their relevant characteristics.

Table 1.1   Components of knowledge environments and their characteristics

---

Task characteristics: short-term/long-term, simple/complex, routine/novel, modularized/integrated

Discipline/field: natural sciences v. social sciences v. humanities, theoretical v. experimental v. modelling, quantitative/qualitative, basic/applied, single paradigm v. multiple paradigms v. pre-paradigmatic, reductionist/'holistic', discipline-based/interdisciplinary or multidisciplinary

Individuals: knowledge, skills, abilities, cognitive style (for example, broad/narrow, focused/eclectic), motivation, interests, career plans, values, beliefs, other personality properties (for example, introvert/extrovert), private life situation

Group characteristics: size, integrated/loosely coupled, inward-looking ('group think') v. outward-looking, leadership style, degree of tension/harmony, heterogeneity/homogeneity of group members, 'chemistry' of personalities in the group, composition of knowledge, skills and abilities, agreed-upon or contested beliefs or underlying assumptions

General work situation for individuals: number of different work tasks or projects, features of time available for research (for example, scant/abundant, fragmented or concentrated), job ambiguity (total autonomy v. narrowly defined goals), quality of information technology (IT) available (including the usability)

Physical environment: facilities, buildings, architecture, location, climate, equipment

Organization: economic situation, organizational structures, reward profile, leadership and managerial style (for example, controlling/allowing), degree of tension/harmony, organizational culture

Extraorganizational environment: expanding/decreasing economy, market characteristics (for example, open/restricted, global/regional, competitive/monopoly), reward profile, information availability (open/closed), job opportunities and mobility, national and cultural characteristics

---

As is clear from Table 1.1, knowledge environments are dependent on a wide range of different conditions and circumstances that overlap and interact. A specific CKE represents a unique combination of these various characteristics. We noted earlier that CKEs can be seen as having physical, social and cognitive aspects, and we also observed that the cognitive and social aspects are difficult to separate in practice. The components in Table 1.1 illustrate this point, in that many of them cannot easily be categorized with respect to being physical, social or cognitive. For example, for each of the components (and perhaps most clearly in the case of 'Task characteristics', 'Individuals', 'Group characteristics', and 'General work situation for individuals'), the cognitive and social aspects are likely to be inextricably linked.

For a given set of CKEs, there will be certain similarities and differences, and at a general level it is important to try to distinguish the main types of CKEs. Hence the construction of a well formulated taxonomy of CKEs is a crucial research task. In the Triple Helix literature, usually only three types of CKEs are acknowledged: academia, industry and government. However there may well be other significant types of CKEs such as various 'hybrids' between these three main types. Research on 'Mode 2' (that is the suggested new mode of knowledge production where research is transdisciplinary and carried out in a context of application), for example, has analysed various different forms of collaboration between university and industry (see, for example, Gibbons *et al.*, 1994; Jacob and Hellström, 2000). In addition, as discussed below for academic and industrial CKEs, it may be useful in certain circumstances to refine the categorization of CKEs with respect to identifying different types of CKEs *within* the three main types of CKEs listed above (academia, industry and government). In brief, in order to achieve a realistic understanding of CKEs, it is important to be aware of their most significant differences.

For example, university CKEs differ from industrial CKEs in several ways. One such difference is the need for researchers in the university context to publish in scientific journals, in contrast with the need for profit in the industrial context. At the same time, we are apparently witnessing increasing heterogeneity within industry CKEs, with publishing also being very important in some industries (for example, the pharmaceutical industry). Likewise some universities are becoming more involved with issues to do with intellectual property and the exploitation of knowledge, further blurring the boundaries between academia and industry. Another obvious difference is that most university researchers carry out other activities besides research (in particular, teaching and administration) whereas researchers in industry can often devote themselves more wholeheartedly to their research activities, as can researchers in research institutes (such as the Max Planck institutes in Germany) who do not teach.

Moreover, as mentioned above, university and industrial CKEs are also heterogeneous within themselves. For example, different types of disciplines (for example the natural sciences, social sciences and human sciences, or theoretical as compared with 'modelling sciences' such as artificial intelligence) may require different CKEs. Thus what makes for a creative knowledge environment in one discipline may be very different from that for other disciplines. It is well known that different disciplines have different cognitive and social styles (Becher, 1989; Whitley, 1984). This means that the nature of innovation (Laudan and Laudan, 1989) and the assessment of what is 'creative' may vary, for example, between natural sciences (many of which are characterized by a single stable paradigm) and social sciences (some of which may be multiparadigmatic, with a certain degree of incommensurability between the various 'paradigms', while others may be 'pre-paradigmatic'). Likewise, different types of industrial research contexts may demand different conditions for a knowledge environment to promote creativity and innovation.

An illustration of the diversity of 'industrial' CKEs can be found in the chapter by Wallgren and Hägglund in the present volume where the authors distinguish and analyse interesting differences between engineering environments and consulting environments for the doctoral students. Another example comes in the chapter by Kaiser, where he describes two sectors, telecommunications and pharmaceutical biotechnology, and their recent shifts in technology paradigms. Together with other changes (national research policy, financing and so on) in the macro-level aspects of CKEs, Kaiser examines how the two industrial sectors are developing in different CKEs.

A third type of knowledge production context, recognized in the Triple Helix literature, is the government or public sector, or the wider society. Again the conditions for CKEs may be quite different in this type of environment compared with those in academia and industry. Knowledge production in the public sector or in society more widely is generally aimed at an improvement in the living conditions and welfare of the population as well as the development and effectiveness of public organizations. This is typically pursued from a political perspective, with society being viewed in terms of a number of relatively discrete 'knowledge sectors' such as education, the economy, social services, defence, agriculture, commerce and so on. In the case of such CKEs, the policies of that society (or, as may be the case, of the ruling party) play a key role. Those policies are based not only on knowledge but also on the prevailing ideology (basically 'values') regarding the development of society. This means that knowledge production in such CKEs has rather different drivers and functions than in industry and academia.

At the same time, the addressing of societal needs is dependent to some extent on the other two types of knowledge environment producing appropriate knowledge and services. In this way, a public or societal CKE can be seen as being embedded in academic and industrial CKEs. This is similar to the starting point in the Triple Helix model in which the three types of organizations (government, academia and industry) are seen as interacting closely with one another. The study of CKEs, like research carried out in the framework of the Triple Helix model, includes analysing the relations between universities, the public sector and industry. The field of CKE research can therefore be said to embrace the Triple Helix area, but it is broader in that it also attempts to analyse the features of each of these specific contexts as CKEs.[2]

In addition to these three main types of CKE (and there may be other types or indeed classifications that are useful in certain circumstances) there are two other important aspects of CKEs that need to be taken into account: the scale level and the stage in the task or problem process. Together with type of CKE, these can be seen as constituting the three 'dimensions' of CKEs, as illustrated in Figure 1.1. (Again, as with the components in Table 1.1, each of these constituent components may have a combination of physical, social and cognitive aspects.)

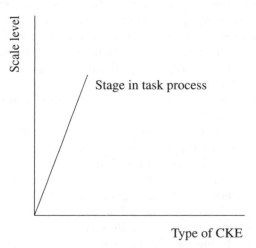

Figure 1.1   Three dimensions of CKEs

We have already discussed how CKEs can be analysed on a number of different scales (in particular, micro, meso and macro levels), so let us focus here on the dimension relating to different stages in the knowledge-production process. All knowledge-production processes incorporate a number of stages,[3] for example problem finding or problem identification, idea generation, idea elaboration, evaluation (including identifying and rejecting poor ideas) and 'selling' (legitimating and convincing others of the value of) the idea. These stages do not necessarily occur in the above order, nor are they always distinct; instead they may overlap (for example evaluating and 'selling' the idea) and be repeated. The appropriate conditions for each of these stages will vary in different types of CKEs.

For example, there is likely to be a considerable difference between the characteristics of a CKE in the problem-identification stage of an industrial task to produce a specified service or product and those for a university research group trying to understand a new physical phenomenon. Whereas the problem-identification phase in many university environments is heavily influenced by factors such as the disciplinary situation and the agenda of senior researchers, in industrial CKEs it is more likely to be influenced by the needs of the company. In the 'selling' (legitimating) phase, the type of legitimation needed when attempting to obtain funding for the problems identified is likely to differ in university, public and industry CKEs. Likewise the evaluation phase might be conducted according to somewhat different criteria between university and industry CKEs. Although in both contexts a great many ideas may be rejected on the way in the knowledge-production process (for a study on rejection of ideas in the industrial context, see Stevens and Burley, 1997), in the industry context the needs of the host company will generally play a greater role than those of the host university in the academic context.

A REVIEW OF THE CREATIVITY LITERATURE RELEVANT TO CKEs

In the following section, we review previous research that has attempted to characterise creativity and to analyse its sources.

Characterizing Creativity

Sternberg (1999) has distinguished between six different approaches that have been used to understand creativity, namely mystical approaches ('divine inspiration'), pragmatic approaches (such as De Bono's 'lateral thinking'), psychodynamic approaches (which are less well developed), psychometric approaches (for instance, Guilford's 'Brick Test'), cognitive approaches (focusing on mental representations and processes in creative thought) and finally social personality approaches (looking at such factors as traits, motivation and the environment). In this chapter, as may be already apparent, we are adopting the last two of these approaches to the study of creativity and the environmental factors that influence it. In our view, the most explicit and persuasive theories of creativity describe creativity in terms of the confluence of a range of different factors. In what follows, we briefly summarize the work of four authors who take a similar approach, along with one who has produced an interesting conceptual analysis of creativity.

The first of these authors is Amabile, who emphasizes three sets of factors – intrinsic motivation, domain-relevant knowledge and abilities, and creativity-relevant skills – as determinants of creativity (Amabile, 1999). Intrinsic motivation is contrasted with extrinsic motivation (such as that engendered by payment) and includes such internal stimuli as a strong interest in the subject and its development. Internal motivation is generally considered to be more important or influential in relation to creativity than extrinsic motivation. Another feature stressed by Amabile is the prior need for often quite extensive knowledge of the domain if creative action is then to take place. Amabile also points out that a degree of practice and learning in relation to creative action is generally necessary for creativity to occur. A consequence for CKEs is that it is vital that individuals be given enough time and opportunities for such practice and learning to occur in the environment.

Secondly, the interaction of the individual, the domain and the field is crucial to creativity, according to Csikszentmihalyi (1999). Hence, in addition to the individual, Csikszentmihalyi emphasizes the domain-specific knowledge and in particular the 'field', included in which are to be found the ultimate judges or evaluators of the creative product or innovation (see also Stoycheva and Lubart, 2001). In his view, it is difficult if not impossible to say that something is 'creative' without its being evaluated as creative by others.[4]

Thirdly, Woodman *et al.* (1993) analysed creativity in organizations with a model based on similar factors to those stressed by Csikszentmihalyi (1999): 'to understand creativity in a social context necessitates an exploration of creative processes, creative products, creative persons and creative situations' (ibid., p.317). This model offers an interactive view of creativity which, although apparently well grounded, nevertheless requires rather extensive empirical studies for it to be used in practice.

Fourthly, according to Sternberg and Lubart (1999), creativity is found in people who are able and willing to 'buy low and sell high'. In other words, such people are virtually alone in believing in the value of an idea while others at that stage do not (that is, they are able 'to buy low'), but after a period of development or persuasion this idea eventually proves successful (making it possible for them 'to sell high'). This view of creativity is derived from investment theory, where success is determined in these terms, and it is consistent with the views of other authors reviewed here, such as Csikszentmihalyi who emphasizes the social identification of a product as creative. However, although the ability 'to buy low and sell high' is probably typical of creative individuals, it does not directly address our main concern here, namely what environmental factors are crucial to creativity.

Finally Unsworth (2001) has recently suggested that creativity is not a unitary construct. She analysed the various concepts of creativity employed in the literature and identified two dimensions, namely the problem type which can be open or closed, and the stimulus or driver for engagement which can be external or internal (see Figure 1.2 below). These two dimensions result in a two-by-two matrix of creativity types, where the open, external type is called 'expected creativity', which entails finding a required solution to a self-discovered problem (such as being asked to write a poem). A second type is the open, internal one, termed 'proactive creativity', which involves a volunteered solution to discovered problems (for example, unprompted suggestions). The third type is a closed, external creativity type named 'responsive creativity', which means finding a required solution to a specified problem (for instance, responses produced by think-tanks). Finally, the fourth, closed, internal creativity type she describes as 'contributory creativity', which involves a volunteered solution to a specified problem (for example, an employee who engages in creative behaviour to solve a problem in a team of which he or she is not a member).

Problem Type

		Open	Closed
	External	Expected creativity	Responsive creativity
Driver for Engagement	Internal	Proactive creativity	Contributory creativity

Source: Unsworth (2001).

Figure 1 2   The two dimensions of creativity

Perhaps the most demanding and therefore the most interesting of the four types is proactive creativity. This type may at least to some extent be dependent on the presence of internal motivation which Amabile regards as the prime component and driver of creative action. In contrast, the more external constraints there are, the less freedom there is to act and behave creatively in line with one's own intentions. This means that the responsive and expected forms of creativity are arguably a little less 'creative', at least if one attaches the same importance to internal motivation for creativity as Amabile. Moreover, the closed internal type of creativity might also be a little less 'creative' in the sense that there is no freedom to choose the problem to solve. However, all four types of creativity are possible aspects of our notion of creative knowledge environments.[5]

Let us conclude this section on creativity by noting that all the above attempts to characterize creativity contain useful elements. Although some of the researchers reviewed here stress more than others the social dimension of evaluating creative products, they all appear to agree that creativity depends on some combination of motivation, domain-relevant understanding, skills, social structures, the actors in the knowledge domain and social interaction. In general, creativity involves interactions between one or more individuals (for instance, interactions between their respective talents and abilities), situations (for example, in meetings between individuals), contexts (for instance, supportive and encouraging circumstances), processes (for example, processes creating a certain amount of constructive tension), products (for instance, a revolutionary scientific article or technology) and evaluators (who assess whether something is creative or not) over different time periods (in which creative acts may happen more or less frequently). Moreover, from the work of Unsworth, it is clear that creativity (or creative tasks) can be classified into at least four types. In this present volume, the primary focus is on the contextual or environmental factors stimulating (or constraining) creative knowledge-based processes and products.

Sources of Creativity

In general, previous research has shown that creativity tends to be enhanced by new influences, for example new knowledge and ideas, new personal contacts or new environments. New combinations of these various components are often a necessary condition for creative results. Given the fact that individuals approach the task of knowledge production from their own perspective, a perspective that is shaped by local conditions (including their disciplinary, institutional, cultural, social, geographical and motivational situation), it is scarcely surprising that groups including members from different cultural or disciplinary backgrounds tend to be more creative than groups with members sharing a more homogeneous background. In addition, a lively and outspoken minority is likely to facilitate group creativity (Wilke and Kaplan, 2001).

Likewise, a common finding in creativity research is that a change of environment or reference frame can often result in creative products. The history of science is replete with examples of researchers moving from one research field to another and making creative advances in that new field.[6] The basic feature in these examples may be the combining of different frames of reference or different preconceptions, or the transfer of a perspective, model or methodological approach from one discipline or subdiscipline into another.

At the same time, it is important to note that it can be difficult to get researchers from different fields to collaborate successfully in the same project (Ancona and Cadwell, 1992, cited in Blackler *et al.*, 1998). This raises the question of what kind of structures and factors act to hinder the development of cross-disciplinary research[7] or the migration of researchers from one field of work to another. Issues here include the extent to which different disciplines may be subject to a 'territorial imperative', and the varying permeability of disciplinary 'boundaries' to external 'colonizers'.

According to Ziman (1987), most scientists, at least in their own perception, only occupy one or two research fields. He notes that a change of research field is often a question of a gradual 'drift' rather than abrupt change. Judging from the limited data available, he concludes that abrupt changes are apparently not very common, involving perhaps only 10 per cent of researchers. However this estimate is very uncertain and may obviously vary across research fields. Ziman points out that slow changes may be more attractive to migrating researchers since the risks taken when changing faster are evidently greater. For example, there may be more of a problem in establishing oneself in a field when one is a total newcomer than if one slowly works one's way into the field.

Given our earlier observations on creativity, researchers who change research fields are, on average, likely to be somewhat more creative, if for no other reason than that they have access to knowledge, understanding and ideas that are unusual compared with those of their colleagues, but which may nevertheless be relevant in their new field. Unusual knowledge may, for example, stimulate creative metaphorical thinking. Furthermore, all other things being equal, abrupt changes, seen from this perspective, may be better in fostering creativity than less abrupt changes since they tend to generate more unusual knowledge. On the other hand, the 'costs' associated with abrupt changes (not only for the individual but also because more effort will be needed to manage a group that involves researchers with very different disciplinary backgrounds and the consequent 'clash' of ideas) may more than offset their positive effects (see, for example, Tierney, 1997).

WHAT DO WE KNOW ABOUT CREATIVE KNOWLEDGE ENVIRONMENTS SO FAR?

This section focuses on an analysis of the literature relating to creative knowledge environments. In the management and psychological literature on CKEs, there tends to be a concentration on studies of research and innovation activities, presumably because such activities are knowledge-based and knowledge-creating.[8] Studies in education on suitable conditions for teaching and learning, which may entail some aspects of creativity, are not included in our review below, simply because they tend to concern a specific environment designed solely for one purpose, namely teaching and learning. Our focus is on general environments for creative human activities and work which include learning as one of several components. The studies that we have identified mostly focus on social and cognitive environmental factors. There are few if any relevant studies on the physical environment and its influence on creativity and innovativeness in work situations for knowledge workers to be found in the databases that we searched. The studies of CKEs discussed here concern social and cognitive factors and are divided into the following three sections, although there is inevitably some overlap: (a) research environment studies, (b) innovation environment studies and (c) work team environment studies.

Research Environment Studies

A number of empirical studies have been carried out to identify the main factors influencing the performance of research groups in universities and other public research organizations and in private R&D laboratories. These studies form a relatively distinct research cluster from those on the innovation environment and work teams presented later. Since successful research performance depends to a greater or lesser extent on creative work processes, these studies are clearly relevant to our analysis of research environments and their effects on creativity. The major findings of these studies can be summarized as follows. A successful creative research environment should have

- clear objectives functioning in a coordinated way for researchers;
- a primary focus on research;
- a genuine research culture built up over a long time period;
- a positive group climate;
- group members who participate actively in the leadership of the group's research;
- a flat and decentralized organizational structure;
- internal and external communications which are lively and supporting;
- basic resources for staff: adequate time, research funding, research equipment, appropriate premises and library materials;
- diversity in size, age and experience of groups and individuals;
- a high level of motivation (and even enjoyment of the job), career structure, promotion and rewards;
- well managed staff selection;
- good individual competencies and characteristics;

- excellent leadership;
- quality control (although not in too excessive or intrusive a form); and
- an institutional base with an established reputation and visibility.

This list of factors is derived from Andrews (1979), Bland and Ruffin (1992), Martin and Skea (1992), Pelz and Andrews (1966) and Stankiewicz (1980), each of which treats a number of the factors mentioned above. It is clear that the factors listed operate at different levels and can be grouped in various categories. First, and not surprisingly, individual researchers and their characteristics are important to research performance. Secondly, a successful research environment must possess a certain sufficient level of basic resources as well as a participative and collegial management and working style. Finally, and very importantly, a creative knowledge environment has specific psychological and organizational characteristics.

Innovation Environment Studies

The characteristics of innovative environments have been widely discussed in the management literature. One prominent author in this field is Kanter (1996, 1997). Drawing on her studies of innovations at the micro level, she concludes that creative organizations tend to have integrative structures, but at the same time they tend to emphasize diversity, to have multiple structural linkages within and outside the organization, to have flexible or permeable boundaries, to have a sense of collective pride and a faith in the talents of individuals, and to emphasize collaboration and teamwork. As can be seen from these characteristics, they are broadly similar to those contributing to successful environments in research, but are stated in rather more general terms. In addition, Kanter describes four stages of innovation in organizations that are helpful when analysing creative environments. First, there is the idea-generation phase, which perhaps is the most crucial part of the creative process. Secondly, there is a coalition-building phase, during which people in a firm are persuaded that the creative idea is a good one.[9] Thirdly, there is a phase where ideas are translated into concrete products or processes. The fourth and final stage is when an innovation is transferred or diffused. Although this is a simplified model of an innovation process, it is of importance for CKEs because different stages may demand rather different environmental conditions.

One would expect that the earlier creative activities leading to innovations in Kanter's four stages would to a large extent be influenced by similar factors to those found in research environment studies. However the process of generating a successful innovation involves certain phases that are not generally relevant to research (for instance, the marketing of products), although there are various similarities between the publication and dissemination phase of research and the marketing phase of products.

In the management and organizational literature, there are several other studies that are relevant to our topic. Often these focus on the micro and meso levels. One of the more comprehensive articles on creative environments is that by Woodman *et al.* (1993), the conclusion of which, ten years later, is still valid: 'researchers still know surprisingly little about how the creative process works, especially within the context of complex social systems such as formal organisations' (ibid., p.316).

Also important is the previously mentioned work by Amabile and co-authors (Amabile *et al.*, 1996; Amabile, 1999). They use the concept of 'climate' to denote a significant component of the social micro environment influencing creativity. Important examples of empirically investigated climate factors include supervisory encouragement, the freedom to choose and to work on different assignments, possessing sufficient resources, workload pressure (which may exert a negative influence if it rises above a certain level[10]) and organizational impediments. The effect of team climate in particular as a significant influence on innovative capacity in organizations has been investigated by a number of authors (for example, Agrell and Gustafson, 1994; Amabile *et al.*, 1996; Anderson and West, 1998). An important concept that is linked to that of team climate is the tension both between individuals and between the individual and the domain. 'Tension' can be thought of here as some degree of unease or discomfort in a social relationship or an ambiguity towards a knowledge claim. Such a tension is not necessarily negative in its effects; it can sometimes be instrumental in bringing about creative changes (Amabile, 1999; Gulbrandsen, Chapter 2 in this book; Pelz and Andrews, 1966).

To gain an overall picture of the environmental factors at work, one could adopt the three categories of factors influencing work group performance that were suggested in a review by Anderson (1992): (a) structural factors, that is, group composition and group development; (b) psychological factors, that is, group or team climate and social relationships; (c) processual factors, that is, institutional processes and interpersonal interactions. However these three sets of factors overlap to an appreciable extent or could perhaps be viewed as different aspects of the same phenomena. For example, psychological factors can obviously also be both structural (such as group developments) and processual (such as interpersonal interactions).

Perhaps the most comprehensive work on individual, group and organizational creativity in relation to innovation that we have found was carried out by Ford (1996). Using an extensive review of the literature, he developed a theory of creative action which takes into account multiple social domains. In the latter he includes subunits and groups at the lowest level, organizations at the next, then institutional environments and, finally, markets. This is similar to our own distinction between CKEs on different scales (micro, meso and macro levels). Ford suggests that individuals draw upon three main resources in undertaking creative actions: (a) sense making (that is, how we initially understand a situation eliciting intentions and expectations), (b) motivation (including goals, 'receptivity beliefs' or how we foresee the reception of our actions, 'capability beliefs' or how we expect our abilities will cope with a given situation, and emotions), and (c) knowledge and ability (including domain-related knowledge, behavioural abilities and creative thinking ability). All three sources of creativity overlap and are fairly familiar from the previous discussion of the definitions of 'creativity' and the other components of CKEs above.

More interesting is Ford's analysis of social environments, or 'social domains' as he prefers to call them. At the organizational level, Ford points to the 'absorptive capacity' (the ability to recognize the significance, and to make fruitful use, of new information) and a predisposition towards taking risks as two key features of the environment that affect creativity and innovation. A general aspect of institutions is that they often consolidate actions into established routines that may then hinder subsequent creativity. However, where there is scope for crossing institutional borders and, where interactions are encouraged, there may well be opportunities for creative action by entrepreneurs. In the market environment, Ford suggests that 'radical innovations will fare best in moderately well-established market domains that provide a basis for consumer valuations but are still equivocal enough to tolerate a substantial degree of diversity' (ibid., p.1132).

Work Team Environment Studies

Most of the empirical studies of work environments have been carried out at the micro level and focus on work teams. In this section, we discuss what is known from these studies about creativity and innovativeness.

Unsworth and Parker (2003), on the basis of a review of the subject, suggest that the following are the main groups of contextual factors influencing creativity and innovation:

- task and work design (for example degree of autonomy, complexity, stresses such as time pressure, work load, job ambiguity, concentration demands, organizational problems);
- social characteristics (for example collegial communication, team working, leadership);
- organizational characteristics (for example climate or culture, human resource practices, organizational design).

Most or perhaps all of these factors are of course valid for our analysis of CKEs, but it must be stressed that our focus is on knowledge-creating and knowledge-intensive workplaces. This means that other characteristics that are not found in general workplaces may play an important role in the environment. For instance, of the components listed in Table 1.1 above, the 'Discipline/field' component is likely to be important, while the impact of the knowledge of individuals may well be more pronounced in CKEs than general work environments.

The first group of studies we review below relate to the first category of contextual factors suggested by Unsworth and Parker (2003), namely the influence of task and work design on creativity. According to reviews from the 1990s (see Anderson, 1992; King and Anderson, 1995), there seems to be little evidence that there is an optimal work group structure, size or form of leadership for creativity. Rather these characteristics appear to be phase-dependent. In other words, these factors differ in importance over time, for instance in the idea-generation phase in comparison to the implementation phase. Another finding from these reviews is that long-term membership of a group appears to be correlated with a lower degree of innovativeness, which implies that innovation is linked to some extent to the turnover of individuals in teams. This is a result consistent with the findings in studies of research group composition and performance presented above.

The second group of studies is related to the social characteristics of work teams, where social interactions have been shown to have an important impact on creativity. The literature about social networks is related to the social psychology of groups and it demonstrates that there are strong links between the two literatures to be explored in further analysis. In an empirical study of 47 work groups in both public institutions (universities) and private institutions (manufacturing firms, distributor companies and consumer products companies), Sparrowe et al. (2001) reported that group members who are central to group advice-sharing activities are more positively rated in terms of individual performance. This supports the hypothesis that a person who is regarded as central in social interactions tends to be judged as performing well. In a somewhat similar vein, Sonnentag (2000) investigated excellent performers (who are presumably also more creative) in the domains of software development and engineering and found that excellent performers, compared to moderate performers, 'more often regarded cooperation as a useful strategy' and more often participated 'in work-related communication and cooperation processes' (ibid., p.483).

A higher level of social interaction influenced the success of new ventures in a study by Lechler (2001). He studied levels of social interaction in 159 entrepreneurial teams (in small knowledge-intensive firms – 80 per cent having fewer than ten employees – in the machinery, construction, electronics, chemicals, construction, and plant and engineering sectors in Germany) to identify success factors. Using a standardized questionnaire on social interaction, he chose to focus on process dimensions rather than on input characteristics such as team characteristics which, in previous studies, have exhibited only a weak correlation with the success of new ventures. His results support the hypothesis that high-quality social interaction in entrepreneurial teams influences the success of new ventures in terms of innovative capacity. The components measured were communication (for information exchange within the team), cohesion (the desire to be a member of the team), work norms (shared expectations in the team about team members' behaviour), mutual support (cooperation between the team members) and coordination (the harmonization and synchronization of time frames, budget lines and deliverables within the team). Lechler concludes that, if we are to explain success in relation to entrepreneurial business and innovation, social interaction should be included as part of a model that also includes team composition and task performance. It is clear from this and other studies reported, for instance Unsworth and Parker (2003), that effective communication appears to be a crucial factor in CKEs.

In an exploratory study based on interviews with 38 scientists in French public institutions (universities) and private-sector institutions (chemicals, pharmaceuticals, electronics, food, glass and cosmetics firms), Bouty (2000) attempted to arrive at an understanding of the individual decision processes in informal exchanges between scientists and across organizational borders. She demonstrates that social capital, as reflected in informal contacts, exerts a strong influence on the process of organizational learning (see also Allwood and Hedelin, forthcoming). Moreover she concluded that equitable exchanges are preferable from an organizational learning perspective, because they are richer than profitable ones and because they limit opportunistic behaviour. This study is interesting because it shows the importance of CKEs that stimulate informal contacts between individuals across organizational borders for the innovative benefit of the organization itself and not only individuals: that is, on both meso and micro levels.

A study by Axtell *et al.* (2000) concerned group and organizational characteristics associated with creativity. With regard to the first phase of innovation, where ideas are generated, 148 machine operators of a beverage manufacturer were asked to complete a questionnaire about suggestions they had made for innovations and whether those suggestions were subsequently implemented in innovations. They were also asked to assess (using a scale) the degree of participative safety (that is, 'members feel able to interact freely and propose new ideas') and support for innovation (two key aspects of the so called 'team climate inventory'). The results show that the suggestion of ideas is more closely related to individual (personal and job) characteristics than to group and organizational characteristics, whereas the implementation of ideas is more strongly correlated with group and organizational characteristics (ibid.). More precisely, self-efficacy (for example, confidence to take the initiative) and autonomy are related to producing a greater number of suggestions, while support from both management and team members as well as participation in decision making are crucial to getting the ideas implemented – that is, to innovation.

The relationship between personal and situational factors with regard to creative management styles and leadership was studied by Vinkenburg *et al.* (2001) using a questionnaire completed by 139 managers, mostly in top and middle management positions in a variety of industry and service organizations. On the basis of vignettes of specific managerial situations, respondents were presented with a number of alternative ways of dealing with the described situations. The results show that, in contrast to the conclusions of most management authors who recommend a certain leadership style based on coaching, exhibiting a degree of flexibility with respect to the situational factors making up the environment is likely to be the most successful style for managers if they are to produce good performance and creative solutions. This study highlights the importance of management styles to CKEs.

Finally, we found one study (Tierney, 1997) concerned with cognitive factors in CKEs. A possible reason for this was suggested above, namely that social and cognitive factors are so closely intertwined that they tend not to be treated separately very often. In a survey of 240 employees in a well-established corporation, Tierney measured cognitive style (by means of the Kirton Adaptation-Innovation Survey), job satisfaction (using the Job Diagnostic Survey) and creative efficacy (assessed by means of a three-item instrument) within work groups. Her results reveal that 'the more innovative the cognitive climate of the work group to which an employee belongs, the lower the level of employee job satisfaction' (ibid., p.840). Furthermore employees in such innovative groups report less satisfaction with their co-workers. This is interpreted as meaning that innovators may often be creative loners who are less concerned with building relationships. This finding is consistent with a number of studies concerning creative researchers' personalities (see Taylor and Barron, 1963), where typical traits besides motivation, ambition, endurance and the like could entail non-supportive, dominant, aggressive and similar not-so-positive traits. It clearly has implications for organisations which wish to foster creativity in their workforce in terms of how they set about achieving this. In particular, they have to monitor innovative groups and compensate for the effects of any dissatisfaction without at the same time reducing any 'creative tensions' which are beneficial for creativity and innovation (see Chapter 2 of the present volume).

To sum up, the above review of previous literature on environments for research, innovation and work teams shows that task and work design as well as social and organizational characteristics at the micro and meso levels can have a crucial influence on creativity and on innovative activities. Few authors describe the effects of the macro-level environment on creativity and innovation (but see Chapter 8 in the present volume for a discussion of some aspects in this context). However the American psychologist Simonton (1999) has discussed the wider influence on creativity and performance with researchers and others. He argues that there is a cultural influence (a 'Zeitgeist') affecting creativity. Moreover, he claims to detect a societal influence from population growth on creativity. He also finds an influence on creativity related to economic growth, and one from political factors such as wars.

Unfortunately there are no clear, simple 'recipes' for promoting creativity by suitably engineering the environment. Nevertheless certain lessons can be drawn. First, individuals are clearly important actors in CKEs in relation to both research and innovation processes, especially in the early phases during which ideas and suggestions are generated. Secondly, a successful CKE embraces certain management and working styles, where the role of managers is de-emphasized, where there is considerable autonomy for teams, and where self-leadership and social interaction are prominent. Thirdly, work teams should emphasize and tolerate diversity among members, so that an element of creative tension exists and conformity is not overemphasized. Fourthly, distinguishing between the different phases of creative work processes and innovation is crucial for understanding CKEs (cf. Paulus and Yang, 2000). One phase may require very different conditions for creativity than another.

In the final chapter of this book, we shall return to the question of what makes for a better creative knowledge environment.

CONTENTS OF THE BOOK

In this book, in addition to this introduction (Chapter 1) and the concluding Chapter 9, we have brought together seven papers that concern the micro, meso and macro levels of creative knowledge environments.

The seven chapters have been divided into two parts, with the first consisting of papers focusing on micro environments while the second deals with meso- and macro-level aspects of CKEs. The former part starts with a paper by Magnus Gulbrandsen (Chapter 2), in which he elaborates on the role of 'tensions' in relation to creativity, drawing on both the creativity literature and on interviews with Norwegian researchers. In a similar vein,

Mika Nieminen (Chapter 3) attempts to assess what impact recent changes in the Finnish research environment have had on the creativity and innovativeness of research groups. He uses a large statistical database from a survey of Finnish researchers, as well as a number of interviews, to address this issue.

The second part of the book consists of five chapters that shed light on the environmental factors at the meso and macro levels that provide a stimulus for creativity and innovation. Two Swedish studies deal with meso-level knowledge environments for creative development. In their case study of the Swedish science park, 'Ideon', Lars Bengtsson and Jan-Inge Lind (Chapter 4) attempt to explain what factors and processes in the knowledge environment may have contributed to the successful development of the science park and to its regional impact through innovative enterprises. The second Swedish study (Chapter 5) is concerned with the interaction between two relatively distinct types of knowledge environment: PhD schools and industry. In an interview-based study of 23 PhD students in applied IT and software engineering, Lillemor Wallgren and Sture Hägglund explore the characteristics of industry environments that are most conducive to a creative PhD programme.

Two chapters consider the influence of national environments in France, Germany and the UK on the development of innovations in electronics, telecommunications and biotechnology. In the first of these two studies, Geoff Mason, Jean-Paul Beltramo and Jean-Jacques Paul (Chapter 6) report on an interview-based survey of matched samples of British and French opto-electronics establishments which was carried out to ascertain the characteristics of, and the differences between, the respective national knowledge environments and their influence on innovativeness in this field. In Chapter 7, Robert Kaiser describes an investigation of the German arena for the two knowledge-based sectors of telecommunications and biotechnology, using a systems and an organizational approach and drawing on data from an EU project.

Chapter 8, by Isabel Bortagaray, is concerned with the creative knowledge environments of South American nations at a number of levels. She analyses co-authorships of scientific papers in order to investigate patterns of research collaboration at the interpersonal, interinstitutional, intersectoral and international levels, and to identify the characteristics of the South American knowledge environment where universities are dominant and industry is a relatively weak actor.

Finally, in Chapter 9, the three editors attempt to summarize the main ideas and findings about CKEs from these seven studies. They identify a number of conclusions and policy implications, as well as highlighting potential topics for further research.

NOTES

1. A societal CKE can also be analysed at a macro level ('state'), meso level ('regional') and micro level ('local').
2. An attempt to provide a description of an actor and its CKE in a Triple Helix context can be found in Hemlin (2001).
3. In a later section, we consider Kanter's differentiation of various stages in the specific case of the innovation process.
4. See also Nieminen (Chapter 3 in the present volume) for a more lengthy discussion of Csikszentmihalyi.
5. It should be noted that problem finding, which is close to proactive creativity, is a similarly creative act that has previously been discussed in the literature (see, for instance, Allwood, 1997; Allwood and Bärmark, 1999; Arlin, 1990; Kantorovich, 1993).
6. To take just one example, the physicist Erwin Schroedinger moved from physics into microbiology, where he made significant contributions and published an acclaimed book on 'the life sciences'.
7. These problems are well illustrated by a case study of a large cross-disciplinary project, the 'Coniferous Forest Project' (see Allwood and Bärmark, 1999; Bärmark and Wallén, 1980).
8. A literature search was carried out using a number of social science databases (such as the *Social Science Citation Index*) and library catalogues at Copenhagen Business School and Göteborg University, and was based on various search terms such as creativity, innovation, research, knowledge, work, environment, context, situation, group and team.
9. There are similarities here with the views of the 'Actor–Network' school in the sociology of science, technology and innovation (e.g. Callon and Law, 1982; Callon *et al.*, 1986; Latour, 1987). The proponents of this theory argue that the scientist or innovator must enlist others and enrol their interests if their scientific discovery or innovation is to prove successful. This view is also consistent with Csikszentmihalyi (1999) and his notion of the 'field' comprising other actors.
10. The Yerkes–Dodson law presupposes a U-shaped curve, where performance is best when there is a moderate arousal (see, for instance, Bernstein *et al.*, 1997).

REFERENCES

Agrell, A. and R. Gustafson (1994), 'The team climate inventory (TCI) and group innovation a psychometric test on a Swedish sample of work groups', *Journal of Occupational and Organisational Psychology*, **67**, 143–51.

Allwood, C.M. (1997), 'The function and handling of research problems in the social sciences', *Science Studies*, **10**, 50–73.

Allwood, C.M. and J. Bärmark (1999), 'The role of research problems in the process of research', *Social Epistemology*, **13**, 59–83.

Allwood, C.M. and L. Hedelin (forthcoming), 'Adjusting new initiatives to the social environment: organizational decision making as learning, commitment creating and behavior regulation', in H. Montgomery, R. Lipshits and B. Brehmer (eds), *How Professionals Make Decisions*, Mahwah, NJ: Lawrence Erlbaum Associates.

Allwood, C.M. and M. Selart (2001), 'Social and creative decision making', in C.M. Allwood and M. Selart (eds), *Decision Making: Social and Creative Dimensions*, Dordrecht: Kluwer Academic Publishers, pp.1–11.

Amabile, T.M. (1999), 'How to kill creativity', *Harvard Business Review on Breakthrough Thinking*, Boston: Harvard Business School Press, pp.1–28.

Amabile, T.M., R. Conti, H. Coon, J. Lazenby and M. Herron (1996), 'Assessing the work environment for creativity', *Academy of Management Journal*, **39** (5),

1154–84.

Anderson. N. (1992), 'Work group innovation', in D.M. Hosking and N. Anderson (eds), *Organisational Change and Innovation: Psychological Perspectives and Practices in Europe*, London: Routledge, pp.149–60.

Anderson, N.R. and M.A. West (1998), 'Measuring climate for work group innovation: development and validation of the team climate inventory', *Journal of Organisational Behavior*, **19**, 235–8.

Andrews, F. (ed.) (1979), *Scientific Productivity. The Effectiveness of Research Groups in Six Countries*, Cambridge: Cambridge University Press.

Arlin, P.K. (1990), 'Wisdom: the art of problem finding', in R. Sternberg (ed.), *Wisdom: Its Nature, Origins and Development*, Cambridge: Cambridge University Press, pp.230–43.

Axtell, C.M., D.J. Holman, K.L. Unsworth, T.D. Wall, P.E. Waterson and E. Harrington (2000), 'Shopfloor innovation: facilitating the suggestion and implementation of ideas', *Journal of Occupational and Organisational Psychology*, **73**, 265–85.

Bärmark, J. and G. Wallén (1980), 'The development of an interdisciplinary project', in K.D. Knorr, R. Krohn and R. Whitley (eds) (1981), *The Social Process of Scientific Investigation*, Sociology of the sciences, Vol. IV, Dordrecht: D. Reidel, pp.221–35.

Becher, T. (1989), *Academic Tribes and Territories*, Milton Keynes: The Society for Research into Higher Education and Open University Press.

Bernstein, D.A., A. Clarke-Stewart, E.J. Roy and C.D. Wickens (1997), *Psychology*, 4th edn, Boston and New York: Houghton Mifflin.

Blackler, F., N. Crump and S. McDonald (1998), 'Knowledge, organizations and competition', in G. von Krogh, J. Roos and D. Kleine (eds), *Knowing in Firms: Understanding, Managing and Measuring Knowledge*, London: Sage Publications, pp.67–86.

Bland, C.J. and M.T. Ruffin (1992), 'Characteristics of a productive research environment: literature review', *Academic Medicine*, **67**, 385–97.

Bouty, I. (2000), 'Interpersonal and interaction influences on informal resource exchanges between R&D researchers across organizational boundaries', *Academy of Management Journal*, **43** (1), 50–65.

Callon, M. and J. Law (1982), 'On interests and their transformation: enrolment and counter-enrolment', *Social Studies of Science*, **12**, 615–25.

Callon, M., J. Law and A. Rip (eds) (1986), *Mapping the Dynamics of Science and Technology*, London: Macmillan.

Carlsson, B. (ed.) (1997), *Technological Systems and Industrial Dynamics*, Dordrecht: Kluwer Academic Publishers.

Collins, M.A. and T.M. Amabile (1999), 'Motivation and creativity', in R.J. Sternberg (ed.), *Handbook of Creativity*, Cambridge: Cambridge University Press, pp.297–312.

Csikszentmihalyi, M. (1999), 'Implications of a systems perspective for the study of creativity', in R.J. Sternberg (ed.), *Handbook of Creativity*, Cambridge: Cambridge University Press, pp.313–35.

Edqvist, C. (ed.) (1997), *Systems of Innovation: Technologies, Institutions and Organisations*, London: Pinter.

Etzkowitz, H. and L. Leydesdorff (eds) (1997), *Universities and the Global Knowledge Economy: A Triple Helix of University–Industry–Government Relations*, London: Pinter.

Ford, C.M. (1996), 'A theory of individual creative action in multiple social domains', *Academy of Management Review*, **21** (4), 1112–42.

Freeman, C. (1987), *Technology and Economic Performance: Lessons from Japan*, London: Pinter.

Hemlin, S. (2001), 'Organisational aspects of mode 2 / triple helix knowledge production', in G. Bender (ed.), *Neue Formen der Wissenserzeugung*, Frankfurt/New York: Campus Verlag, pp.181–200.

Hemlin, S. and S. Wenneberg (2003), *The shift in academic quality control*, manuscript. Copenhagen Business School.

Gibbons, M., C. Limoges, H. Nowotny, S. Schwartzman, P. Scott and M. Trow (1994), *The New Production of Knowledge: The Dynamics of Science and Research in Contemporary Societies*, London: Sage Publications.

Gross, A.G. and W.M. Keith (eds) (1997), *Rhetorical Hermeneutics*, Albany, NY: State University of New York Press.

Jacob, M. and T. Hellström (eds) (2000), *The Future of Knowledge Production in the Academy*, Buckingham, UK: The Society for Research into Higher Education and Open University Press.

Kanter. R. (1996), 'When a thousand flowers bloom: structural, collective and social conditions for innovation in organisations', in P.S. Meyers (ed.), *Knowledge, Management and Organisational Design*, Boston: Butterworth-Heinemann, pp.93–131.

Kanter, R.M. (1997), *Rosabeth Moss Kanter on the Frontiers of Management*, a Harvard Business Review Book, Boston, MA: Harvard Business School Press.

Kantorovich, A. (1993), *Scientific Discovery, Logic and Tinkering*, Albany: State University of New York Press.

King, N. and N.R. Anderson (1995), *Innovation and Change in Organizations*, London: Routledge.

Latour, B. (1987), *Science in Action: How to Follow Scientists and Engineers through Society*, Cambridge, MA: Harvard University Press.

Laudan, L. and R. Laudan (1989), 'Dominance and the disunity-of-method: solving the problems of innovation and consensus', *Philosophy of Science*, **56**, 221–37.

Lechler, T. (2001), 'Social interaction: a determinant of entrepreneurial team venture success', *Small Business Economics*, **16**, 263–78.

Leydesdorff, L. and H. Etzkowitz (1996), 'Emergence of a triple helix of university–industry–government relations', *Science and Public Policy*, **23**, 279–86.

Leydesdorff, L. and H. Etzkowitz (eds) (1998), *A Triple Helix of University–Industry–Government Relations: The Future Location of Research?*, New York: Science Policy Institute, State University of New York.

Lundvall, B.-Å. (ed.) (1992), *National Innovation Systems: Towards a Theory of Innovation and Interactive Learning*, London: Pinter.

Martin, B.R. and J.E.F. Skea (1992), 'Academic Research Performance Indicators: An Assessment of the Possibilities', Science Policy Research Unit, University of Sussex, Brighton.

Mumford, M.D. and S.B. Gustafson (1988). 'Creativity syndrome: integration, application and innovation', *Psychological Bulletin*, **103** (1), 27–43.

Nelson, R. (ed.) (1993), *National Innovation Systems: A Comparative Analysis*, Oxford: Oxford University Press.

Paulus, P.B. and H.-C. Yang (2000), 'Idea generation in groups: a basis for creativity in organisations', *Organisational Behavior and Human Decision Processes*, **82** (1), 76–87.

Pelz, D. and F. Andrews (1966), *Scientists in Organisations: Productive Climates for Research and Development*, New York: Wiley.

Simonton, D.K. (1999), 'Creativity from a historiometric perspective', in R.J. Sternberg (ed.), *Handbook of Creativity*, Cambridge: Cambridge University Press, pp.116–33.

Sonnentag, S. (2000), 'Excellent performance: the role of communication and cooperation processes', *Applied Psychology: An International Review*, **49**, 483–97.

Sparrowe, R.T., R.C. Liden, S.J. Wayne and M.L. Kraimer (2001), 'Social networks and the performance of individuals and groups', *Academy of Management Journal*, **44** (2), 316–25.

Stankiewicz, R. (1980), 'Leadership and the performance of research groups', PhD thesis, Research Policy Institute, University of Lund.

Sternberg, R.J. (ed.) (1999), *Handbook of Creativity*, Cambridge: Cambridge University Press.

Sternberg, R.J. and T.I. Lubart (1999), 'The concept of creativity: prospects and paradigms', in R.J. Sternberg (ed.), *Handbook of Creativity*, Cambridge: Cambridge University Press, pp.3–15.

Stevens, G.A. and J. Burley (1997), '3,000 raw ideas = 1 commercial success!', *Research Technology Management*, **40** (3), 16–27.

Stoycheva, K.G. and T.I. Lubart (2001), 'The nature of creative decision making', in C.M. Allwood and M. Selart (eds), *Decision Making: Creative and Social Dimensions*, Dordrecht: Kluwer Academic Publishers, pp.15–33.

Taylor, C.W. and F. Barron (eds)(1963), *Scientific Creativity: Its Recognition and Development*, New York: John Wiley and Sons.

Tierney, P. (1997), 'The influence of cognitive climate on job satisfaction and creative efficacy', *Journal of Social Behavior and Personality*, **12** (4), 831–47.

Unsworth, K. (2001), 'Unpacking creativity', *Academy of Management Review*, **26** (2), 289–97.

Unsworth, K.L. and S.K. Parker (2003), 'Promoting a pro-active and innovative workforce for the new workplace', in D. Holman, T.D. Wall, C. W. Clegg, P. Sparrow and A. Howard (eds), *The New Workplace: A Guide to the Human Impact of Modern Work Practices*.

Vinkenburg, C.J., P.L. Koopman and P.G.W. Jansen (2001), 'Managerial behaviour and decision making: personal and situational factors', in C.M. Allwood and M. Selart (eds), *Decision Making: Creative and Social Dimensions*, Dordrecht: Kluwer Academic Publishers, pp.211–38.

Weick, K.E. (1995), *Sense Making in Organizations*, London: Sage.

Whitley, R. (1984), *The Intellectual and Social Organization of the Sciences*, Oxford: Clarendon Press.

Wilke, H. and M. Kaplan (2001), 'Task creativity and social creativity in decision-making groups', in C.M. Allwood and M. Selart (eds), *Decision Making: Social and Creative Dimensions*, Dordrecht: Kluwer Academic Publishers, pp.35–51.

Williams, W.M. and L.T. Yang (1999), 'Organisational creativity', in R.J. Sternberg (ed.), *Handbook of Creativity*, Cambridge: Cambridge University Press, pp.373–91.

Woodman, R.W., J.E. Sawyer and R.W. Griffin (1993), 'Toward a theory of organizational creativity', *Academy of Management Review*, **18** (2), 293–321.

Woolgar, S. (1988), Science: The Very Idea, Chichester: Ellis Horwood; London: Tavistock.

Ziman, J.M. (1987), *Knowing Everything about Nothing: Specialization and Change in Scientific Careers*, Cambridge: Cambridge University Press.

PART I

Creative Micro Environments

2. Accord or discord? Tensions and creativity in research

Magnus Gulbrandsen

In this chapter the central argument is that research units that produce creative outputs can be characterized by a certain degree of tension. Organizational tensions may in some cases, if they are 'balanced' and 'maintained', contribute to increased creativity. The goal and ideology of much modern management and policy is, however, rather to remove frictions like tensions and ambiguities than to support or balance them, or to introduce pressures that are not conducive to creativity after all. Tensions that can contribute to creativity may stem from the central role of originality in research work, from the fact that originality is not the only criterion of quality, and from processes of personal and organizational learning, change and maintenance of motivation. A good working climate appears to be a central element in tolerating and benefiting from tensions.

INTRODUCTION AND OVERVIEW

Something close to a paradox emerges in the literature on creative knowledge environments, as well as in the interviews that form the empirical basis of this chapter. Some authors and informants emphasize that creativity in research is the result of what can be termed a *process of discord*: a process characterized by tensions, ambiguities, conflicts and resistances. One of my informants, an institute researcher working with vaccines, argued that creativity is often the result of 'depression', a personal struggle related to the work itself but also to the scientist's relationship with research managers, colleagues and other actors. Kuhn made a somewhat similar point in an essay on creativity, stating, 'the ability to support a tension that can occasionally become almost unbearable is one of the prime requisites for the very best sort of scientific research' (Kuhn, 1963, p.342). This seems particularly oriented towards originality in research work; Kuhn names the phenomenon 'creative tensions'. These tensions arise from the work itself, and are not related to external demands or pressure. At the individual level, an even stronger point is made by Kwang (2001). On the basis of an empirical study of creativity among students, the author claims that creative people are dogmatic, conflict-seeking and not 'nice' in the sense that they are able to get along with other people with a minimal amount of friction. Earlier psychological investigations confirm this picture (cf. Hemlin, 1991).

However parts of the literature, and the majority of informants in my study, gave a completely different picture of creativity, which can be termed a *process of accord*. In my empirical statements, creativity is the result when ('creative') scientists are given a large amount of freedom, little interference and much general support from managers and outsiders, a positive and collaborative working climate and a fair amount of resources. Discord, for example in the form of tensions and conflicting demands or unfriendly people, was in these cases viewed as ruining creative performance. This fits well with a few other investigations; Jacobsen *et al.* (2001) may serve as a good example. In this questionnaire study it was concluded that a good working climate, pleasant atmosphere, mutual acceptance, positive assessments of differences and leadership were the central factors in creative research units. The general discussion about creativity, for instance in policy documents about science and innovation, also views this as something that should be encouraged and admired.

I will discuss this possible paradox and try to explain why both these perspectives may be useful, especially when viewed together to form a 'tension' perspective on research units and creativity. The following section elaborates on earlier studies where this perspective has been applied or developed, ending with a description of my empirical data. The next sections deal with originality in research work, followed by a discussion of creativity and how it can be influenced by factors in the research environment. Analyses of my informants' statements along with a balanced selection of quotations are used to elaborate and exemplify the argument. The final section aims to expand on the concept of tensions and how a fruitful balance of opposing forces is constantly challenged by individual preferences, group developments, management and policy initiatives and perhaps also by intrascientific processes.

TENSIONS AND CREATIVITY: EARLIER STUDIES

The response to the accord/discord paradox described in the introduction is that creative research units (and perhaps individuals as well) can, of course, be portrayed in both ways. Creative research environments can have a lot of 'positive' characteristics such as a supportive working climate and a high degree of freedom, but they may also be characterized in a 'negative' fashion by different forms of tensions and pressures. Some features may even be seen as both types, for instance high ambitions and expectations. Ambitions and expectations can be a source of inspiration for the individual researchers, but also a source of stress.

This was the main result of one of the earliest empirical investigations of productive research organizations (Pelz and Andrews [1966] 1976).[1] The authors adopt Kuhn's term 'creative tension' and discuss factors of 'challenge' and 'security' that together constitute tensions. They assert that all organizational aspects of research units may have a stabilizing and destabilizing side, and that both have to be present in order to create an environment that makes the individuals perform to the best of their ability. Research performance was found to be highest under conditions that seemed 'antithetical', such as simultaneous high levels of autonomy and dependency upon others: 'It seemed reasonable to say that the scientists and engineers of our study were more effective when they experienced a "creative tension" between sources of stability or security on the one hand and sources of disruption or challenge on the other' (ibid., p.xv).

Some of the most distinct tensions were related to time use (the researchers' distribution of time spent on non-administrative tasks across five different professional activities) and communication. Pelz and Andrews found that the highest performers in all types of settings devoted a relatively large share of their time to other activities than what could be described as the main goal of their laboratory or organizational unit. Effective scientists did not spend their time in basic science or in the world of application alone. Pelz and Andrews discuss seven broader tensions surrounding research units: science versus application, independence versus interaction, specialization versus breadth, autonomy versus external demands, influence on others versus control by others, intellectual harmony versus intellectual conflict and young versus old. The authors generally prescribe an approach to management and organization where these opposites are simultaneously supported.

One implication of balancing security and challenge could be that university departments/research groups can be described as 'nice places to work' without necessarily making high-quality research products (Jacobsen, 1990). Having a good and friendly working climate contributes to a feeling of security among the researchers, but does not provide the challenge necessary to produce very good research. It is perhaps typical that the literature that gives a more 'ideal' picture of good research units focuses almost exclusively on challenge factors; see, for example, Asmervik *et al.* (1997), who depict good research units as 'dynamic, demanding and courageous'.

Studies of innovation also focus on tensions, not least related to empirical investigations of innovativeness and creative climate. A creative climate questionnaire has been developed (cf. Ekvall *et al.*, 1983, applied for example in Mohamed and Rickards, 1996) with ten different dimensions. Some of the dimensions are 'positive', such as playfulness/humour, liveliness, trust and idea support, while others can be more 'negative' or 'destructive'. It has for instance been found that the dimension 'conflicts', that is the presence of 'personal and emotional tensions' (Mohamed and Rickards, 1996, p.113), can be beneficial to creative climates.

One last example can be taken from more general investigations of creativity per se. Following three interview studies, the largest one concerning industrial R&D scientists, Amabile (1988) has elaborated on environments that influence creativity. Not surprisingly, freedom appears at the top of the list of promoting factors while various types of constraints figure prominently on the list of inhibiting factors. More interesting in the study is the fact that the two aspects 'time pressure' and 'competition' appear on both the list of creativity inhibitors and the list of creativity promoters. Amabile concludes that 'a balanced amount of pressure is appropriate to creativity' (ibid., p.149). Also other issues require careful balancing acts, particularly reward systems and evaluation. Evaluation pressure and a strong presence of award systems for creativity can lead to reduced risk taking and motivation, and hence creativity, but the absence of evaluation and creativity rewards is not beneficial either. A large review of creativity research originating in psychology concluded that creativity always involves some kind of tension (Tardif and Sternberg, 1988). Such tensions can be envisaged in the process (stick to traditions or enter unknown ground), in the ideas themselves, as well as 'in the constant battle between unorganized chaos and the drive to higher levels of organization and efficiency within the individual, or the society at large' (ibid., p.431).

The findings mentioned here are perhaps not very surprising in light of recent developments in organization theory. Here terms like 'tension', 'ambiguity', 'friction' and 'paradox' have been popular for several decades, and a general preference is that tensions and dualities should be dynamically balanced and used to produce newness and inspiration (Evans, 1999). There may be a fundamental tension in all organizations between the need for efficiency, control and collective action, and the need for learning, renewal and individuality. There are many different perspectives or 'paradigms' in the realm of organization theory, all stating that some organizational elements and processes are more important than others, and thus, implicitly, frequently only centring on one 'side' of a tension. Many authors have argued that empirical investigations therefore need to incorporate several frameworks or views in order to capture a more complete picture of organizations, as each perspective most often gives a logically coherent but still insufficient view of organizational elements and processes. This also corresponds well with older perspectives in disciplines like psychology and anthropology, for example stress–performance studies and the 'equilibrium' approach of Gluckman (1968).

Discussing research evaluation and research environments, Foss Hansen (1995) has proposed a 'paradox perspective' in which the inconsistencies and paradoxes of organizations are defined as their central element, constituting an alternative to utilizing many different inconsistent or mutually exclusive perspectives simultaneously. She argues that all organizations can be characterized by contradictory traits, for example concerning tasks, processes and structures. These contradictions are elaborated as tensions that 'keep organisations breathing and alive' (ibid., p.41) because they 'release energy' and thus improve performance. It is claimed that organizational effectiveness in fact rests largely on the ability to maintain and manage the balance in relevant dichotomous dimensions. Hence research evaluations should, for instance, look for the existence of paradoxes and the ability of the organization to sustain them. Foss Hansen provides three examples of tensions in research organizations: norms of elitism versus norms of egalitarianism, international versus local integration and renewal versus the maintenance of current paradigms and problems. She underlines that the perspective seems fruitful both to get an improved understanding of organizations and to suggest methods for improving quality.

Dougherty (1996) has proposed a similar framework. Here 'tension' is the key word for understanding how innovation is organized. Dougherty distinguishes between four main types of tension: inside versus outside, old versus new, strategic determination (top-down) versus strategic emergence (bottom-up) and responsibility versus freedom. Innovation typically implies a focus on outside orientations, originality, emergent strategies and freedom, while the rest of the organization may be better served by an orientation towards the opposite. It is indicated that tensions stem from the activities themselves, but the theme is not elaborated much further. Dougherty stresses that tensions cannot be eliminated, but that they must be balanced throughout the organization as the activities of innovation extend beyond a project, and are inextricably bound up with the organization as a whole. Weick (1979) suggests that, even if the objective of the organizing process is to reduce ambiguity, some ambiguous features have to remain to make the organization able to survive the transition to a new and different future. Tension can furthermore be linked with theory on 'organizational learning', because learning is seen as disorganizing and increasing variety, while organizing implies forgetting and reducing variety (Weick and Westley, 1996). It is claimed that these two opposites should be connected (that is, maintaining the tension) and that a focus on informal organisational aspects is necessary to accomplish this.

To conclude this section, we have seen that a tension/paradox perspective is consistent with earlier findings in empirical studies of research units: good research organizations seem to be characterized by many such ambiguous aspects. These may be tied to aspects of creativity and research performance, but can also be seen as more fundamental aspects of learning and change in organizations. Still the tensions are often described at a conceptual or abstract level only (like elitism versus egalitarianism) and there is a need for more concrete empirical elaborations. This will be done in the following sections. Two other problems with the tension literature will be discussed at the end of the chapter. These are the many different and only partly synonymous terms that are used, and the somewhat 'normative' underpinnings in the literature that balanced tensions are constructive, energy releasing and stimulating.

Data Used in This Chapter

The empirical basis of the chapter is an interview study of research quality and organizational factors.[2] A total of 64 Norwegian senior researchers were interviewed from ten different disciplines: basic biomedicine, biotechnology, chemistry, clinical medicine, economics, engineering cybernetics, French language, mathematics, philosophy and sociology. The intention was to get at least two disciplines from all fields of learning (the humanities, social sciences, natural sciences, medicine and technology), partly to see if the relationship between organizational factors and creativity could be similar across different research settings. The informants represent universities (30), research institutes (22) and industry (12). Interviews were semi-structured around the theme of research quality and how this can be influenced, and lasted on average two hours.

My goal with the investigation was to find organizational aspects that promote and restrain the quality of research outputs, and I did not have any initial questions on tensions and similar characteristics. However such issues entered the discussion in most of the interviews. Earlier investigators have found that, in interviews (and other types of studies where researchers are asked their opinions), researchers tend to make 'ritualistic' references to the need for resources and other 'beneficial' aspects (cf. Martin and Skea, 1992). Despite a general message of autonomy and freedom, quite understandable from the creativity literature, my informants were surprisingly frank about many 'problematic' aspects of good research units. They mentioned many conflicts, dilemmas and tensions, and did not, for example, see a high degree of resources as a typical characteristic of good units. During the analysis phase, it was also found that tensions were a topic in many of the earlier empirical and theoretical investigations, without being a major issue or framework in most of the texts. The following, will elaborate on such aspects, using the empirical evidence to exemplify and elaborate.

Three assumptions lie behind the choice of method. First, research quality is largely a tacit concept, and explicating the tacit dimension may require a less structured method of gathering data. Second, research quality is defined by central researchers in each discipline, for example through decision making related to publications, projects and appointments. Third, organizational tensions may often be unrecognized and suppressed, thus requiring a careful and indirect collection of data. Concerning the last assumption, several investigations have found that subjective indicators of, for instance, a research unit's resources display stronger correlation with performance than more objective indicators (for example resource levels taken from budgets) (see, for instance, Harris and Kaine, 1994; Stolte-Heiskanen, 1979; Visart, 1979). The type of motivation and dedication of researchers may be a central influence on whether the organizational environment is seen as evocative or as a barrier to performance. Thus qualitative interviews are likely to yield useful information about research quality and relevant organizational characteristics. A major weakness is my focus on senior researchers: the elaboration of creative environments should be improved in later studies by also including other personnel categories.

My analytical approach follows long traditions in the social sciences. I have looked for broad similarities and differences in the statements of researchers, who were asked to talk about research quality and research organizations. The similarities and differences are initially taken at face value, that is, seen as a reflection of the motivations and actions of researchers. I have then constructed a more generalized version of creativity and its relationship with organizational factors. The NUDIST software package was applied in the data analysis. This was particularly helpful, as the relevant statements about creativity were found in many different discussions in the interviews, not only related to specific questions about it. Few 'revolutionary comments' emerge from the interviews, the researchers largely confirm earlier investigations concerning creativity. Their comments may nevertheless prove a useful guide to earlier findings, as well as being exemplars of a less frequently applied tension perspective.

ORIGINALITY, CREATIVITY AND QUALITY IN RESEARCH WORK

Taken for granted in much of the literature on science is that problems, claims and/or results should be new in one way or another. Science is a progressive or accumulating enterprise and a demand for originality is a necessary condition for renewal. Prestigious awards like the Nobel prize are to a large extent awarded on the basis of originality. It has even been suggested that the term 'quality' should be replaced by 'creativity', because the latter is central in research work (Premfors, 1986). Originality is also a key norm in the literature on norm systems in science (for example, Merton [1957] 1973), as well as a top-ranked attribute in earlier investigations of scientists' conceptions of research quality and use of quality criteria (cf. Chase, 1970; Hemlin and Montgomery, 1990; Hemlin, 1993; Kaukonen, 1997; Gulbrandsen and Langfeldt, 1997).

The literature suggests that there are degrees of originality in science, from providing new theories and discovering new phenomena to improving current theory and giving more precise descriptions of known phenomena (Buchholz, 1995). Distinctions can also be made between improving the fit between existing theory and observation, extending existing theory to new areas and collecting the concrete data required for the application and extension of existing theory (Kuhn, 1963). The concept is relative: originality is judged on the basis of current knowledge and, by definition, a certain result is only regarded as novel once. This is probably particular to science; the innovation literature often underscores the fact that an innovation only needs to be new to the adopting firm (see van de Ven 1986). The literature on creativity in science may therefore not always be generalized to other domains.

My informants gave many examples of originality. Two dimensions were emphasized in particular. First, we can distinguish between a theoretical or 'academic' novelty, and the original application of theories/methods to practical problems, the latter also important to many university professors. Second, many talked about degrees of originality with examples of both radical and incremental novelty. Originality was perceived as very important in all disciplines studied, and several of the informants stated that a lack of creativity is often a characteristic of mediocre or poor research units. In disciplines like philosophy and sociology, we found researchers who said that research may be 'too creative' and that there may be a 'narrow line between the genius and the madman'. In most of these cases, the informants added that originality detached or isolated from scholarly tradition often gets 'too wild' and fails to display 'critical originality'.

Originality, however, is not the only quality criterion in any of the studied disciplines. Only in rare cases of radically new theories or methodologies is originality by itself a sufficient criterion of 'good research', the informants stated. Other processes than creativity are of course also important in research organizations, a point to remember when discussing creative knowledge environments. Research outputs have to satisfy demands for solidity, which means that claims have to be substantiated. This includes aspects like stringent arguments, data quality and analytical depth. In addition the informants stressed that research has to be relevant, either to other researchers through being accumulative and/or general (scholarly relevance) or to various types of users (external relevance or utility).

Several tensions were described between the quality criteria. An often experienced dilemma is between solidity and originality. Systematic work and a thorough and long training contribute to solid results, but may hamper creativity, and thus reduce originality. Many also stated that some researchers are much more creative 'by nature', while others are conscientious and patient, and that people rarely combine these two features.

Originality and scholarly relevance may both presuppose each other and conflict with each other. Research which shows itself to be scholarly relevant by discovering general principles, filling holes in the stock of knowledge or opening new areas, is by definition also original. However scholarly relevance may also be judged in a narrower sense, based upon contemporary research trends. The research community does not always value the originality that implies breaking with prevailing traditions. This is close to Kuhn's (1963) notion of creative tension: creating something new that simultaneously 'absorbs' existing knowledge.

The relation between originality and utility also has more than one side. On the one hand, several informants emphasized that the potential utility is proportional to the degree of originality. A mathematician with relations to both university and institute sectors thought, 'Originality and utility most often are positively correlated, and the best researchers often are successful both in academia and in industry'. On the other hand, many informants claimed that 'unoriginal research' can be far more useful than original research. For example, 'yet another survey on living conditions' (a sociologist) can be important and useful, but is not especially original and perhaps not even regarded as 'research' in the stricter German and Scandinavian sense of the word. The negative relation seems particularly connected with short-term utility. Some emphasized that, the less original research projects are, the less future utility may be expected. Others said that demands for short-term utility result in less original research.

CREATIVITY: AN INDIVIDUAL CHARACTERISTIC ONLY?

Many studies of creativity and research performance have been carried out from a psychological perspective where 'inner motivation' and related concepts have been central. This has been called the 'sacred spark' theory (Cole and Cole, 1973) because of the focus on strong individual motivation, dedication or 'inner compulsion' to carry out research, even in the absence of external rewards. That the most eminent or productive researchers are a highly motivated group has been confirmed in several studies (for example Merton

[1968] 1973, Pelz and Andrews [1966] 1976; Harris and Kaine, 1994; also Andrews, 1979a, where motivation is seen as a characteristic of the research unit as a whole). High performers are generally much more dedicated to research work than to teaching, solving social/economic problems and other activities (Blau, 1973; Blackburn *et al.*, 1978; Bailey, 1994; Harris and Kaine, 1994).

More recent reviews tend to emphasize that the creative individual is but one of several necessary components in a long-lasting process (Tardif and Sternberg, 1988). There is still disagreement related to the significance of 'sudden insight' and how random the creative process is. One can also distinguish between different views on how rare creativity is: whether it is commonly available or only seen in special individuals in special contexts (with Edison, Freud and Einstein mentioned frequently). Inner motivation is still regarded as central: 'People will be most creative when they feel motivated primarily by the interest, enjoyment, satisfaction and the challenge of the work itself – not by external pressures' (Hennessey and Amabile, 1988, p.11). Expectations or promises of monetary or other tangible rewards in most cases will reduce the individual's inner motivation for the activity. It is not the reward in itself that functions this way, but rather the significance of making one's activities subject to a form of external control.

Also studies of research unit performance have found that expectancy of financial rewards has a negative influence on research performance (Spangenberg *et al.*, 1990). 'Threats' of upcoming evaluations have for instance been shown to undermine creativity in R&D laboratories (Amabile *et al.*, 1990). Similar negative effects on inner motivation and creativity have been found connected with supervision, time limits and evaluation (Hennessey and Amabile, 1988; see also the section on tensions, above). However, a few studies have shown that some individuals manage to view rewards as an additional motivational factor: good role models seem to be necessary for people to maintain inner motivation during varying circumstances (see ibid., pp.17–35, for a discussion of these studies). Furthermore it has been found that there are large variations between individuals (and even within individuals' careers) in what rewards are expected and how these influence productivity (Tien and Blackburn, 1996).

It can also be added that the researchers' inner motivation can influence how the environment is perceived. Less motivated individuals are more likely to see constraints and problematic aspects in their environment than those with high inner commitment to research (cf., for instance, Harris and Kaine, 1994, who found that 'objective' resource levels were perceived very differently by differently motivated economics professors). Finally motivation can be tied to issues other than creativity. An example is Andrews (1979b), who postulated and found a strong link between motivation and hard work/persistence.

Not all studies have used the 'sacred spark' perspective. Other investigations have, for example, found a relationship between performance and 'stamina' or the capacity to work hard in the pursuit of long-term goals. There is, furthermore, a set of studies looking at abilities such as IQ and grades from secondary school, and others that have concentrated on the cognitive, emotional and perceptual styles and work habits of scientists (see Reitan, 1996; Fox, 1992 for a review). In general, however, many of these investigations have failed to show significant relations between indicators of research excellence or performance and indicators of individual abilities. Because scientists are a highly select group of people, it is much harder to obtain significant correlation coefficients. This is perhaps the most straightforward explanation for the results, and in general one of the most problematic aspects of the literature that studies individual characteristics in search of explanations for performance differences: abilities and traits are not likely to be as unevenly distributed as productivity/performance (Fox, 1992). Even tests of creative abilities have failed to correlate with 'R&D innovativeness' as judged by peers (Pelz and Andrews [1966] 1976). Certain environmental factors have to be present for a creative ability to be transformed into an innovative output (Andrews, 1976; see also Fox, 1992). The studies clearly point to the necessity of viewing social and personal factors together. Personality traits do not exist in a vacuum, but are affected by the social environment in various ways. It should also be added that Amabile (1988) argues forcefully that personal factors like motivation, general intelligence, experience in the field and ability to think creatively are major influences on the output of creative ideas. She nevertheless argues that these traits are systematically used as criteria in hiring decisions in organizations where creativity is important and, hence, that the variation among individuals who exhibit relatively high levels of these qualities may be accounted for by factors in the work environment.

This is perhaps the clearest result from my informants as well. Despite the current rhetoric of group creativity and creativity techniques (to which many informants referred), almost all of them maintained that creativity is an individual trait, not a group phenomenon. Most of the informants, furthermore, explicitly or implicitly stated that creativity mainly is a 'given' characteristic of certain people, something that you are born with or that is made possible in early childhood. Nevertheless a few claimed that it is possible to learn how to be more creative, for instance by consciously attempting to be open towards new ideas. This openness does not come easily, but was rather seen as a personal struggle to be self-critical and to 'think innovatively'.

More than half of the informants, furthermore, claimed that creative researchers have nothing in common, and did not want to elaborate further (they were still probed for examples and so on). A chemist from the institute sector specified: 'I don't think you'd recognise them from behind. (...) They belong to all groups in society, all kinds of backgrounds.' Another institute researcher, from mathematics, problematized the question: 'This also has to do with your own ability to recognise creativity. Sometimes you're just not able to see it.' Nevertheless, from the final answers (after probes) I received, some typical traits of creative researchers emerge. They are 'by nature a little more difficult to control than others', and they have 'an unusually high level of energy' and productivity. An intense work effort was often elaborated, for example by a biotechnology professor: 'They're very difficult to describe, but I believe that they are extremely preoccupied with what they're doing. They have problems and puzzles in their subconscious for a long time, they ponder while they're skiing and things like that, they quite simply give it priority in their minds.'

A recurrent specification was the terms 'curiosity' and 'imagination', often coupled with other traits: 'Imagination, but combined with knowledge, and maybe audacity; some audacious people are extremely creative' (professor, engineering cybernetics). Openness to other fields, domains and ideas was another frequent comment, for instance from a mathematics professor: 'There's often a connection between being open and being creative. (...) It's a bit like Espen Askeladden [a famous figure from Norwegian folk tales], you gather something here and you gather something there, and maybe you'll find some use for it in the future.' This means that creative researchers are often not seen as very structured: 'They're ill-structured, and they easily transfer knowledge from one area to another' (an economist, institute).

However this does not mean that creative researchers are not knowledgable. On the contrary, the most common specification of all was that creativity is based on an extremely broad and/or in-depth knowledge of the relevant speciality. This confirms Simon's (1985) claim that the prior possession of relevant knowledge is a necessary condition for creativity, as it permits linkages and relations that would not have been considered without this knowledge. A cybernetics engineer from the institute sector said, 'A very profound and good understanding of your field is necessary to be creative. I used to believe that these untidy heads were creative, but (...) not anymore.' Creativity is thus not seen as random or accidental: 'Sometimes just before you fall asleep at night, something occurs to you. But that's always based on the knowledge that you already have' (a medical scientist, institute). A medical professor said, 'I like this idea about lateral thinking, that you have the ability to extrapolate from seemingly totally irrelevant things. Creativity in today's complexity depends upon good previous knowledge. Creative ideas don't strike as lightning just in any individual.' A few added that good researchers often have interests outside research, for instance in the arts. This was described as a potential source of creativity as well as a fruitful way of relaxing.

Some emphasized that creativity alone is insufficient to become a good researcher. A chemistry professor said, 'Creativity isn't enough, you need the will to test the ideas.' Another professor, from clinical medicine, made a similar point. He said that fruitfully creative scientists 'manage to *create* something. They don't just have an idea, but they're also able to implement it'. A sociology professor claimed that creativity is focused on too strongly, and he said that 'you can't sacrifice solidity and other quality aspects to get originality'. Although almost all informants described good researchers with terms like 'bright', 'clever', 'analytically sharp', 'intelligent' and so on, some also claimed that the most intelligent (and so on) individuals are not always very creative. Several of the informants were thus sceptical about judging potential post-doctoral and doctoral students on their grades, because these were not seen as an adequate reflection of the necessary skills and traits. The point was elaborated by a chemistry professor: 'It doesn't necessarily mean very much that you graduate with the best grades in the world. Very often we see that the grades don't mean much, it's more those skills that are very complex, the ability to do something to an idea and the will and capability of [seeing it through].' A biotechnology professor exemplified, 'good grades are a nice starting point, but not enough to become a good scientist. On the contrary, I would say in some cases. (...) The two or three best of my graduate students were too much "A4" [standard size sheet of paper] to become good scientists'.

Regarding individual traits other than creativity, a somewhat unexpected finding is the many strong claims made in the interviews about communication skills and 'general social skills'. Earlier studies often portray good scientists as not very preoccupied with people and not necessarily equipped with good interpersonal skills (Jackson and Rushton, 1987; Fox, 1992; Reitan, 1996). My informants clearly saw the 'ideal scientist' as quite sociable. One reason could be that the growth in group work and other types of collaboration has increased the need for researchers that are good not only at the research work per se. These communicative skills need to be given weight when hiring new researchers, it was claimed. Some informants were critical as to whether today's criteria and mechanisms for recruitment are able to capture interpersonal skills and abilities to a satisfactory extent.

As mentioned in the introduction to this chapter, some informants made more atypical comments. An institute researcher from clinical medicine said, 'I believe there are many more creative people among the depressed than among the happy psychopaths.' This statement constitutes a contrast to the many positive images of creative scientists as energetic, highly visible professionals. A few others emphasized that research groups need members who can play the devil's advocate or who otherwise contribute negative and/or highly critical comments even in the idea stages.

This latter point received a lot of general comments. Since not all (good) researchers are creative, this is an argument for diversity in research units; not all personnel need come up with new ideas. Some informants elaborated different personality types or group roles, like leaders versus 'others', creative versus thorough people, initiators versus people who 'carry things all the way through', visionaries or theorists versus more 'down-to-earth' or practically oriented workers, and extrovert versus introvert people. A medical researcher elaborated such dimensions at length: 'You need someone who's not original on the team who's willing to repeat boring tasks to get solid statistics and things like that, and of course the original people with crazy ideas. (...) You need some enthusiasts who can drive things forward and have dreams, but you need much more, and that is often overlooked, people who are depressed and negative and crabby and see dangers and difficulties all the time. And you need at least one parent with small kids who has to go home early to pick them up at the day nursery; if not you risk that a good working team wears itself out in no time.' Those who were concerned with such issues generally spoke about the inclusion of both 'opposites', or of the importance of considering such matters when hiring new researchers. When asked why diversity may be important, the informants mainly pointed at synergy effects and 'positive stress' factors like forcing oneself to present things more clearly and stringently. It is often a greater challenge to interact with people somewhat different from yourself, it was claimed. The same point applies to diversity of tasks. Many informants stated that involvement in other tasks (like teaching and supervision, collaboration with users, cross-sector cooperation) can create both strain and creativity by being intellectually challenging. On the other hand, this also generates time pressures that may or may not be seen as fruitful. The issues of diversity of people and tasks can be seen as organizational aspects, leading us to the next section, dealing with influences on creativity.

ORGANIZATIONAL INFLUENCES ON CREATIVITY

The literature on creativity defines autonomy as a fundamental prerequisite for creative work, as seen above (cf. Tardif and Sternberg, 1988; Hennessey and Amabile, 1988). Autonomy is often named as a basic characteristic of good research units, frequently in addition to a 'loose organizational structure' (for example, Pelz and Andrews [1966] 1976; Premfors, 1986). It can be expected that researchers generally do not like 'bureaucracy', particularly if it takes time away from the research activities (see Spangenberg *et al.*, 1990; Martin and Skea, 1992). However a strong focus on individual autonomy has also been described as typical of low-rated university departments (Andrews, 1979a; Bennich-Björkman, 1997) and poorly performing industrial and governmental R&D project units (Kim and Lee, 1995). It seems that, in high-performing units, autonomy is coupled with a common vision, strong group cohesiveness, active supportive leadership, an unusually high degree of interaction, or external pressure (for example, Pelz and Andrews [1966] 1976; Kim and Lee ,1995; Bennich-Björkman, 1997). Some authors have argued that researchers may use their autonomy for many other purposes than creating (good) research (Bennich-Björkman and Rothstein, 1991). Earlier studies also find that good project management, sufficient resources, encouragement, recognition, a climate marked by collaboration and a certain degree of challenge and pressure can be beneficial to creativity (cf. Amabile, 1988). On the constraints side, we find organizational disinterest, poor project management, evaluation, insufficient resources, time pressure, overemphasis on status quo and competition. It bears repeating that, although Amabile in general finds that individual traits are principal to creativity, the selection of relatively creative individuals for certain types of work (like research) implies that organizational factors may still account for much of the difference in creative output.

Some of my informants emphasized recruitment initiatives as the only practical way of promoting creativity. One chemistry professor, furthermore, stated that some people manage to be creative in extremely bad circumstances. To him, this did not imply that one should not try to promote creativity, but that the most creative and motivated scientists are able to flourish in almost any organizational environment. This was not indicated by any of the other informants. Most of the others talked about 'bureaucracy' and (poor) leadership as the main destructive aspects, and of freedom or autonomy and aspects of the organizational or research culture as beneficial to creativity. The answers are strikingly similar across sectors and disciplines. The processes by which creativity was reported to be influenced appear to be the same in all settings.

'Bureaucracy' in its popular sense was the most recurrent theme when discussing factors that destroy creativity. A medical scientist from a clinical institute, for instance, said, 'The standard way of killing all creativity nowadays is modern management, where you have to complete forms with goals and subgoals and plans for just about everything.' The source of such bureaucracy was often described as external to the institution, or at the department level and above: 'At the department level one technique of ruining creativity is to swamp people with bureaucratic trivialities' (a chemistry professor). Too 'strong' or top-down control was frequently mentioned as an aspect of a bureaucratic organization. A few added that reduced creativity rarely is intended. For instance, a professor of engineering cybernetics stated, 'a tight and inflexible organization surely restrains it, and I think that, in many R&D organisations, restrained creativity is an unintended consequence of other [goals]'. Needs/rights of students and university employees in general may be a source of rules and routines that have negative effects on creativity. Some also mentioned Research Council programmes as a source of bureaucracy, particularly as these often include non-researchers in the programme boards and regular ('bureaucratic') reporting demands.

Poor leaders/leadership was mentioned by about ten informants. An economist from the institute sector said, 'The conservative seniors that oppose all new ideas can very easily destroy creativity.' Regarding creativity, poor leaders are those who are too 'authoritarian', 'unpredictable' or 'conservative' both in organizational and in scholarly matters. 'Shifty and unpredictable leadership is occasionally worse than authoritarian', a medical professor exclaimed. However another medical scientist (institute) claimed that leaders often face a dilemma because 'young and inexperienced researchers often have poor ideas'. Encouraging the young may be difficult to combine with what this informant regarded as necessary criticism of poor ideas. 'If I sift good and bad ideas too much it's only my little brain that contributes to creativity, and that can't be the best for the unit', was a technology professor's judgment, indicative of the prevalent view that creativity has to do with producing ideas, while other skills contribute to exploiting the ideas.

It is interesting that, also in the open questions on leaders and leadership in the interviews, this was mainly viewed as a factor that does not influence quality and creativity a lot, or that has a negative influence only. There are probably many reasons for this (cf. Gulbrandsen, 2000, for a discussion). What is relevant for the discussion in this chapter is that some informants claimed that junior researchers have different needs for support, supervision and other (leadership) processes than the senior personnel. They indicated a tension based on varying needs between types of personnel, and a few claimed that managers (too) often adapt to the seniors' expectations of non-interference or 'screening' rather than the juniors' requirements of supportive leadership and balanced feedback. Also the juniors' needs can constitute a dilemma. About ten professors mentioned a difficult balance between support and criticism. A technology professor found it useful to be 'too kind' at the start of a PhD or post-doctoral project, and then increase the level of 'strictness' and critical feedback as the final deadline approached.

Organizational aspects that promote creativity are largely the opposite of what was described above. To most of the informants, freedom or autonomy is the antithesis of 'bureaucracy' and top-down control: 'You have to provide people with freedom, you can't be voted down every time you propose something new' (a medical scientist, institute). Many informants discussed the issue of autonomy versus other characteristics, which indicates an important tension or dilemma in the design of an efficient organization of research work. An economist from the institute sector said, 'If the decision-making structure is relatively flat, you can instigate some creativity among the researchers. (…) But of course you need some structure (…) we once applied for the same project from two different groups.' Some informants talked at length about the need for freedom, but also at the same time about effective coordination and efficient utilization of equipment and resources. 'You should have individual freedom to come up with ideas, start your own projects and select your collaborators. Group composition must be flexible, but resources, money, equipment, technicians and other support must be utilised optimally as well, also across traditional departmental boundaries' (clinical medicine, university). A similar tension was sketched by a biotechnology professor: 'A loose structure is particularly important, it does much to creativity and results in really good and original research. But it does not always make the department the best suited for external contracts, and we struggle with that, because it is not always popular in industry that wishes we were organised in a more structured way.' It should be added that this professor saw industrial funding as fundamental for all the department's research activities.

Autonomy and freedom were often tied to the organizational culture and the working climate, which preferably should be open and tolerant. A professor of economics stated, 'The organization can't be too dogmatic, it has to be open to new ideas', and a sociologist (institute) said that the central element is 'tolerance – you get so easily pushed down by formal demands'. Tolerance was mainly tied to being able to do 'stupid' things, which was seen as a precondition for creativity by many. An economist from industry said, 'It's (…) trust and encouragement and so on. One must be allowed to act a bit stupid, (…) or rather to try the opposite of what's common without being regarded as stupid.' The same was specified by a chemist in the institute sector: 'If people feel insecure, unsafe, they won't be creative. You need tolerance and generosity.' This implies that lack of tolerance can be negative: 'What may restrain [creativity] is the fear of making a fool of yourselves. You should always remember people for the best they did and not for the blunders they've made, and judge them on their best work' (an economics professor). Only a few of the informants made more 'negative' comments about the working climate and other informal organizational characteristics. These all said that a 'certain degree' of internal competition may be good for creativity. However two scientists also discussed negative effects of 'too hard internal competition'.

When asked why informal aspects are important, a majority pointed to the motivation of the unit members. A medical professor said that because 'Basic research demands an enormous dedication and it demands mutual enthusiasm,' the informal aspects are central. Informants from all disciplines and institutional settings mentioned this relationship. 'If you feel part of a team, (…) it can give you more inspiration', a philosophy professor maintained. It may thus be claimed that, where there is no formal teamwork, the informal sense of belonging and of collegiality becomes even more central. Some also mentioned that a good working climate makes it easier to cope with the downsides of international interaction. A professor of clinical medicine elaborated: 'People work best, and now I think mainly of doctoral students, in a unit where they get a suitable blend of challenge and support. You do get large challenges from the international research community (…). So we can be more on the support side here, because [we are] the base from which our young people go out into the world and present, write and do their projects. [And they] return here to lick their wounds, and they get encouraged to go out there again.'

Other informants said that a sense of humour, non-scholarly interaction and friendliness were aspects of the organizational climate that helped relieve the stress of ambitious professional work: 'We go home (…) early [in Norway], while elsewhere they go to the pub together with colleagues and drink beer (…). And for research, beer drinking would be better' (clinical medicine, institute). This informant did not want to switch, he said it was a 'choice' of values, which also indicates that (of course) not all scientists have ambitions of becoming 'eminent' and/or displaying unusual amounts of creativity.

Time was also mentioned by a considerable proportion of respondents, not least in the applied sectors where researchers often get tied up in projects with very specific goals and methods. A chemist in industry said, 'You should leave some slack to be able to test out new ideas. If you can't test out new ideas all creativity will be killed.' The same argument was stated by a chemist in another company, who underlined, 'I don't think creativity can be learned, but I think it's important that you (…) at least have the time and the right conditions to be creative.' The 'right conditions' were elaborated in terms of, for example, how much of the individuals' time should be 'free', that is, not allocated to any specific projects. Some basic researchers also made this point, praising sabbaticals in this respect. An economist from a research institute stated laughingly, 'At least I have to *believe* that I have some freedom and some time to exploit it.'

A few informants suggested communication as beneficial when asked about influences on creativity. 'You need active professional discussions to promote creativity', a sociology professor maintained. 'It has to do with communication – to have good seminars and lunchtime discussions about big problems, not details,' a mathematics professor elaborated. A very high degree of interaction was generally seen as a fundamental aspect of good research units, and not particularly related to creativity. 'Collaboration, collegiality (…) I believe it is very important, without well-being both work effort and productivity decrease. When you have team spirit and chemistry between people in the department and on the project, everything goes much easier' (mathematics. industry). A cybernetics engineer from the institute sector said that the organizational culture 'influences collaboration which is at the heart of good research', and a professor of the same discipline talked about 'synergy effects' of having a common culture and a good working climate.

It was repeatedly stressed that the working climate and the relationship between the research unit members affect the level of communication. An economist in the institute sector said, 'If you have a nice social climate you feel better and then it's easier to go and ask others for help and advice.' A similar argument was made by a professor of French language: 'People must not only have [professional] respect for each other but also sympathy. (...) Because the other then feels recognised and you get a scholarly discussion and exchange.' In my interviews, there are hardly any examples of units with non-collaborative or 'hostile' climates that produce good research, but a few claimed that a good climate does not necessarily lead to good research. A few also stated that communication involves tension. As scientific communication is a form of social exchange (and thus involves a certain friction), it carries with it expectations of reciprocity and balance that constitute a source of challenge rather than security for many researchers. A few institute researchers saw their dual links with universities and users as a source of creative tensions.

Two natural scientists from the same private company mentioned a prize for creativity that is awarded annually to a researcher in the firm (the same informants talked negatively about 'brainstorming' and similar attempts at increasing group creativity). Other traditional quality assurance mechanisms, like commenting on your colleagues' manuscripts, were not seen as an influence on creativity. A sociologist in the institute sector said, 'We read and comment on each other's manuscripts, that's a duty (...) and we also have some kind of board of editors for our own publications. That's excellent, but a bit controversial because people think that too little is done to assure quality in earlier phases of the research process.' Even the creativity prizes that were mentioned above are awarded ex post. It is probably natural that the first phase of the research process should be the most autonomous and the least bureaucratic, hence few formal quality routines in the idea phase make sense. Several comments from the informants indicate, however, that research units are on the constant lookout for tools that can enhance creativity and increase the number of ideas, despite their disappointment with brainstorming and similar techniques.

It is interesting to note that formal organizational aspects like the level of resources (apart from time resources) and size of research units were hardly mentioned at all in the discussion of creativity. My informants emphasized that a certain level of resources is needed to be able to do research at all, but that you can never 'buy' creativity with a lot of funding, even in disciplines that demand expensive equipment and a fair size. Several gave examples of their own or other people's creative work that had been done with few resources and 'old-fashioned' equipment. The informants generally wanted research units to be 'sufficiently' large to promote increased personnel stability and steady access to funding, but small enough to avoid fission and subgroups. Margins seem to be quite wide, however: for instance, 'more than two' and 'less than ten' scientists in the group. A few applied researchers mentioned a dilemma in formal promotion criteria: should the best researchers become research unit leaders or should these positions be reserved for people with more management ambitions? Two expressed the view that it is an advantage to keep the best researchers full-time with concrete scientific/technological work, but also stated that this could yield leaders who fail to recognize and support creativity.

CONCLUDING DISCUSSION: CREATIVITY AND ORGANIZATIONAL TENSIONS

This chapter started out by linking creativity to various types of organizational tensions, followed by a literature review and an empirical investigation of originality, creativity and organizational aspects. My informants pointed out tensions and strain factors at many points in the discussion of good research units. Some of the most frequently mentioned in all settings (university, institute, industry; different disciplines) were the following:

- autonomy/freedom versus structure/control,
- social support versus critical professional feedback,
- ambiguous leadership role (non-interference/screening versus more active role),
- diversity of people and tasks (creates more challenging interaction, intellectual trials, a certain time pressure),
- high degree of professional communication (a tension in itself for example through demands of reciprocity and balance in social exchange),
- positive drive towards larger units versus advantages of being small.

These tensions were to some degree tied to creativity, but they reflect perhaps even more the fact that creativity alone is insufficient to produce good research. Scientific quality also depends upon processes that contribute to relevance and solidity – quality criteria that conflict somewhat with originality. In addition tensions can be linked with the maintenance of motivation and inspiration, not least for researchers early in their careers. At the heart of this issue is the balance between challenge and support. Some informants gave examples of talented PhDs and postdoctoral researchers who 'wasted' their skills and abilities in a research unit that only provided challenge or only provided support. This blend of challenge and support is most likely important for senior researchers as well, but they may to a larger extent assume responsibility for it as well as finding themselves in a 'virtuous circle' in this respect. The early years in a scientist's career were described by some as crucial for the quality of future research products, or for the desire to do scientific work at all. Because formal systems for taking care of young researchers are often lacking, much can depend on colleagues and not least on one's supervisor/mentor. As Thagaard (1991) has described, one can perhaps sketch a mutually reinforcing process in early years between motivation and the support from the organization, and subsequent creative involvement in science.

Autonomy versus control is probably the tension most directly tied to creativity per se. This is likely to involve a continuous balancing act in many research organizations. The autonomy that promotes creativity and security could and should lead to risky ideas, which on the other hand may elicit organizational responses and resistances that undermine autonomy and security. It can be added that the informants gave a picture of some good research units as 'tension-seekers', for instance by aiming to employ somewhat different people, focusing on an array of professional tasks and by combining strong social support with ambitious standards and expectations of international excellence. Tension, furthermore, is not the same as personal conflicts. Severe personal conflicts were unanimously seen as disastrous and destructive to the working climate of an otherwise possibly good unit. Scholarly disagreement is, of course, not negative unless it escalates into a clear personal conflict.

Finally a short discussion of the term 'tension' as opposed to the very popular terms 'paradox' and 'ambiguity' in management and organization studies can be fruitful. As indicated in my discussion of tensions at the beginning of the chapter, I see paradox and ambiguity as conceptual terms dealing with tensions at an abstract level. Two examples are elitism versus egalitarianism and stability versus change. More generally, paradox denotes contradictory ideas or beliefs that are simultaneously held to be 'true', while ambiguity may refer to multiple rather than strictly antithetical interpretations of phenomena. 'Tensions', as I have used the term throughout the chapter, is an empirical concept and is the subjective embodiment of paradoxes and ambiguities, and also friction/resistance and conflicts of interest, in research units. Thus the concept is related to the way individuals and groups interpret their wider organizational surroundings. The subjectivity of tensions is central and it demands advanced research methods in later investigations that seek to focus on organizational tensions. This also means that tensions may appear as creative or destructive relative to individual characteristics and norms in the research units.

Later investigations may want to measure tensions in a way similar to that by which other organizational constructs are measured, such as 'organizational culture' or 'creative climate'. The dichotomies of Pelz and Andrews ([1966] 1976) could prove a good starting point (see the section 'Tensions and creativity', above). A tension perspective turns some traditional ideas from organization theory upside-down. One traditional idea is seeing an organization as a stable or balanced system that will only change when the external conditions make it impossible to continue in the same manner (this is a governing idea in strategic management and other disciplines, cf., for example, Gluckman, 1968). The tension perspective focuses instead on the way in which the internal level of 'balance' along various dimensions may decrease over time and make changes necessary in order to remain creative, motivated, productive and so on. Behind the claim that organizational tensions need to be balanced or maintained lies perhaps an assumption that there is a curvilinear relationship between performance and tension (which corresponds well, for instance, to the stress–performance curve studies known from psychology). This was found in Pelz and Andrews ([1966] 1976) but has not been much focused on since, and could be the theme of future studies.

Åkerman (1998) claims that the 'modern rationality project' is based on removing obstacles like tensions and friction, believing in perfection and efficiency. This can perhaps also be seen as the continuing goal of the scientific endeavour, which then carries a difficult duality with it: to solve puzzles and problems, yet maintain an ambivalent stance towards the knowledge that is produced. However the normative underpinning in literature on organizational paradoxes, friction, ambiguities and tensions is that these should *not* be removed but rather 'maintained' or 'balanced' to allow for flexibility, change, learning and creativity. Although these suggestions may sound a bit simplistic, they are well reflected in many of the informants' statements made in this study. Remarks such as 'not too small, not too large', 'different people but not too different', 'freedom but we need *some* structure', 'a good mix of collaboration and competition' are not naïve expressions of moderation and a 'golden mean', but rather highlight a strong emphasis on balance between the various forces in research organizations. As Pelz and Andrews ([1966] 1976) argued, it is possible to promote tensions by focusing leadership efforts on a balanced support for organizational aspects and developments that may seem counter to each other. Still it can also be argued that many of the creative tensions develop in good research units without conscious leadership attention, as a result of characteristics like high scientific ambitions, international orientation, diversity and scholarly criticism.

Researchers are probably not very different from other professionals in that they need a blend of challenge and support to remain motivated and productive. What is particular about researchers is that they have a dual membership, representing both an institution (university, institute, company) and a discipline or speciality. A balance of opposing forces therefore does not have to be seen as something 'internal' to research units. As many informants noted, they saw a good working climate as a secure haven that balances the challenges the unit members encounter in their interactions with the international research community and perhaps in other arenas as well. In addition, to maintain diversity of people and tasks, to work with several time perspectives in mind and to have high professional ambitions is, as mentioned, most likely a tremendous challenge to individuals who often may prefer stability, predictability and less uncertainty. For most of my informants, a decent local working climate was seen as a good way to cope with this.

It can be argued that achieving a good balance is very difficult. Individual researchers probably have many different preferences, but some may desire organizational surroundings that are less uncertain and ambiguous than is desirable from a creativity viewpoint. A well-known feature of many research and development organizations is the 'Not-Invented-Here' syndrome (Katz and Allen, 1982). This group process, the tendency for a group of stable composition to believe it possesses a monopoly of knowledge of its field, can contribute to the dominance of single perspectives and perceptions rather than maintaining a balance between opposing views. New ideas from outsiders are rejected, to the detriment of creative performance. Political processes, for example if the senior researchers' views on, and needs for, leadership determine the leadership style and activities in a research unit, can also lead to reduced tension.

More generally, Rochlin (1998) claims that most modern management ideologies, including the ones behind public policy, have a 'neo-Taylorism' resonance, particularly the belief that there is 'one best way' to perform any task. This means that the focus is on removing obstacles, even if these have positive benefits. It has been argued that policy goals and techniques of standardization and best-practice can be considered as 'grandiose attempts' at minimizing tensions and frictions (Nowotny, 1998). The end result may be lessened pluralism or heterogeneity, one of the prime sources of tension in the research system as a whole. It is unclear how the development of 'post-academic science' with increased demands of utility and accountability (see Ziman, 2000) may affect tensions in research organizations as a whole. Following Rochlin (1998), it could be argued that some of the change processes related to increased monitoring and top-down control contribute to reducing creative tensions. More research is needed on these issues.

There are also intrascientific processes that can contribute to removing tensions or making it difficult to achieve a good balance. One example is the Matthew effect (cf. Merton [1968] 1973). This effect implies an accrual of recognition to scientists of considerable repute, and lesser recognition to those of limited repute. Eminent scientists are particularly favoured: both in collaboration and in multiple discovery, disproportionate credit is given to the already eminent. Merton thus seems to indicate that the process of cumulative advantage has negative effects, that it is non-meritocratic. The repetitive strengthening of authority implied in this process and, thus, the increased difficulties for new entrants or alternative approaches, may also lead to reduced heterogeneity. In addition the increasing specialization in research work and, hence, more limited contact with neighbouring disciplines creates a set of conditions where creative tensions perhaps are of less and less importance. When the researchers to a lesser extent are challenged or informed by perspectives from other specialities, this may reduce the conditions for creativity that Simon (1985) describes. Policy mechanisms like centres of excellence and increased competition for funding probably contribute to some of these processes.

Maintaining organizational tensions implies sustaining forces that play both a stabilizing and a destabilizing role. On the one hand, frictions and tensions destabilize interactions, sweep away social capital and open up new pathways of development (Nowotny, 1998). Yet tensions and frictions also have a stabilizing side as they slow down the decision process and make for a slower, yet more creative and holistic, development process (Rochlin, 1998). A focus on quality and creativity in science thus demands a shift in the focus from the efficiency with which research organizations carry out their tasks to the nature of the outcomes.

NOTES

1. The discussion of tensions occurs mainly in the introduction to and new chapters in the second edition of this book, published in 1976 (the original appeared ten years earlier).
2. For a longer discussion of the methodology of the investigation, as well as a longer treatise on aspects of good research units, cf. Gulbrandsen (2000).

BIBLIOGRAPHY

Åkerman, N. (1998), 'A free-falling Society? Six introductory notes', in N. Åkerman (ed.), *The Necessity of Friction*, Boulder, CO: Westview Press, pp.3–27.
Amabile, T.M. (1988), 'A model of creativity and innovation in organizations',

Research in Organizational Behavior, **10**, 123–67.

Amabile, T.M., P. Goldfarb and S. Brackfield (1990), 'Social influences on creativity: evaluation, coaction and surveillance', *Creativity Research Journal*, **3**, 6–21.

Andrews, F.M. (1976), 'Creative process', in D.C. Pelz and F.M. Andrews (eds), *Scientists in Organizations. Productive Climates for Research and Development*, Ann Arbor, M1: Institute for Social Research University of Michigan. pp.337–65.

Andrews, F.M. (ed.) (1979a), *Scientific Productivity. The Effectiveness of Research Groups in Six Countries*, Cambridge and Paris: Cambridge University Press and Unesco.

Andrews, F.M. (1979b), 'Motivation, diversity, and the performance of research units, in F.M. Andrews (ed.), *Scientific Productivity. The Effectiveness of Research Groups in Six Countries*, Cambridge and Paris: University Press and Unesco, pp.253–89.

Asmervik, S., B. Cold and B. Reitan (1997), 'The life of good research units', report, The Scientific Advisory Board of the Swedish Council for Building Research, BVN 1997:3, Stockholm.

Bailey, J.G. (1994), 'Influences on researchers' commitment', *Higher Education Management*, **6**, 163–77.

Bennich-Björkman, L. (1997), *Organising Innovative Research: The Inner Life of University Departments*, Oxford: IAU/Pergamon Press.

Bennich-Björkman, L. and B. Rothstein (1991), 'A creative university: is it possible?' report, Council for Studies of Higher Education and Research, 1991:4, Stockholm.

Blackburn, R.T., C.E. Behymer and D.E. Hall (1978), 'Research note: correlates of faculty publications', *Sociology of Education*, **51**, 132–41.

Blau, P.M. (1973), *The Organization of Academic Work*, New York: John Wiley and Sons.

Buchholz, K (1995), 'Criteria for the analysis of scientific quality', *Scientometrics*, **32**, 195–218.

Chase, J.M (1970), 'Normative criteria for scientific publication', *American Sociologist*, **5**, 262–5.

Cole, J.R. and S. Cole (1973), *Social Stratification in Science*, Chicago, IL: University of Chicago Press.

Dougherty, D. (1996), 'Organizing for innovation', in S.R. Clegg, C. Hardy and W.R. Nord (eds), *Handbook of Organization Studies*, London: Sage Publications, pp.424–39.

Ekvall, G., J. Arvonen and I. Waldenström-Lindblad (1983), 'Creative organizational climate. Construction and validation of a measuring instrument', report, The Swedish Council for Management and Work Life Issues, Stockholm.

Evans, P.A L. (1999), 'HRM on the edge: a duality perspective', *Organization*, **6**, 325–38.

Foss Hansen, H. (1995), 'Organizing for quality – a discussion of different evaluation methods as means for improving quality in research', *Science Studies*, **8**, 36–43.

Fox, M.F. (1992), 'Research productivity and the environmental context', in T.G. Whiston and R.L. Geiger (eds), *Research and Higher Education. The United Kingdom and the United States*, Buckingham: SRHE/Open University Press, pp.103–11.

Gluckman, M. (1968), 'The utility of the equilibrium model in the study of social change', *American Anthropologist*, **70**, 219–37.

Gulbrandsen, M. (2000), 'Research quality and organizational factors: an investigation of the relationship', Dr.ing thesis 90/2000, Department of Industrial Economics and Technology Management, Norwegian University of Science and Technology, Trondheim.

Gulbrandsen, M. and L. Langfeldt (1997), 'Hva er forskningskvalitet? En intervjustudie blant norske forskere', Rapport 9/97, NIFU, Oslo.

Harris, G. and G. Kaine (1994), 'The determinants of research performance: a study of Australian university economists', *Higher Education*, **27**, 191–201.

Hemlin, S. (1991), 'Quality in science. Researchers' conceptions and judgments', Department of Psychology, University of Gothenburg.

Hemlin, S. (1993), 'Scientific quality in the eyes of the scientist: a questionnaire study', *Scientometrics*, **27**, 3–18.

Hemlin, S. and H. Montgomery (1990), 'Scientists' conceptions of scientific quality: an interview study', *Science Studies*, **3**, 73–81.

Hennessey, B.A. and T.M. Amabile (1988), 'The conditions of creativity', in R.J. Sternberg (ed.), *The Nature of Creativity. Contemporary Psychological Perspectives*, Cambridge: Cambridge University Press.

Jackson, D.N. and J.P. Rushton (eds) (1987), *Scientific Excellence. Its Origins and Assessment*, Newbury Park, CA: Sage Publications.

Jacobsen, B. (1990), *Universitetsforsker i Danmark*, Copenhagen: Nyt fra Samfundsvidenskaberne.

Jacobsen, B., M.B. Madsen and C. Vincent (2001), *Danske forskningsmiljøer. En undersøgelse af universitetsforskningens aktuelle situation*, Copenhagen: Hans Reitzels Forlag.

Katz, R. and T.J. Allen (1982), 'Investigating the Not Invented Here (NIH) syndrome: a look at the performance, tenure and communication patterns of 50 R&D project groups', *R&D Management*, **12**, 7–19.

Kaukonen, E. (1997), 'Science policy and research evaluation facing the diversity of science', in M. Hyvärinen and K. Pietilä (eds), *The Institutes We Live By*, Publications 17/1997, Tampere: University of Tampere, Research Institute for Social Sciences, pp.167–201.

Kim, Y. and B. Lee (1995), 'R&D project team climate and team performance in Korea: a multidimensional approach', *R&D Management*, **25**, 179–96.

Kuhn, T.S. (1963), 'The essential tension: tradition and innovation in scientific research', in C.W. Taylor and F. Barron (eds), *Scientific Creativity*, New York: John Wiley and Sons, pp.341–54.

Kwang, N.A. (2001), 'Why creators are dogmatic people, "nice" people are not creative, and creative people are not 'nice''', *International Journal of Group Tensions*, **30** (4), 293–325

Martin, B.R. and J.E.F. Skea (1992), 'Academic research performance indicators: an assessment of the possibilities', report to the Advisory Board for the Research Councils and the Economic and Social Research Council, Swindon, ESRC.

Merton, R.K. ([1957] 1973), 'Priorities in scientific discovery', reprinted in *The Sociology of Science: Theoretical and Empirical Investigations*, Chicago and London: University of Chicago Press, pp.286–324.

Merton, R.K. ([1968] 1973), 'The Matthew effect in science', reprinted in *The Sociology of Science*, Chicago and London: University of Chicago Press, pp.439–59.

Mohamed, M.Z. and T. Rickards (1996), 'Assessing and comparing the innovativeness and creative climate of firms', *Scandinavian Journal of Management*, **12** (2), 109–21.

Nowotny, H. (1998), 'Rediscovering friction: not all that is solid melts into air', in N. Åkerman (ed.), *The Necessity of Friction*, Boulder, CO: Westview Press, pp.287–311.

Pelz, D.C. and F.M. Andrews (eds) ([1966] 1976), *Scientists in Organizations. Productive Climates for Research and Development*, rev. edn, Ann Arbor, MI: Institute for Social Research, University of Michigan.

Premfors, R. (1986), 'Forskningsmiljön i högskolan – en kunskapsöversikt', report no. 36, Group for the Study of Higher Education and Research Policy, University of Stockholm.

Reitan, B. (1995), 'Creativity and innovation in research groups – a literature review', Swedish Council for Building Research, Scientific Advisory Board, BVN 1996:3, Stockholm.

Rochlin, G.I. (1998), 'Essential friction: error-control in organizational behavior', in N. Åkerman (ed.), *The Necessity of Friction*, Boulder, CO: Westview Press, pp.132–63.

Simon, H.A. (1985), 'What we know about the creative process?', in R.L. Kuhn (ed.), *Frontiers in Creative and Innovative Management*, Cambridge, MA: Ballinger, pp.3–20.

Spangenberg, J.F.A., R. Starmans, Y.W. Bally, B. Breemhaar, F.J.N. Nijhuis and C.A.F. van Dorp (1990), 'Prediction of scientific performance in clinical medicine', *Research Policy*, **19**, 239–55.

Stolte-Heiskanen, V. (1979), 'Externally determined resources and the effectiveness of research units', in F.M. Andrews (ed.), *Scientific Productivity. The Effectiveness of Research Groups in Six Countries,* Cambridge and Paris: Cambridge University Press and Unesco, pp.121–53.

Tardif, T.Z. and R.J. Sternberg (1988), 'What do we know about Creativity?', in R.J. Sternberg (ed.), *The Nature of Creativity. Contemporary Psychological Perspectives*, Cambridge: Cambridge University Press, pp.429–40.

Taylor, C.W. and F. Barron (eds) (1963), *Scientific Creativity: Its Recognition and Development*, New York: John Wiley and Sons.

Thagaard, T. (1991), 'Research environment, motivation and publication productivity', *Science Studies*, **4**, 5–18.

Tien, F.F. and R.T. Blackburn (1996), 'Faculty rank system, research motivation and faculty research productivity', *Journal of Higher Education*, **67**, 2–22.

van de Ven, A.H. (1986), 'Central problems in the management of innovation', *Management Science*, **32**.

Visart, N. (1979), 'Communication between and within research units', in F.M. Andrews (ed.), *Scientific Productivity. The Effectiveness of Research Groups in Six Countries,* Cambridge and Paris: Cambridge University Press and Unesco, pp.223–52.

Weick, K.E. (1979), *The Social Psychology of Organizing*, 2nd edn, Reading, MA: Addison-Wesley.

Weick, K.E. and F. Westley (1996), 'Organizational learning: affirming an oxymoron', in S.R. Clegg, C. Hardy and W.R. Nord (eds), *Handbook of Organization Studies*, London: Sage Publications, pp.440–58.

Ziman, J. (2000), *Real Science. What It Is, and What It Means*, Cambridge: Cambridge University Press.

3. Changing academic research environments and innovative research*

Mika Nieminen

Numerous changes have taken place in the academic research environment during recent decades. Because of profound economic, political and cultural changes, the whole research system seems to be in flux, ranging from governmental policies to the reorganization of research. These transformations have also provoked wide debate over the possible consequences of changes for scientific research.[1] There has, however, been relatively little debate on whether such obvious changes as increasing external funding and short-term project work undermine the potential for the best possible quality in scientific work.

In the following I approach this question tentatively from the perspective of innovativeness, which is usually considered as one of the focal, if not the major, hallmarks of high-standard academic research (Gulbrandsen, 2000; Hemlin and Montgomery, 1990). It can be claimed that, besides individual characteristics, organizational characteristics and processes such as resources and organizational communication affect the likelihood of innovativeness. The environment may be an even more salient factor for researchers than individual factors in innovativeness (Amabile, 1994; Hurley, 1997). If so, what kinds of consequences might one expect in academic research from the perspective of innovativeness when the research environment changes? Have the changes in research environments perhaps diminished possibilities for conducting high-standard research?

The first section of the chapter deals with innovativeness theoretically. The section is heuristic, addressing the question, how should we understand the phenomenon called innovativeness in science? The following sections approach the above-mentioned questions empirically by reinterpreting some recent research results concerning Finnish universities (Nieminen, 2003; Nieminen and Kaukonen, 2001, 2003) from the perspective of the innovative research organization. The data comprise the results of a survey that was sent out to the heads of university departments and research units in Finland

(n=369), and 19 semi-structured interviews with senior researchers in university departments and research units that cooperate on a continuous basis with non-academic partners.[2] The analysis is framed by the assumption that the major changes that took place in the Finnish science and technology system during the 1990s also affected the organizational dynamics under which researchers have to operate. Accountability pressures increased throughout the system, university research became predominantly financed by external, competitive sources and researchers were urged to pay more attention to the utility aspects of knowledge (for more details, see Nieminen and Kaukonen, 2001, 2003).

The problem is complex and does not open up to easy conclusions. My argument is that changing research environments in Finland have had both detrimental and positive consequences for the development of research. By approaching these changes from the perspective of freedom in research, research cooperation and problems of research organization, only a little evidence can be found that changes would have had major detrimental effects on research. On the other hand, some problems have indeed resulted from these changes, and the analysis provokes further research questions concerning the relationship between changing research environments and the dynamics of scientific research.

INNOVATIVENESS AND HIGH-STANDARD RESEARCH

In general, innovativeness can be defined as creative activity that produces new and/or unique scientific knowledge and applications.[3] Much of the literature on creativity in science represents psychological research in which the focus is usually on personal traits and qualities (such as motivation and IQ) or on such environmental factors as upbringing and school experiences (Jackson and Rushton, 1987; cf. Taylor and Barron, 1963). It is evident, however, that innovativeness is also an attribute of a social system that makes judgments about individuals. In the arts the criteria for innovativeness are different from those in science. Therefore it is as important to study the symbolic and cultural environment in which the criteria for innovativeness are embedded as well as individual traits of creativity.

Mihaly Csikszentmihalyi (1990, pp.200–208) proposes that creativity is actually the result of the interaction among the social subsystems that he calls a domain, a field and a person. In his vocabulary a domain is 'any symbolic system that has a set of rules for representing thought and action'. A domain specifies mental or physical performances, preserves desirable performances and transmits them to new generations of people to learn. For example, music, religion or football is a domain. In order to apply Csikszentmihalyi's ideas to science, any field of science or subspeciality would be a domain. The domain functions as a source of knowledge and practices for individuals to be trained in a certain discipline or subspeciality. They are socialized to the norms and values upheld by the domain and they learn to distinguish between relevant and irrelevant knowledge in that particular domain. The domain is not a totally self-sufficient entity but its existence is affected by society's varying needs for knowledge, the valuation of knowledge and what is generally considered as an acceptable and usable form of knowledge. Naturally the effects are not unidirectional, but science and its development affect the surrounding society as well.

The field, in turn, is 'that part of the social system that has the power to determine the structure of the domain'. The field consists of knowledgable people who have the power and possibility to define what kind of mental or physical performances belong to a domain. A field has a gate-keeping function: it assesses and selects those works that might be valued as creative. In relation to the existing stock of knowledge, the position of peers and established scientists is decisive in science. They decide whether the produced piece of knowledge shows such qualities that it can be accepted for preservation in the domain, and whether it shows originality or creativity. It is also typical that there is no general consensus on the uniqueness of certain results or ideas, but even bitter debates and quarrels may emerge over their value (cf. Bourdieu, 1988).

The person brings a dynamic dimension into the model. Even though innovativeness is understood as a social phenomenon, personal qualities, knowledge, skills and motivation also have an important role to play. Currently some scholars understand creativity as part of a wider phenomenon that is called 'giftedness'. Giftedness includes, among others, such factors as motivation, personality, intelligence, creativity and affective and motor abilities. Gifted persons may become, in turn, talents in some specific domain through learning and practising if environmental factors support their development (Gagné, 1995; Uusikylä, 1996, pp.66–70). In science an innovative researcher is, besides being well trained and knowledgable concerning his field, likely to have such personal characteristics as insistence and strong intrinsic motivation in research (Hurley, 1997).

An essential point in the model described above is that scientific innovativeness is not only a personal quality, but a phenomenon that develops in the interaction of the field of science, peers and individuals. Also institutional arrangements for science and society's knowledge needs as well as culture provide for constructing and sustaining a system that makes innovativeness possible.

Innovativeness is, then, a relational concept. Unambiguous or universal criteria for innovativeness do not exist since they are socially constructed in varying social contexts. Consequently manifestations of innovativeness cannot be studied before one has explored the criteria to be applied. This also concerns science. Since innovativeness is assessed on the basis of performance, we should ask the experts from different fields whose work they consider innovative or especially fruitful for the development of their own field of study. On the basis of their answers, we could analyse the criteria applied and also possible tensions between assessments. From this we could go further by analysing the individual and social environment-related factors affecting the work of researchers that were considered to be innovative.

This view also emphasizes the fact that science is not a uniform phenomenon but a field with endless internal variation. Disciplines have different cognitive and social 'styles', which are mirrored in their varying modes of working, research orientation, problems and values (Becher, 1989; Whitley, 1984). It is sensible to assume that the assessment of innovativeness may vary accordingly. For instance, in natural scientific or technical research, the aim of the study is usually to convince the reader of the truthfulness of the research in relation to objective reality and a relatively stable paradigm functions as a point of reference in the evaluation. In contrast, in soft and multiparadigmatic fields, the existence of several theories and approaches may make it difficult to compare results in a commensurable way (Kekäle and Lehikoinen, 2000, pp.39–40). This is not to say that natural scientists do not get into disputes, but to point to possible differences and problems in ways of determining the scientific value of research results. Definitions of what counts as a true innovation vary from one scientific context to another, and they are often subject to dispute (Laudan and Laudan, 1989; Mertcn, 1973).

The domain is also a conservative social structure. In order to be admitted into the domain, the performance must follow certain existing rules and criteria. Besides originality, the methodological soundness of the work, its high validity and reliability are such criteria. The work must be convincing in terms of already existing knowledge and fit into this tradition somehow (Gulbrandsen, 2000; cf. Hemlin and Montgomery, 1990).

A major share of the changes in scientific knowledge comprises, however, relatively small specifications of existing knowledge or revisions of interpretations, 'small innovativeness'. Connotations of the term 'innovativeness' easily focus too much attention or radical breakthroughs. Therefore it might be sensible to talk more moderately about high-standard research and factors that affect its occurrence. This kind of perspective would also include the wider criteria and pay attention to 'small innovativeness'.

CHANGING RESEARCH ENVIRONMENTS: COMPROMISING ACADEMIC RESEARCH?

It is reasonable to think that, if individual abilities and personal characteristics as well as organizational resources and dynamics are all on an optimal level, the likelihood of high-standard research – and innovativeness – increases (cf. Hurley, 1997). If the individual factors providing for innovativeness are taken for granted, what kind of social factors might then contribute to innovativeness in science?

It has been pointed out that an organizational culture that supports innovativeness is characterized by freedom in deciding how to do one's own work, good project management, sufficient resources, encouragement, organizational characteristics like communication and cooperation, and a culture where innovation is the norm. In contrast, innovativeness would be undermined by poor communication, a hierarchical command mode, constraints on freedom in the work, unclear goals, overcontrolled work assignments, evaluation pressure, insufficient resources and time, a status quo mentality and overemphasis on extrinsic motivation (Amabile, 1994; Boxenbaum, 1991).

Against this background it is rather easy to conclude that such major changes in science and higher education policy as the application of accountability principles should have changed the organizational premises of academic research rather profoundly. For instance, accountability and the constant evaluation of teaching and research signal mistrust and may divert attention to the fulfilment of external evaluation criteria. The moderate development of general university funds and increasing dependence on external funding sources increase, in turn, short-term employment and may decrease possibilities for long-term commitment to research as concurrently the significance of such extrinsic motivational factors as securing one's livelihood becomes more important. When a researcher does not have to worry about securing income, he or she is able to concentrate better on the work and extrinsic motivators do not disturb intrinsic motivation.

It is possible, however, that these kinds of conclusions simplify the situation too much. Evaluation may bring out problems to which nobody has paid attention and lead to improvements. External funding increases research possibilities and resource competition may select the best researchers to continue research. Amabile (1994, p.326) has noted that we cannot simply judge that all evaluation and constraints undermine creativity. Instead she suggests that any excessive pressure or incentive that leads scientists to focus on extrinsic motivators may undermine creativity: 'Thus, for example, organizational apathy towards a project or lack of any clear goal for work may convey to the scientist that the work itself is unimportant. Lack of equitable pay and reward for good effort can lead individuals to focus on those extrinsics just as surely as the frequent dangling of reward "carrots" can'. It is also important to note that we should not overemphasize the significance of organizational factors; researchers' personal motivation and ambitions may compensate effectively for poor organizational conditions.

However, as the heads of departments in the Finnish universities regard the lack of basic funding (general university funds), tight schedules and accountability pressures as the most serious problems that aggravate their department's research activity (Table 3.1), it is possible to claim that such organizational conditions can undermine possibilities for conducting high-standard research. In our recent postal survey (Nieminen, 2003; see the data description in the introduction), at least half of the respondents, covering all the major discipline groups,[4] considered these factors as great or very great problems in their research environment. Clearly smaller problems were, for instance, deficiencies in the know-how of research personnel, and insufficient research equipment.

Table 3.1   Problems in the research environment

	Mean	Great or very great significance (%)	N
Insufficient basic funding	3.97	70.3	350
Hurry, insufficient time resources	3.96	73.0	356
Insufficient number of research personnel	3.72	60.9	348
Difficulties in combining teaching, research and administrative duties	3.72	60.2	362
Accountability pressures, increased efficiency requirements	3.43	49.0	347
Funding competition	3.39	45.8	347

Note: The questionnaire rubric was as follows: 'Research is often affected by various research environment-related problems. How important do you consider the following factors to be in your department?' On this basis, the six most significant problems were identified and are presented here. Scale used: 5 = very great significance, 1 = no significance at all.

The results are hardly surprising. Universities have faced a number of new requirements and tasks during the last decade. Increasing student numbers, constant evaluation of activities, accountability and continuous pressure for various structural developments have characterized everyday life in the universities. Time became a scarce resource or, at least, the experience of rushing became stronger. More time had to be spent in applying for research funding as general university funds increased only moderately (cf. Nieminen and Kaukonen, 2003). It is noteworthy that the respondents, regardless of their disciplinary background, were unanimous about the central problems. Therefore there are grounds to ask whether the changes in the research environment have emphasized, for instance, competition to the extent that, in spite of a competitive academic tradition, it is detrimental to research activities.

The results of our recent interview studies (Nieminen and Kaukonen 2001, 2003; see the data description in the introduction) indicate also that strong dependence on external funding sources may create problems in pursuing widely accepted academic goals. For instance, the continuity of the research is always at stake. For researchers it is backbreaking to apply continuously for funding, as the length of contracts can be rather limited. Therefore project work is very time-consuming for the personnel and attempts to maintain a balance between academic activities and contract research activities may create problems. Even though project activity may be experienced as satisfying, there is a danger of the workload becoming too big, endangering, at the same time, scientific development. Projects come and go and, as deadlines can be rather strict, researchers' time is spent on a continuous 'project treadmill'.

The responses suggest problems in dimensions that might be regarded as decisive for the development of research. There is a lack of basic resources which, in turn, endangers continuity and researchers' personal development. From the lack of resources it also follows that researchers cannot give their undivided attention to what they are doing. These results differ to some extent from studies concluding that productive researchers usually have large workloads and work on several topics simultaneously (Gulbrandsen, 2000; Pelz and Andrews, 1976). Clearly, workloads and the diversity of the work may become too big. Results presented by Nieminen and Kaukonen (2001) also suggest that research funding plays a bigger role than is reflected in other studies concluding that resources do not play such a decisive role for innovative research. It seems that sufficient basic resources are crucial for the development of academic research and that a lot depends also on the 'nature' of research funding: what kinds of normative expectations it involves and whether it provides a sufficient time frame for research.

Dependency on extramural funding sources does not necessarily undermine possibilities for high-standard research, however. It depends on the leadership whether a department or research unit is able to develop its research activity under heavy dependence on external funding. Graversen *et al.* (2002) point out interestingly, in their study on Danish innovative research departments and units, that these kinds of departments and units have relatively many sources of external funds and that the leadership uses considerable energy to secure these funds. From this it can be concluded that, if leadership is able to secure funding and guarantee appropriate working conditions for researchers (who do not have to participate in time and energy-consuming fundraising), high-standard research does not necessitate extensive basic funding and that external funding can also stabilize and create continuity for research.

FREEDOM IN RESEARCH

It is not very surprising that, from the researchers' perspective, freedom in research seems to be one of the most important factors supporting innovativeness. For instance, in John Hurley's (1997, pp.81–93) study on discovery in science, the Nobel laureates appreciated freedom of thought and being able to choose what they work on. In contrast, they thought that pressure from peers and being under the pressure of evaluation are the worst working conditions for creativity. Thus the approach taken by the Nobel laureates in their laboratories was not 'management by results operations at all; rather researchers used their own judgment, worked on what they thought best and shared it all in public view so that each colleague could learn from others' (ibid., p.93)

It is also possible to claim that freedom in research is an ideological manifestation of the prevailing academic research culture. Thus, if researchers are asked, the significance of freedom is emphasized since they believe it is important. Some studies point out, however, that innovative research units usually have clearly formulated research strategies and objectives in addition to well-defined profiles (Hollingsworth, 2000). Pelz and Andrews (1976, pp.8–34) have shown that some combination of coordination and freedom is helpful for the researchers if the researchers themselves can participate in and influence the decision-making process. In particular, they suggest that innovative research organizations are characterized by 'creative tensions' on both the individual and organizational levels. They indicate in their study, for instance, that, on the level of organization, the departments with minimum coordination, autonomous individuals and maximum security were ineffective, while those with stimulation from a variety of challenging elements were more effective.

Freedom is articulated during the research process in several ways: in the formulation of a research problem, the selection of an approach, the implementation of the research plan and the publication of results. The formulation of a problem may be more important in creative work than its solution. Problem solving may involve only the application of accepted methods until the desired solution is achieved. Instead, in problem discovery, the problem has yet to be defined and there is no agreed-upon method for solving it (Csikszentmihalyi, 1990). Therefore the formulation of a research problem can be considered as a fundamental element in scientific research, even though there is also variation among researchers as to how important they consider the role of the problem to be in the research process (Allwood, 1997). Contract research, however, is usually understood as an activity in which there are limited possibilities for free problem setting, and which comprises, more or less, technical problem solving (e.g. Ziman, 1996). Increasing external funding of research, in general, and contract research, in particular, would then be expected to deteriorate freedom of research.

If the selection of research problems is used as an indicator of freedom, the survey shows that researchers' personal interest in a research subject and the scientific importance of the problem are still more important selection criteria than the availability of funding and financiers' steering, while the availability of funding is a condition that nonetheless has to be taken into account when research projects are planned. In other words, the growth of external funding has not replaced the significance of personal motivation in the choice of research problems, even though the significance of external funding and research contracts has increased almost dramatically over the last decade.

However, since many other factors were estimated to be effective as well, the result suggests that researchers choose their topics in a multidimensional and complex decision-making context (Table 3.2). In current research environments a successful researcher has to be able to combine both sets of incentives: intrinsic and extrinsic. Researchers must be able to 'sell' their ideas to several other actors, such as fellow researchers, financiers and publishers. Research problems are also used 'strategically' to promote research careers and guarantee funding (Allwood, 1997; Knorr-Cetina, 1982). Thus the ability to take into account various interests in the formulation of research problems may also mark a successful and innovative researcher.

A rather similar picture can be drawn on the basis of our interview study (Nieminen and Kaukonen, 2001, 2003). Partners and financiers may have a significant role in project design, but overall the results show researchers have an important role in the formulation of problems. Researchers' interests are not superseded, but they coincide with other interests. Externally funded project research is often a negotiation process necessitating compromises.

> It is not just a joke that the project idea of these partners, who come to suggest project co-operation, is very unspecified. (...) Here and now I can't remember any research that we would have been given a framework for and instructions that this kind of research is needed, but we have mostly ourselves shaped it – both methods and research questions. (Head of research unit)

Table 3.2   Factors shaping research topic selection

Factor	Total mean
Personal interest in research problem	4.25
Problem's scientific significance internationally	4.05
Availability of research funding	3.85
Problem's practical relevance	3.77
Problem's scientific significance nationally	3.59
Department's research tradition	3.50
Partners' interests	3.29
Targets set by the department	3.13
Financiers' wishes	3.06
Science and technology policy priorities	2.68

Note: The questionnaire rubric was as follows: 'Assess to what extent the following factors affect the selection of research topics in your department/research unit.' A 5-point scale was used: 5 = affects very much, 1 = no effect at all (N = 347).

Another way to test the idea that external constraints would have been detrimental to the academic research is to scrutinize publication rates and citation indexes. The freedom to publish results and innovativeness manifest themselves in publications. In journals the gatekeepers of a scientific field, peers and established scientists, assess and select works that might be valued as original and fruitful. In other words, a decreasing publication rate and citations in a scientific community may reflect problems in maintaining quality and other problems that derive from the research environment. The latest information on the productivity of Finnish science indicates, however, that publishing increased during the 1990s. During the period 1991–99, the number of publications by researchers in Finland increased on average by 6.4 per cent a year. Likewise the citations received by Finnish publications as a proportion of world citations increased during the 1990s. While in 1990 the share was approximately 0.7 per cent, in 1999 it was over 1 per cent (Husso *et al*. 2000, pp.72–93).

Even though there are problems that relate to the use of publications and citations as indicators, this result suggests that such changes in the research environment as increasing external contract funding and accountability pressures did not necessarily diminish the likelihood of conducting high-standard research and publishing. On the other hand, it is also possible to claim that the aggregate productivity increased in Finland simply because the number of researchers and resources increased and because increasing scientific competition forced researchers to become more productive.

RESEARCH COOPERATION

Besides freedom of work, stimulating and open communication is a perceptibly important characteristic for an innovative working environment. Thus, for instance, Graversen and his colleagues (2002, pp.7–8) emphasize in their study on innovative research environments that 'there is an intensive and an ongoing dialogue in dynamic and innovative research environments, both internally and externally', and furthermore that 'the high level of external communication and knowledge transfer is a precondition for both innovation and quality assurance in the environments'. It is rather evident that colleagues are important for the discussion of ideas, project design and encouragement, and that networking with other scientists in related areas may strengthen a researcher's capacity to handle complex problems (Hurley, 1997, p.78).

Usually it has been claimed that organizations producing major innovations are characterized by a certain degree of scientific diversity combined with a high degree of communication. Interdisciplinarity is seen as a prerequisite for high-standard research in many research areas since the increasing complexity of research problems requires cooperation across disciplines (Gulbrandsen, 2000; Hollingsworth, 2000; cf. Klein, 1990). The bulk of recent studies on innovation systems or on the role of research in innovation systems also puts emphasis on the growing interaction among scientific research communities with different disciplinary backgrounds and between research communities and their wider environment. The general assumption in these studies is that this new type of interaction will result in both organizational innovations and new kinds of knowledge and applications that have more socioeconomic relevance (Miettinen, 2002; Schienstock and Hämäläinen, 2001).

Changing research environments may either open up new possibilities for cooperation or set limitations on it. One condition is whether there are sufficient resources for cooperation. Also science policy measures may have a significant role in creating incentives and frameworks for cooperation (an example is research programmes that support and presuppose cooperation). On the other hand, cooperation also depends crucially on researchers' own activity. Human resources make cooperation happen, and it is sometimes impossible to increase cooperation since such resources have their natural limits. For instance, there may be a shortage of time owing to other duties, or the number of personnel may limit possibilities for starting cooperation. Cooperation begins and continues also most likely when both partners benefit from it; cooperation should involve such qualitative aspects that partners appreciate it.

It may be claimed that science policy in Finland has strongly supported research cooperation. Increasing external funding, on the one hand, and extensive use of such funding instruments as research programmes, on the other, have increased rather than diminished possibilities for cooperation. The survey results indicate clearly that university departments are collaborating actively with various actors, from domestic and foreign university departments to non-university research institutes and companies (Table 3.3). Even though the cooperation is most active within the university system, there is also a lot of cooperation with non-academic research institutes and companies.

Table 3.3 Project research partners

Our projects include/involve researchers from:	*Proportion of all respondents (n)*
Other departments of our university	66 (242)
Other Finnish universities	72 (263)
Foreign universities	71 (259)
Finnish non-university research institutes	41 (151)
Foreign non-university research institutes	14 (50)
Finnish firms	40 (146)
Foreign firms	13 (49)

Note: Respondents were asked, 'What kinds of partners do you currently have in your department/research unit's research projects? Please circle the alternatives that describe your department' (% of 'yes' answers of all respondents, N = 369).

Upon closer examination, however, significant differences among disciplines appear (Nieminen, 2003). It is possible to cluster discipline groups roughly into two categories on the basis of the extent of project cooperation. The social sciences and the humanities comprise a group that collaborates mainly within the university system. The focal research partners are from domestic and foreign universities (in the social sciences also to some extent from domestic research institutes and companies). The other disciplines comprise a group whose cooperation partners range from research units/departments in other universities to research institutes and companies. Cooperation is, however, extensive in every discipline group and the variation more likely indicates differences in the societal exploitability of the research than in the research activity itself. On the other hand, differences are also due to varying research contents, orientation and cultures. The tradition of the humanities or social sciences does not involve, for instance, strong involvement in industrial development.

In addition cooperation with non-academic partners seems to have positive rather than negative knowledge effects in research (Nieminen and Kaukonen, 2001, 2003). The flow of knowledge is not a one-way street from university research to companies or other utilizers; rather cooperation makes an evident knowledge impact on university research as well. Besides financial opportunities, external cooperation provides access to knowledge that would otherwise be difficult or impossible to obtain, such as like access to a partner's tacit knowledge and to data or databases, and diversifies the knowledge production framework outwards from the disciplinary context. A professor in the interview study expressed the benefits in the following way:

> We are awfully small actors; we have some 3–5 persons or 10 persons in a group to conduct research in some research domains, which is negligible on a global scale – a totally marginal thing. But if there is company X with us (...) From there comes a lot of knowledge we would not get otherwise. If we would not get that basic knowledge, we possibly should work for five years first in order to get to that starting level we now get at once.

Therefore it cannot be claimed that the changes in the environment of university research have been detrimental to cooperation as an element of innovativeness. Even non-academic cooperation seems to have had a positive impact on research quality. It is evident, however, that there are a number of different kinds of collaborative relationships and it is difficult to judge on the basis of the available data the extent to which a specific kind of collaborative relationship actually enhances innovativeness and the development of new ideas.

CONCLUSIONS

On the basis of this analysis, it is not possible to give a straightforward and unambiguous answer to the question whether changing research environments have affected detrimentally the organizational dynamics of Finnish research. On the one hand, a number of changes have taken place that are obviously experienced as negative in university departments and research units. The lack of basic funding, insufficient numbers of personnel and growing student numbers have led to constant rushing and funding competition, which is regarded as negative from the perspective of research. Interviews indicate also that dependency on external project funding may endanger the long-term continuity of the research and individual-level scientific development. In addition it is possible to claim that constant evaluation and performance assessment may shift attention from pursuing purely scientific goals to meeting external evaluation criteria.

On the other hand, increasing external funding (and the new networks it has created) may also have positive consequences for the dynamics of research. Thus the growth of funding has extended research opportunities. External funding does not seem necessarily to endanger freedom in research or diminish publishing and the quality of publications. External funding has also increased research cooperation, which is active both within academia and with non-academic actors. Non-academic cooperation may even support academic research if it provides a wide knowledge production framework, where information flows freely between the partners.

Even though we are quite familiar with the general organizational factors that may contribute to innovativeness in research, the tentative conclusions from this analysis suggest that the changing research environment may create new kinds of problems and supporting elements in research. Combined with earlier research results, the perspective of changing research environments also stimulates a number of further research questions. Among other things, it seems obvious that more often than not research groups and individuals have to cope with multiple incentives and demands coming from, for instance, disciplinary cultures, external financiers and users of knowledge. From this follows the question, how do research communities deal with possibly conflicting pressures and motivations? What are the means by which conflicts may lead to positive outcomes? Is there really such a thing as 'creative tension' (Pelz and Andrews, 1976) and, if so, what is the 'optimum' balance of psychological security and challenge? Furthermore how can an academic organization maintain continuity in this kind of dynamic environment regarding, for instance, long-term basic research commitments and the training and socialization of PhD students? What is the role of personnel policy and leadership? What kinds of strategies do departments and research units apply, if any, and how do they provide for organizational performance as the research environment changes?

Last of all, the crucial question seems to concern the relationship between continuity and change. On the one hand, the role of stabilizing and maintaining elements seems evident from the perspective of long-term commitment in research. The probability of high-standard research increases if researchers have the time and resources with which to focus on their research. On the other hand, the avoidance of a status quo mentality, challenges and continuous change characterize dynamic and innovative research environments. The problem is, perhaps, how to control and balance these elements. Where is the optimum balance between continuity and change?

NOTES

*   This chapter is a revised version of an article previously published in Finnish in H. Aittola (ed.) (2003), *EKG? Eurooppa, korkeakoulutus, globalisaatio?*, Jyväskylä: Koulutuksen tutkimuslaitos, Jyväskylän yliopisto [Europe, Higher Education, Globalization? Research Institute for Education, University of Jyväskylä], pp.85–101, The Research Institute for Education has kindly given permission to publish the revised version in this book.

1. Observers have pointed to a wide variety of changes in university-based research, ranging from increasing applied research and changing quality criteria to tightening competition and the erosion of traditional norms and the ethos of science (Nowotny *et al.*, 2001; Clark, 1998; Slaughter and Leslie, 1997; Ziman, 1996, 1994; Gibbons *et al.*, 1994). Some other observers have criticized these views as exaggerations and claimed that the change is actually much more moderate, as viewed from a wider historical perspective (Martin and Etzkowitz, 2000; Shinn, 1999; Godin, 1998; Weingart, 1997) and that the academic community is able to resist external pressures and maintain its relative integrity (Behrens and Gray, 2001; Prichard and Willmott, 1997). All in all, the analyses dealing with the transformation of university research have ended up with rather different conclusions and interpretations, the validity of which is sometimes hard to judge.

2. The survey data in the empirical section are based on a questionnaire, which was sent out to the heads of all university departments and research units in Finland (n=696), of whom 369 responded (53 per cent). As the response rate was the same as in other comparable studies in Finland, it can be considered as satisfactory. The sample is representative from the perspective of both universities and disciplines. The data include all the universities in Finland (17, excluding three universities of art) and discipline groups (natural sciences, engineering, medicine, agriculture and forestry, social sciences, humanities). Only in the technical field (41 per cent) and in two Swedish speaking universities (40 and 31 per cent) was the response rate clearly below the average. The dropout analysis did not reveal any other specific pattern of non-respondents. The aim of the study was to examine changes in academic research. The questionnaire included questions on four different themes: resources, research organization and cooperation, research targets and quality, and international cooperation. The aim of the interview data used here was to examine how researchers see non-academic research cooperation and what kinds of consequences it has had for the research enterprise. The data consisted of 19 semi-structured interviews. The interviewees were selected from among senior researchers in university departments and research units that cooperate on a continuous basis with non-academic partners. In terms of academic background, five interviewees were social scientists, four had a technical background, four were from a medical faculty, two were from a natural science faculty and one was from a faculty of business administration. Altogether the interviewees represented five different research units and seven departments. In addition three research liaison officers from two universities were interviewed.

3. In this context 'innovativeness' and 'creativity' are understood as interchangeable terms.

4. Including natural sciences, engineering, medicine, agriculture and forestry, social sciences and humanities.

REFERENCES

Allwood, C.M. (1997), 'The function and handling of research problems in the social sciences', *Science Studies*, **10** (2), 50–73.

Amabile, Teresa M. (1994), 'The "atmosphere of pure work": creativity in research and development', in William R. Shadish and Steve Fuller (eds), *The Social Psychology of Science*, London: The Guilford Press.

Andrews, Frank M. (1976), 'Creative process', in Donald C. Pelz and Frank M. Andrews (eds), *Scientists in Organizations. Productive Climates for Research and Development*, rev. edn, Institute for Social Research, Ann Arbor, Michigan: The University of Michigan.

Becher, Tony (1989), *Academic Tribes and Territories*, Milton Keynes: The Society for Research into Higher Education & Open University Press.

Behrens, T.R. and D.O. Gray (2001), 'Unintended consequences of cooperative research: impact of industry sponsorship on climate for academic freedom and other graduate student outcomes', *Research Policy*, **30**, 179–99.

Bourdieu, Pierre (1988), *Homo Academicus*, Cambridge: Polity Press.

Boxenbaum, H. (1991), 'Scientific creativity: a review', *Drug Metabolism Reviews*, **23**, 473–92.

Clark, Burton R. (1998), *Creating Entrepreneurial Universities: Organizational Pathways of Transformation*, Guildford: Pergamon.

Csikszentmihalyi, Mihaly (1990), 'The Domain of Creativity', in Mark A. Runco and S. Albert Robert (eds), *Theories of Creativity*, Newbury Park: Sage.

Gagné, F. (1995), 'Hidden meanings of the "talent development" concept', *The Educational Forum*, **59**, 350–62.

Gibbons, Michael, Camilla Limoges, Helga Nowotny, Simon Schwartzman, Peter Scott and M. Trow (1994), *The New Production of Knowledge. The Dynamics of Science and Research in Contemporary Societies*, London: Sage Publications.

Godin, B. (1998), 'Writing performative history; the new Atlantis?', *Social Studies of Science*, **28**, 465–83.

Graversen, Ebbe K.,Evanthia K. Schmidt, Kamma Langberg and Per S. Lauridsen (2002), 'Dynamism and innovation at Danish universities and sector research institutions. An analysis of common characteristics in dynamic and innovative research environments', Summary of report 2002/1 from the Danish Institute for Studies in Research and Research Policy.

Gulbrandsen, Johan M. (2000), 'Research quality and organizational factors: an investigation of the relationship', Department of Industrial Economics and Technology Management, Norwegian University of Science and Technology, Trondheim.

Hemlin, S. and H. Montgomery H. (1990), 'Scientists' conceptions of scientific quality: an interview study', *Science Studies*, **3**, 73–81.

Hollingsworth, R. (2000), 'Why do some research organizations make multiple breakthroughs in the development of new knowledge but most make none?', lecture given at the seminar 'Research Programme on the Finnish Innovation System' organized by SITRA, Helsinki, 13 January.

Hurley, John (1997), *Organization and Scientific Discovery*, Chichester: John Wiley & Sons.

Husso, Kai, Sakari Karjalainen and Tuomas Parkkari (eds) (2000), 'The state and quality of scientific research in Finland. A review of scientific research and its environment in the late 1990s', publications of the Academy of Finland, 7/00.

Jackson, Douglas N. and Philippe J. Rushton (eds) (1987), *Scientific Excellence. Origins and Assessment*, Newbury Park and Beverly Hills: Sage.

Kekäle, Jouni and Markku Lehikoinen (2000), 'Laatu ja laadun arviointi eri tieteenaloilla' (Quality and evaluation of quality in different disciplines),

psychological reports, no 21, Faculty of Social Sciences, University of Joensuu.
Klein, Julie T. (1990), *Interdisciplinarity : History, Theory and Practice*, Detroit: MI
Wayne State University Press.
Knorr-Cetina, K.D. (1982), 'Scientific communities or transepistemic arenas of
research? A critique of quasi-economic models of science', *Social Studies of
Science*, **12**, 101–30.
Laudan, R. and L. Laudan, L. (1989), 'Dominance and the disunity of method: solving
the problems of innovation and consensus', *Philosophy of Science*, **56**, 221–37.
Martin, B.R. and H. Etzkowitz (2000), 'The origin and evolution of the university
species', *VEST Journal for Science and Technology Studies*, **13**(3–4), 9–34.
Merton, Robert K. (1973), *The Sociology of Science, Theoretical and Empirical
Investigations*, Chicago and London: University of Chicago Press.
Miettinen, Reijo (2002), *National Innovation System, Scientific Concept or Political
Rhetoric*, Helsinki: Edita.
Nieminen, Mika (2003), 'Muuttuva yliopistollinen tutkimus – tehokkaammin,
soveltavammin, organisoidummin?' (Changing university research – more efficient,
applied, organized?), in Johanna Hakala, Erkki Kaukonen, Mika Nieminen and Oili-
Helena Ylijoki (2003), *Yliopisto – Tieteen kehdosta projektimyllyksi? Yliopistollisen
tutkimuksen muutos 1990-luvulla (University – From the Birthplace of Science to a
Project-mill? Change of University Research in the 1990s)*, Helsinki: Gaudeamus.
Nieminen, Mika and Erkki Kaukonen (2001), *Universities and R&D Networking in a
Knowledge-Based Economy. A Glance at Finnish Developments,* Sitra reports series
11, Helsinki: Sitra.
Nieminen, Mika and Erkki Kaukonen (2003), 'Universities and Science–Industry
Relationships: Making a Virtue out of Necessity', in Gerd Schienstock (ed.),
*Embracing the Knowledge Economy: The Dynamic Transformation of the Finnish
Innovation System*, Cheltenham, UK and Northampton, MA, USA: Edward Elgar,
pp.196–218.
Nowotny, Helga, Peter Scott and Michael Gibbons (2001), *Re-Thinking Science.
Knowledge and the Public in an Age of Uncertainty*, Cambridge: Polity Press.
Pelz, Donald C. and Frank M. Andrews (eds) (1976), *Scientists in Organizations.
Productive Climates for Research and Development*, rev. edn, Ann Arbor,
Michigan: Institute for Social Research, The University of Michigan.
Prichard, C. and H. Willmott (1997), 'Just how managed is the McUniversity?'
Organization Studies, 18, 287-316.
Schienstock, Gerd and T. Hämäläinen (2001), *Transformation of the Finnish
Innovation System: a Network Approach*, Sitra reports series 7, Helsinki: Sitra.
Shinn, T. (1999), 'Change or mutation? Reflections on the foundations of
contemporary science', *Social Science Information*, **38**, 149–76.
Slaughter, Sheila and Larry L. Leslie (1997), *Academic Capitalism*, Baltimore and
London: The Johns Hopkins University Press.
Taylor, Calvin W. and Frank Barron (1963), *Scientific Creativity: Its Recognition and
Development*, New York and London: John Wiley & Sons.
Uusikylä, Kari (1996), *Isät meidän. Luovaksi lahjakkuudeksi kasvaminen (Fathers of
Ours. Growing up into a Creative Talent)*, Juva: Atena & Tampereen yliopiston
opettajankoulutuslaitoksen julkaisuja A7.
Weingart, P. (1997), 'From "finalization" to "mode 2": old wine in new bottles?',
Social Science Information, **36**, 591–613.
Whitley, Richard (1984), *The Intellectual and Social Organization of the Sciences*,
Oxford: Clarendon Press.

Ziman, John (1994), *Prometheus Bound. Science in a Dynamic Steady State*, Cambridge: Cambridge University Press.
Ziman, J. (1996), '"Post-academic science": constructing knowledge with networks and norms', *Science Studies*, **9**, 67–80.

PART II

Creative Meso and Macro Environments

4. Strategizing for regional advantage: a case study of Ideon Science Park in Lund, Sweden

Lars Bengtsson and Jan-Inge Lind*

INTRODUCTION

In her study of Silicon Valley and Route 128 in the Boston, USA area, Saxenian (1996, pp.165–8) proposed a model for the creation of a network-based system for regional development. For the first step she proposed the creation of a community of interests and for the second the creation of a decentralized network-based system requiring collective action on two levels. On the first level a pool of necessary service firms must be present or developed in the region. The specialist firms in a regional industrial system depend on the external provision of a wide range of collective services including capital, research, technical education, managerial education, market knowledge and training. These services can be provided by private as well as public actors or a mix of these. On the second level Saxenian asserts that the intense localization of economic activity in a limited geographical area places huge demands on the region's infrastructure such as transport, land availability and telecommunication, as well as on the environment. These problems have to be dealt with at the regional level and involve several local and regional private and public sector organizations.

While Saxenian's interesting analysis gives us some understanding of the sources of regional advantages, it is not so forthcoming about the process of creating regional advantages. Moreover, for many students of regional advantage, Silicon Valley, Route 128, Austin and other well-known high-tech areas represent a far greater concentration of industrial resources and competence than is imaginable in smaller countries or areas with a more normal concentration of industries. There is thus a great need for further knowledge about upgrading regions and creating regional advantage, both for researchers and for practitioners.

* The authors wish to thank the editors for constructive comments on the chapter and The Swedish Research Council for financial support for parts of this research.

Silicon Valley and Route 128 are regional systems for innovation based on extensive interaction between industry, university and government. The complex interactions of these three subsystems, with the university taking a leading part, can play a major role for innovation in increasingly knowledge-based societies according to the Triple Helix approach (Etzkowitz and Leyersdorff, 2000, p.111; Etzkowitz *et al.*, 2000, p.314). This focuses on the interaction and expectations of the three actors and how they mutually shape and reshape institutional arrangements. Combining the reasoning of Saxenian and the Triple Helix would lead us to believe that new or rejuvenated systems for regional innovation and advantage would arise in such institutional arrangements created by the three Triple Helix actors. One of these institutional arrangements is clearly the science park.

In many European countries the setting up of science or technology parks is an important strategy when starting a process of regional development and creating territorial attractiveness and advantage (Storey and Tether, 1998, pp.1037–41). In the Nordic countries there are now some 50 science or technology parks (Bengtsson and Löwegren, 2002, p.155). Generally these are seen as growth engines giving impetus to economic growth, not only in the park itself but also in the region where the science park is located.

One of the most interesting Nordic science and technology parks is the Ideon Science Park in Lund, Sweden. Ideon formally started operating in 1983, as the first science park in Sweden and the second in the Nordic countries, at the end of a serious national and regional financial recession. The aim was to exploit the research and higher education at Lund University to support the establishment of new businesses and firms. Today the park has about 150 high-tech companies and some 50 service firms (including banks, solicitors, patent firms, restaurants and so on) with about 2200 employees. This may sound modest, but the effect on the region in terms of new companies, new jobs and the creation of relatively well developed information technology (IT) and biotechnology clusters has been profound.

In this chapter we will argue for a better understanding of how new regional innovation systems and regional advantage are created by design. Saxenian's studies, the Triple Helix studies and studies of clusters (Porter, 1990, 1998) all provide us with a better theoretical understanding of why a certain region or system has a competitive advantage. They do not, however, tell us much about the way such systems have been created or how the process has unfolded over time (cf. Lind, 2002). By means of a case study of Sweden's first science park, we will argue that the creation of a regional innovation system can be described as a process where a new regional vision is created and different key actors and regional competencies are linked together to realize this vision (ibid.).

THE AIM AND STRUCTURE OF THE CHAPTER

The aim of this chapter is to describe and analyse the process of starting and developing Sweden's first science park, Ideon Science Park, in Lund in order to better understand the dynamics and quality of the process of creating a new regional innovation system. The structure of the chapter is based on some methodological assumptions, the most basic being that order or disorder in the social world is created by human actors and that more complicated patterns develop above all through the actors' interplay. Often this order is the result of conscious efforts by actors to organize larger social systems, which we call 'strategizing', but it can occasionally be quite unintentional and only possible to observe in retrospect.

The rest of the chapter has six sections. In the first we describe the Ideon case in terms of milestones and critical incidents. In the second and third sections there is an analysis on two levels: a concrete actor level and a theoretical level. The actor analysis basically seeks to understand the actors' behaviour from their own subjective perspective. The theoretical analysis has an innovation system approach (see, for example, Edquist, 1997). In the fourth section we compare Ideon's development with that of other science parks. In the fifth section we discuss the role of a science park in composing a new regional high-tech based innovation system. The chapter ends with some conclusions.

THE IDEON CASE

The case is based primarily on a recently published account (Westling, 2001) of the 'Ideon story' by the former rector of Lund University, Håkan Westling. He was loosely connected to the starting process of Ideon at the beginning of the 1980s but became more actively involved during his period of office at Lund University (1983–92). Westling bases his book on documents and interviews with various key people who were involved in the founding and development of the Ideon Science Park. As the book does not cover the more recent developments we have added information from various public documents as well as from interviews with the current CEO of Ideon Center, Gertrud Bohlin. Limited space necessitates a very brief description of the case. The interested reader is referred to Westling's book, the most comprehensive source of the history of the Ideon Science Park.

First, some general information about Lund University and the city of Lund may be useful. At the time of the founding of Ideon, Lund University was (and it still is) one of Scandinavia's biggest higher education organizations in terms of number of students, which is currently some 37 000. It was founded in 1666, making it one of the oldest universities in Sweden. It is a state-owned and largely state-funded organization with some research funding coming from the private sector. Education and research are carried out in nine faculties. Lund is a city with a population of around 80000 dominated by the university and the university hospital. But some major firms also have their home here, most prominently Tetra Pak (packaging), Alfa-Laval (food processing equipment) and Gambro (blood dialysis).

At the beginning of the 1980s the climate for cooperation between university and industry was still very sensitive. After the rise of the left-wing movement at the end of the 1960s, any relations between industry and university were still regarded with great suspicion by students and many of the faculties. Industry was also a bit wary of any invitation from the university to cooperate; it was not long since they had been called 'capitalistic pigs and robbers'. But some initiatives had been taken. At the end of the 1970s, Lund University established several liaison offices for university–industry contacts, and the university board included members from industry and the trade unions. At the end of the 1970s and the beginning of the 1980s, the recession hit the industry in southern Sweden particularly hard. Here the big industries, confectionery and textiles, rubber and plastic, shipbuilding and building materials all found themselves in great difficulty. For confectionery, textiles and shipbuilding it was by and large the beginning of the end.

Against this background a certain amount of contact had been made between the county governor, Nils Hörjel, and professors at the School of Engineering in Lund to discuss new ideas, firms and areas which could form the foundation of future industries in the south of Sweden. Nils Hörjel had a civil service background with many years of important positions in various government departments in Stockholm. He was also a board member in a number of companies. At the end of the 1970s, he realized that new measures directed against the recession were better than trying to prop up industries that had no future in Sweden. In that perspective Lund University and its research were of singular importance. Hörjel also had experience of higher education issues from his time as a high-ranking civil servant in the employ of the central government. For example, he had been a key mover in the founding of Umeå University in the north of Sweden, at the beginning of the 1960s. After some initial contacts with the rector of Lund University, Nils Stjernquist, he became involved in various activities related to the university, especially those based on good contact with the central government. He arranged, among other things, for government financing of the building of a new section of Lund University, the Chemistry Center, which was vital for research related to biotechnology.

In 1981, a professor of chemistry, Sture Forsen, happened to read an article in the *Financial Times*, 'The case for another science park' (5 June 1981) about the establishment of a new park outside Manchester. Science parks had previously been established in Cambridge and in Edinburgh, and of course Stanford in California had been established before these. The article reported that science parks were turning out to be successful, in contrast to many other industrial policy projects. The *Financial Times* speculated that the prestigious university environment, the proximity to high-class research and the possibility to recruit good students explained this success. Sture Forsen, a member of the Nobel Prize committee and an internationally highly reputed professor of chemistry, later introduced the idea to the rector of Lund University, Nils Stjernquist. He, in turn, gathered together the board of the university and a group of researchers for a day of policy discussions, in November 1981. Two areas were singled out as having a special future potential: computer/electronics and biotechnology. Professor Forsen introduced the biotechnology discussion when he also pleaded for a science park in Lund.

In 1982, the man behind the second science park in Great Britain, at Heriot-Watt University in Edinburgh, Ian Dalton, visited Lund at the invitation of Sture Forsen. Dalton spoke at the university to an audience of industry, university and government/municipality representatives. He also visited the university's Chemistry Center. Dalton reached the conclusion that Lund University and Lund itself possessed good potential for a science park and that it was vital that it be located close to the campus. That same year, the new organization, SUN (the foundation for cooperation between university and industry) was formed. The initiative came from the county governor, Nils Hörjel, and the county administration. SUN's objectives were to activate contacts between industry and the university, to facilitate the exchange of information between them and to support relevant education and development programmes and research. SUN, which comprised Lund University, the county of Skåne, the regional development fund and the commercial chamber of Skåne, became the organization that, from the end of 1982, took over the planning of a science park in Lund. The initiator, Professor Forsen, went back to working full-time at the university. SUN's small staff, Ulf Andersson and Sven-Thore Holm, together with the county governor, Nils Hörjel and his chief of staff, Lennart Linder-Aronson, and the rector of Lund University, Nils Stjernquist, together with his chief of staff, Sverker Oredsson, became the prime movers of the project. SUN's main project soon became the establishment of Ideon Science Park, even though its activities also included other industrial projects in cooperation with scientific research.

During the autumn of 1982 another important event occurred. Until 1982, Ericsson and British Marconi had jointly owned a radio communication company called SRA. In 1982, Ericsson acquired the whole company and planned for quite a considerable expansion of SRA's operations in the 1980s related to the development of mobile phone communications. However the firm had difficulty in finding the number of engineers needed for this expansion. Ericsson and SRA were Stockholm-based but also had some units, mainly defence products, in Göteborg. However neither Ericsson nor SRA had any operations in the south of Sweden and recruited only marginally from the Engineering School in Lund. Nils Hörjel, who was a member of the board of SRA, knew about the plans and proposed that a new location in Lund be investigated. SRA's top management undertook several visits to the Engineering School in Lund and looked at possible location sites. Hörjel also knew one of the main owners of Ericsson, Marcus Wallenberg, the head of the most important finance family in Sweden. Thus Marcus Wallenberg was also informed about the plans. Hörjel's initiative succeeded and SRA decided to locate a development unit for mobile phones in Lund. Thus Ericsson/SRA, or Ericsson Radio Systems as it was named later, became the first tenants of the Ideon Science Park, even though it was not yet in operation or even planned in detail.

In late 1982, the construction planning of the science park started the first part, mainly for computer/electronics firms and the second part, for chemistry and biotechnology firms. Ericsson's decision to localize its development of mobile phones in Lund made it a matter of urgency to start operations as soon as possible. Ericsson had been promised that it could start up in mid-1983 at the latest. The municipality of Lund and its politicians were persuaded to reserve municipally owned land between the Engineering School and large companies like Astra Draco and Gambro for industrial and university use. The location was just a few hundred metres from the Engineering School. There was no time to construct new buildings if the promise to Ericsson was to be kept. The park had to start with temporary prefabricated buildings. These were installed during the summer of 1983 and the Ideon Science Park was officially opened on 29 September of the same year. Ericsson became the first computer/electronics tenant and another major Swedish company, Perstorp, the first chemistry firm. However the financing of the permanent buildings had not been secured. Skanska, a major Swedish construction company, that handled and rented out the temporary buildings, was unwilling to finance the new buildings. Other potential financiers in the region were also negative.

In late 1983, the county governor learned that IKEA had substantial amounts of capital tied up in so-called 'investment funds'. Profits paid into these investment funds were exempt from tax. The capital could be used for later investments but carried no interest as long as it was not used for investments. Normally such funds could only be used for investment in the same company in Sweden unless there were special reasons. At the time IKEA did not have any use for its investment funds in Sweden. Nils Hörjel contacted Ingvar Kamprad, the owner of IKEA. Kamprad was willing to invest in the

Ideon buildings as long it was acceptable to the tax authorities and the tax deduction was not jeopardized. It was the central government, more specifically the social democratic finance minister, who handled issues of exemptions from the investment fund rules. Hörjel, who had worked with the finance minister at the time, Kjell-Olof Feldt, managed to negotiate an exemption for IKEA. In January 1984, IKEA signed a contract for an investment of 109 million Swedish Krona (SEK) in a real estate firm, Första Fastighetsbolaget Ideon (FFI). The board of FFI consisted of two members from IKEA, one member from each of the municipality of Lund and SUN and a fifth member was jointly appointed by IKEA and SUN. FFI also bought the temporary buildings and decided to let them remain on the site. These were inexpensive and had a lower rent than the permanent buildings. FFI thought these facilities would suit smaller firms with limited resources. FFI also started the service organization, Ideon Center, which handled, among other things, reception, the switchboard and conference service.

When IKEA started FFI it was already evident, at least to the county governor, that the facilities built by FFI would not meet the demand for offices in Ideon. A second real estate firm, Ideon AB, was set up soon after FFI to finance some additional buildings in the park. In this case the money came from a private investor and former law student at Lund University, Eric Penser, a few major firms in the south of Sweden and bank loans. The construction of the first two buildings in the park, Alfa and Beta, started in 1984 and was completed in April 1986. To coordinate the decisions of the two real estate firms, the municipality of Lund, the university and local industry signed an agreement stipulating that a special Ideon board should be set up consisting of representatives of all these parties. The board started to operate in May 1984. The two most important issues for this board were the admittance of new tenants (only firms undertaking research and development were allowed as tenants) and decisions on rent subsidies for certain younger and smaller firms. In April 1986, the inauguration of the first two buildings took place; these represented a total investment of 250 million SEK. In total 55 000 square metres were available and at the time of the inauguration Ideon had 62 tenant firms.

The success of Ideon also led to approaches from the county administration responsible for healthcare to propose a new park in Lund based in an old mental hospital that was then vacant because of a new psychiatric therapy regime. The idea was to convert the buildings into offices and production facilities for the use of Ideon firms when they were to start manufacturing their products because this was not allowed in the science park. The county administration acted as financier for the conversion of the buildings and in October 1985 Ideon Industriparken opened. However this park had no formal relations with SUN or the board of Ideon Lund. After a while it became evident that Ideon Industriparken wanted to act as a real estate firm renting out offices and production facilities to any company willing to locate there. At the beginning of 1988, SUN, which owned the rights to the name Ideon, terminated the agreement.

Nils Hörjel, the county governor, retired from his position in 1984 but stayed on in SUN and the Ideon board until the end of 1987, when he reached the age of 70.

In 1986, the service organization, Ideon Service, became reorganized and changed its name to Ideon Center; it was then owned by the two real estate firms FFI and Ideon AB. Ideon Center provided normal office and real estate services, restaurant services, administration of the leasing of the offices in the buildings, arrangement of seminars and conferences, marketing of Ideon Science Park and contacts with firms that might have an interest in establishing themselves at Ideon. The new CEO of Ideon Center was Sven-Thore Holm, a former employee of Nils Hörjel at the county administration of Skåne. He was also one of the key people in SUN and in the establishment of Ideon Science Park. Sven-Thore Holm did not limit himself just to providing services to the firms in Ideon. He also took other initiatives such as creating contact networks at the university and finding seed and venture capital for new firms, not only those interested in Ideon. After a few years Ideon Center had grown substantially, partly because of Sven-Thore Holm's ability to raise money from various national state funds supporting technology and small business development activities. The real estate firms were critical of this expansion.

In 1988, the second real estate firm, Ideon AB, put up new buildings even though their existing ones were not fully occupied. However they forecast a higher demand. Instead the financial crisis hit Ideon AB at the beginning of 1990s. In 1991, the financial situation became alarming and some of the bank loans were reorganized, transferring loans into foreign currency with lower interest rates. Eric Penser, the finance man and part-owner of Ideon AB, also pledged another 20 million SEK in order to avoid bankruptcy. However, after the drastic devaluation of the Swedish currency in the autumn of 1992, the financial situation became worse. The other owners, three construction firms, did not want to invest more money. Lund University, Eric Penser and the local bank, Sparbanken Finn, wanted to avoid bankruptcy at almost any cost. To resolve the situation, Lund University acquired 60 per cent of the real estate firm for six million SEK and Eric Penser acquired another 15 per cent (he already owned 25 per cent) and Sparbanken Finn wrote off part of their loans. After 1992, the economy picked up and the number of tenants in Ideon AB increased again.

In 1991, Ideon Center split into two parts: Ideon Vision, an organization for the support of commercialization of research and technology development projects as well as financial support, and Ideon Center, a service organization for Ideon Science Park. Ideon Vision became financed to a considerable degree by the wage-earner funds established by the Social Democratic government in the 1980s. At the beginning of the 1990s, the conservative-led coalition government transferred these funds into foundations to support research and commercialization of research and new technology. These were called Technology-bridge foundations. Ideon Vision, which had the task of supporting new firms in the south of Sweden, worked with new and small firms. The Ideon name was therefore not representative of its task and was subsequently changed to Teknopol, headed by Sven-Thore Holm. Teknopol became an organization independent of Ideon as it was 45 per cent owned by the Technology-bridge foundation, 45 per cent by Lund University's development company and 10 per cent by the state development organization ALMI. Through Teknopol and its own organizations, Lund University could provide researchers interested in commercialization with advice and support in patenting, licensing, seed money and other services.

In 1988, there were about 100 firms in Ideon Science Park. Because of the strong growth of (particularly) Ericsson Radio Systems and the fact that only minor additions were made to the facilities, the number of companies remained at this level until 1996. At this time Ericsson Radio Systems, with its then 750 employees, decided to move to its own building near the Ideon complex. The Alfa building, where Ericsson had its offices, was partly renovated to accommodate smaller firms. Because of this and the IT boom at the end of the 1990s the number of firms started to increase again.

During the remainder of the 1990s and the beginning of the 2000s, some new buildings were added to the complex. This now consists of five buildings in the Alfa-complex (owned by FFI), five buildings in the Beta-complex (owned by Ideon AB), one Gamma building (owned by FFI) and one new building in a new complex called the Delta-complex (owned by FFI with room for expansion into six buildings), and the first temporary buildings, known as Kuvösen (the Incubator) (owned by FFI).

In 1999, Ideon Center recruited a new CEO, Gertrud Bohlin, a former part-owner of one of the first Ideon firms, Bohlins Reologi. In collaboration with the university and Teknopol, Ideon focussed on more intensive support and development of a few (10–15) small high-growth firms in the so-called 'Incubator'. This is located in the inexpensive part of Ideon, the old temporary buildings.

As noted above, Ideon today (2003) consists of some 150 high-tech firms and 50 service firms, about one-third in IT, one-third in biotech and the rest in other high-tech areas. Ericsson is still a tenant in Ideon. Even though it has moved most of its organization in Lund to a building nearby, it still retains a smaller unit in Ideon, called Ericsson Mobile Platforms, a unit developing and selling Ericsson's technology in the mobile internet. Ericsson's major financial problems in the mobile phone business have caused them to enter into a joint venture with Sony, forming Sony Ericsson. So far this has saved Lund and Ideon from experiencing any major reduction of the mobile phone development operations in Lund. Among the largest of the other firms in Ideon are Anoto, Axis, AU-system, BioInvent, Framfab, Precise Biometrics, Probi and Sigma. All these firms are listed on the Stockholm Stock Exchange. In total some 500 firms are or have been located in Ideon Science Park.

AN ANALYSIS OF THE ACTORS IN THE IDEON CASE

In this part of the chapter the Ideon case is briefly interpreted from the point of view of the three major actors in the Triple Helix, the government, the university and industry. Our initial question is: why did Sweden's first science park develop in Lund in the early 1980s, given a rather hostile environment with the divide between university and industry, the mature regional industry and politicians looking for fast new employment rather than long-term and risky high-technology projects? Can we understand the answer to this question by understanding each actor's subjective rationality?

The government, especially through its county administration office in Malmö and the county governor Nils Hörjel, took a very active part in the creation of the Ideon Science Park. A county governor is normally a former politician with special affiliation to the county where he or she is appointed. Thus their role mostly concerns administration of the central government's regional organizations but also protection of the interests of the region vis-à-vis the central government. Nils Hörjel was an unusual county governor. Born in Skåne, he was a former high-ranking civil servant, with special links to the social democratic government but also to the industry where he was a member of the boards of a number of important large Swedish firms, most notably in this context Ericsson Radio Systems.

Hörjel was determined to fight the recession and unemployment in the region but, maybe more importantly, to build a new industry structure there. The government was working on a national scale to combat unemployment and recession in Sweden, using defensive tools such as subsidizing industries such as steel, shipyards and confection. Ideon, the first science park in Sweden, promised the development of new and perhaps more competitive industries in the future. Hörjel could provide interest and support from the central government. He could also organize much of the infrastructure needed to start the park. Through his network of contacts he managed to obtain the first important tenant, Ericsson Radio Systems. Furthermore he secured the financing needed for the first buildings from IKEA and Ingvar Kamprad and made the municipality of Lund change the town planning of the area and sell their land to the two Ideon real estate companies. Finally he organized construction firms to build and part-own the second real estate firm. Thus Nils Hörjel acted as a relational entrepreneur in the Triple Helix linking the interests and the resources of its actors, government–university–industry, in order to achieve the goal of starting Sweden's first science park.

However the central government's support for Ideon decreased after Hörjel's retirement at the end of 1984 and the national recession became transformed into a boom economy in the mid-1980s. It was not until the conservative coalition came into power in 1990 that there was renewed interest from the government manifested by the Technology-bridge foundations and their task of supporting new firms and commercialization of research and new technology. However these services were not designated uniquely for science park firms but more generally for new and small firms. Again the interest in Ideon and this type of university–industry relations came at the time of a general recession. After 1994, the interest from the government in Ideon or science parks in general decreased again. Science parks were not mentioned at all in the government's industrial or small businesses policy. However, in 2001 and 2002, the government began to turn its attention to innovation issues and established a new government agency, Vinnova, that is to focus on research, policy development and actions aiming at strengthening the Swedish innovation system. Thus the central government became aware of a more offensive and forward-looking policy instrument than the normal defensive ones aimed at keeping problem companies and industries going. It was the county governor of Skåne who brought this instrument to the attention of the central government.

The local government of the municipality of Lund generally supported Ideon. There was a political struggle at the beginning of the 1980s over Ideon. Some political parties wanted the land to be reserved for housing. However the larger political parties in Lund, the Social Democrats, the Liberals (Folkpartiet) and the Conservatives (Moderaterna) have supported Ideon at all times. In terms of more direct support, the change of town planning arrangements and the selling of land (at market price) were the most important contributions. The municipality of Lund has not invested any money in Ideon.

Lund University, through some of its professors and its rector, Nils Stjernquist, initiated the idea of a science park and also early on identified its profile as consisting of computer/electronics and chemistry/biotech. The promotion of industry-related projects was a very controversial matter for the university organization. For ideological reasons, but also because of a fear of losing key people to the industry, the top management of the Engineering School voiced concerns, about starting a science park. The rector, however, joined forces with the county governor and managed to handle these concerns and Lund University was able to support the project. This was especially important with regard to the town planning of the municipality, the central government and the firms interested in locating in Ideon, most notably Ericsson.

Lund University did not want to invest any money in the project since it was considered too sensitive vis-à-vis the social democratic central government. It was not until the end of the 1980s and the beginning of the 1990s, when Ideon had become a success and most of the ideological concerns relating to interactions with industry had disappeared, that Lund University started to establish its own organizations for industry–university interaction: an investment firm and ownership of Teknopol. By then Sweden had a conservative-led coalition government that advocated more independent universities. Then Lund University was prepared to take up a financial position in the project. This became a reality when the second real estate firm, Ideon AB, had to be reconstructed financially in 1992.

The interest of the university in Ideon and university–industry interaction increased particularly during the latter half of the 1990s. One reason was the large budget cuts for the universities during the end of the 1990s which forced Lund University and other universities to look for alternative revenue streams. One of these is part-ownership of patents and firms based on spinoff research from that of the universities. Lund University now has an organization for investing in research firms (Lunds Universitets Utvecklings AB), a listed firm developing and selling distant learning software (LUVIT) and has part-ownership of Teknopol and Ideon and a patent firm (Forskarpatent). Apart from returns on investments from these firms, Lund University has recently hired a fundraising consultant to increase the amount of money coming from private donations and sponsorship.

Industry was from the beginning very sceptical about the Ideon project. While some large companies like Ericsson and Perstorp showed interest in the project there was no general understanding or support for the concept of a science park from industry. Westling (2001) noted in his book that, when Hörjel tried to raise money for the first real estate firm, only one of some 20 top managers he talked to expressed any support for the project, and no one was prepared to invest money in it. Part of the reason for this lack of support could probably be attributed to the regional structure of the industry at the time. In Skåne, low- and medium-tech industry dominated. Very little high-tech industry existed at the time, apart from some pharmaceutical and medical equipment firms. These latter firms often need very specialized facilities, not normally provided by a science park.

In general industry's interest in Ideon became somewhat greater after the initial success of the park. This interest grew even stronger during the latter half of the 1990s, when a substantial group of firms in the IT and biotech sector became established in the region. In 2003, private real estate firms now offer new facilities nearby Ideon Science Park. The high-tech firms developed in Ideon and elsewhere in the region are usually staffed by university graduates. Thus it has become more natural for these firms to interact with the university than for those with staff with little or no higher education. For the group of firms that have developed together with Ericsson Radio Systems, some of Ericsson's suppliers and partners, it has become evident that continuous innovation is the key to maintained competitiveness. An inspiring environment has become more important to many firms and the industry perceives Ideon as providing this.

Thus the Ideon case shows how the actors in the Triple Helix have collaborated in order to create and develop Sweden's first science park. However the three actors have involved themselves with varying intensity in the Ideon project. Starting out as a project largely led by the county administration, with additional initiatives from the university, the project received more support from the university and industry during the 1990s. The central government seems to have been mostly active in times of recession. An initial economic crisis, a relational entrepreneur bringing the three actors together with a new vision of developing high-technology industry in the region, and a commitment from the big high-tech multinational company, Ericsson, are some of the more significant answers to the question why Ideon was established in Lund despite the lack of any traditions of university–industry relations, and a very limited presence of high-tech industry in the region.

PATTERNS IN THE STRATEGY DEVELOPMENT PROCESS OF CREATING AND MOBILIZING REGIONAL ADVANTAGE, IN RETROSPECT

The Ideon Science Park project could be seen as the first step in a strategy development process to create a new regional innovation system or a creative knowledge environment in the south of Sweden. In this new system the university, and its output in terms of research, technology development and higher education, played a more important role. Furthermore, with the united efforts of the university, industry and government, new expectations, relationships and institutions had to be developed. While Ideon Science Park, according to most observers, can be considered a success and has been a role model for many other science parks in the Nordic countries, the case shows that it has had its downturns and less fortunate times, for example the financial crisis of Ideon AB (the second real estate company) at the beginning of the 1990s. However it is not the success of Ideon as a real estate company that is of interest; rather it is the process and the barriers against and the driving forces towards the development of the first embryo of a new regional innovation system that is the most interesting aspect of the case.

A characterization of the quality of the strategy development process could be fruitful in terms of specific patterns in the interplay between actors taking different roles in the development process. First of all, our observations suggest a tentative differentiation between the variety-generating and variety-reducing phases of the process. In the former phase the case illustrates that the strategy is based on an understanding of the driving forces and opportunities in the emerging knowledge-based economy. In terms of actor roles, the case suggests the importance of a frame breaker in mature regional economies and creation of opportunity spotting arenas both to mobilize and focus actors and resources, based on an interplay between emerging structural changes and identification of regional competence clusters. In the later variety-reducing phase, the case suggests that the strategy was based on linking new visions and key actors together in the science park arena in order to start a movement and a snowball effect. It is also important to create a physical manifestation and a brand name to link the physical manifestation with the vision. In terms of actor roles, the case suggests the importance of the relational entrepreneur to link different key actors to each other in order to start a realization of the vision.

The Variety-generating Phase

Destabilizing the current system: creating regional crisis and awareness
Recession plagued the regional economy in Skåne in the mid-1970s. The traditional strong shipbuilding, textiles and construction industries were all in crisis. The general view was that the recession would eventually disappear and the traditional industries would do well again. However the county governor and members of Parliament from the region interpreted the situation differently: it was a structural crisis, not a temporary one. They pointed out that the structure of the regional economy was considerably inferior to that of the rest of the country. The county governor and some other politicians started to change their opinion about the regional economic situation. The perception and interpretation of a region in structural crisis became after a while shared by industry, politics and academia. Thus the context preceding the start of Ideon Science Park was the perception of a structural crisis for the region of Skåne. This interpretation and view of the economic situation led to a search for new opportunities and new visions for the region. The county governor decided to contact Lund University and some of its professors.

Creating opportunity spotting arenas and new regional visions
In a series of talks over two to three years with professors at Lund University,

the county governor and the university administration became convinced that the future growth areas lay in computer/electronics and chemistry/ biotechnology. These areas and their connected industries depended to a much greater degree on higher education and research than the traditional industries in the region. A new regional vision of a future regional economy with substantial components of high-tech industries in computer/electronics and chemistry/biotechnology began to take form. In terms of how to start to build such industries, the idea of a science park came up.

The key actor role in the variety generating phase: the frame breaker

In an environment with considerable vested interest in mature industries, a university of the traditional research type and a government mostly administering a traditional defensive industrial policy, a frame breaker is needed to force the key actors into new thinking and action patterns. Even though a few individuals have been prominent in the Ideon project, we do not necessarily think only of individuals. The case also tells us about groups of people as well as whole organizations. The county governor is obvious in this case, but so also is the rector of Lund University, as well as some of its professors. Indeed they challenged not only cognitive frames of the regional economy's current shape and future development, but also Lund University's role in the development of the regional economy: Lund University should engage not only in higher education and research but also in innovation activities in the region.

The Variety-reducing Phase

The science park arena: creating links between a new vision and key actors

Several new links were created once the idea of a science park and development of two high-tech clusters had begun to receive support in the variety-generating phase. These new links became organizations like SUN, the board of Ideon, the two real estate firms, Teknopol and liaison offices. In particular the links between the central government, finance capital (Kamprad and Penser), the university and industry (some large multinational firms) were important in the Ideon case. It provides many examples of relations created and facilitated by the Ideon Science Park later on. Without Ideon, these new relations might not have been realized, or would have developed much later. Among the examples are biotech firms acting as service R&D firms to larger pharmaceutical firms. Some biotech firms have managed to create and exploit relations with the regionally important food industry, collaborating on functional foods. Relations between science and the generally low-tech food industry are otherwise rare.

The importance of large multinational firms

In Sweden the large multinational firms are very important institutions as they dominate the national economy. Sweden has one of the highest rates of multinational corporations per capita. They dominate in terms both of legitimizing actions in the Swedish industry and of having large networks of suppliers, customers and partners. Two broad areas were the focus of interest in Ideon: computer/electronics (later called information technology) and chemistry/biotechnology (later called biotechnology). This proved attractive to companies like ABB, Ericsson and Perstorp which established research and development units in the park. Ericsson's unit for the development of their mobile telephones was the most important localization for the continued development of Ideon. At the time, the Ericsson unit was quite small, but its importance in legitimizing Ideon, as well as for the subsequent development of many local suppliers of high-tech companies, was quite significant.

Creating a physical manifestation of the vision

The Ideon case suggests that creating an early physical manifestation of the vision, a science park, in terms of securing a land area and putting up buildings on it, was important. A rapid concrete result stabilized the new regional vision and added momentum to the change process. Fortunately for the Ideon project, the first tenant, Ericsson, demanded a fast pace in this respect and land was secured and buildings erected in record time.

Creating the Ideon brand

Today Ideon is well known in the Nordic countries as a park with strong capabilities in the IT and biotech industries. Lund University, regional and municipal organizations, firms in the park and the Ideon Park management have continuously tried to market the park and its name both at home and abroad. Drawing on the general image of the science park concept (high-tech, R&D, growth firms) Ideon has succeeded in becoming a brand name among science parks. It has managed to develop a widespread reputation in the Nordic countries as well as in a wider international context (Dahab and Cabral 1998). This is very important for the firms in the park, especially those that are new and small. The image and reputation of the Park lends credibility to these firms, enhancing their chances to survive and grow.

The key actor role in the variety-reducing phase: relational entrepreneurs

The entrepreneurs that create favourable links and relations between the state, the municipality, relevant government organizations, the university, the industry and financiers we call 'relational entrepreneurs'. These entrepreneurs have as individuals or as organizations good and trustful relations in both the private and the public sector. By means of these, the relational entrepreneur tries to connect key actors and key resources to the new vision. At a later stage other relational entrepreneurs create relations between different firms, between firms in the science park, between firms and their customers, suppliers and finance capital. If successful, the relational entrepreneurs facilitate the construction of relational assets that are transformed into a community of interest, knowledge and innovation.

THE IDEON CASE COMPARED WITH THE ESTABLISHMENT OF OTHER EUROPEAN SCIENCE PARKS

Ideon was the first science park to be established in Sweden and, since then, another 27 such parks have been established in this country up to the present year (2003). Ideon was established despite the lack of any tradition of university–industry relations as well as a very limited presence of high-tech industry in the region. We have explained this process by differentiating between a variety-generating and a variety-reducing phase with actor roles of frame breakers and relational entrepreneurs and their creation of opportunity-spotting and resource-linking arenas. How does this compare with the establishment of other science parks? Is Ideon a unique case or a fairly typical one?

Two precursors in their respective countries, in terms of establishing science parks, are Grenoble in France and Cambridge in the UK (Druilhe and Garnsey, 2000, pp.163ff). In 1970, Trinity College in Cambridge founded Cambridge Science Park and in 1972, ZIRST Technopole was set up in Grenoble. While these parks were established more than ten years earlier than Ideon they are still interesting for comparison. All three parks were the first to be established in their respective countries and all started well before the boom of science park establishment. Prior to the establishment of Ideon only three parks in the UK (Cambridge, Edinburgh and Manchester) and two in France (Grenoble and Sophia-Antopolis) had been set up. The first in the Nordic countries, Oulu in Finland, was set up only months before Ideon.

According to Druilhe and Garnsey (ibid., p.164) the Grenoble area had a strong industrial heritage with thriving industries in the fields of electrical equipment, cement, metallurgy and chemicals, but very little activity in high-tech industries. Higher education in Grenoble reflected this heritage in the shape of several engineering schools and applied research institutes. The relations between industry and higher education had a long tradition in the area and were considered to be a part of the local identity. In Cambridge, the university and its colleges had a strong scientific base but limited industry. A few companies in electronics and scientific instruments had spun off from the university laboratories. However further industrial development was looked upon with suspicion by the city and was restricted by the planning authorities; for example, IBM was refused permission to locate an office in Cambridge in the 1960s.

Compared with Grenoble and Cambridge, Lund was somewhere in between in terms of its industrial base. There was a certain amount of industry in Lund, including some high-tech companies, when Ideon started. Lund's leading industries were packaging and the manufacture of food processing equipment, both being connected to the regionally important food industry. These had very limited interaction with research and science. In the high-tech sector, Lund had a relatively large medical equipment company and a larger pharmaceutical company. These two companies worked in close cooperation with the Medical School at Lund University and the University hospital. In terms of university–industry interaction, Lund resembled Cambridge, lacking a tradition of industry–university relationships. Instead both places had strong traditional academic values.

One initial condition that was unique to the Ideon case was the regional economic crisis. Even though the city of Lund was better off than the rest of the county, the crisis was evident here as well, with the hard-hit county capital of Malmö only 20 kilometres from Lund. Neither local nor regional economic crises seem to have been present at the initiation of science parks in Grenoble or Cambridge.

In Cambridge, influential scientists at key colleges, well-acquainted with experience from MIT and Stanford in the USA, were the key drivers of the process. Among them the bursar of Trinity College, John Bradfield, became the champion of a science park. In 1970, Fellows of Trinity College decided to create Cambridge Science Park. Apart from regulating land use, the local government had a very limited role in the establishment of this park. In Grenoble, local government politicians with a background in science and research, a few local industry managers and research institute directors played key roles in establishing their first science park. Local government and local authorities, in particular, had a decisive role in the process. Also in Grenoble they were aware of US experiences. In both cases, the central government played an insignificant role; it was local initiative that started the process.

Regional authorities and the rector of Lund University, in collaboration with some of its professors, took the initial leading roles. The local and central governments played minor roles in the starting process. The science park process in Lund, as well as in Grenoble and Cambridge, was the result of action taken primarily by the local and regional administration. The fact that regional authorities played an important role in Lund, in contrast to Cambridge and Grenoble, could probably be explained by the regional economic crisis in Skåne. For the county governor, Lund and Lund University were not the problem, it was other parts of the region that were the problem. On the contrary, Lund and its university were the solution. In Lund it is very uncommon for researchers and scientists to be involved in local government as politicians. In Grenoble, local government politicians acted as relational entrepreneurs with good relations to academia, the political system and industry. In Cambridge, the colleges often have good relations with industry in terms of maintaining contacts with alumni and receiving donations for Chairs and other academic activities. Lund University received the largest part of its budget from central government, and other sources of income were unusual. Alumni activities were, and still are, fairly uncommon in the Swedish university system and thus not a major source for industrial relations. Lund University was probably more isolated from industry than both the Cambridge colleges and the higher education institutions of Grenoble. By chance, the county governor in the Ideon case, with his background in national authorities and industry, happened to be in the best position to act as a relational entrepreneur.

In both Grenoble and Cambridge the first businesses to be located in the parks were primarily spinoffs from established companies in electronics. Cambridge Science Park is still dominated by larger and foreign-owned companies, while other, later-established college science parks in Cambridge, for example St Johns Innovation Centre, have substantially more spinoffs from researchers and scientists for which Cambridge is now renowned. In Grenoble it was not until well into the 1980s that spinoffs from the university became more prevalent. Grenoble still has much fewer university spinoffs than Cambridge. At both Grenoble and Cambridge parks the IT sector dominates, with a relatively small component of biotechnology firms. In Lund, the initial localization of some larger company spinoffs resembles the development in Grenoble and Cambridge. The IT sector dominates in Lund as well, but there is also a strong telecom component reflecting Ericsson's importance in the park. However the biotechnology sector has also been strong in Lund, perhaps reflecting the strong scientific base at Lund University as well as the increased number of opportunities in the sector when it was established in the 1980s. At Ideon the university spinoffs also became more prevalent in a later phase in the 1990s. Ideon now reports that 75 per cent of the firms there are university spinoffs. In this regard Ideon resembles the Cambridge rather than the Grenoble situation. Our comparison of the three parks is summarized in Table 4.1.

Table 4.1   *Comparison of the science park establishments in Grenoble, Cambridge and Lund*

	Grenoble/ZIRST	Cambridge/Cambridge Science Park	Lund/Ideon
Initial conditions	Strong industry base, small high-tech industry strong applied research base, strong university–industry interaction	Weak industry base, strong scientific base, some university–industry interaction	Some industry base, small high-tech industry, strong scientific base, weak university–industry interaction
Economic situation at founding of park	Good	Good	Regional economy in crisis
Key actors in initiation of process	Local government and authorities in collaboration with some company managers and research institute directors	Influential professors at key colleges, primarily Trinity College	Regional authorities, i.e. county governor and university rector in collaboration with some influential professors
Frame breaking	Need more high-tech and science-based firms in the region	Need high-tech and science-based firms in the region and new role university in innovation	Need more high-tech and science-based firms in the region and new role of university in innovation
Relational entrepreneurs in early phase	Local government politicians	College professors	County governor
First tenants in park	Large company spinoffs or R&D units in IT	Large company spinoffs or R&D units in IT	Large company spinoffs or R&D units in IT and biotech
University spinoffs	More prevalent in later phase, still in minority	More prevalent in later phase, now in majority majority in the Cambridge area	More prevalent in later phase, now majority

THE SCIENCE PARK'S ROLE IN THE CREATION OF A NEW REGIONAL HIGH-TECH INNOVATION SYSTEM

The aim of this chapter is to describe and analyse the process of starting and developing Sweden's first science park, Ideon Science Park in Lund, in order to better understand the dynamics and quality of the process of creating a new regional innovation system. The latter part of the aim has been achieved by relating our findings to Saxenian's (1996, pp.165–8) model of development of regional innovation systems. While our findings to a great extent confirm Saxenian's model, we believe that they also generate a model that increases our understanding of the way a new high-tech regional innovation system is actually created.

It is evident from our case study of Ideon Science Park and from the comparisons with Grenoble and Cambridge that the start of a science park can play a major role in the process of creating a new regional high-tech innovation system (cf. Druilhe and Garnsey, 2000). The focus of this chapter has been on the early processes of the start-up of a science park and how different actors and organizations are organized and integrated by key actors, frame breakers and relational entrepreneurs, in order to support the vision of a new regional high-tech innovation system.

The creation processes of regional innovation systems in the three cases have developed differently, subject to different local initial conditions. Thus the development of the process depends both on the available local resources and on the initiatives of local actors. In the Ideon case, there was a strong research-oriented university (as in Cambridge), an industrial base with some high-tech companies (as in Grenoble, but on a smaller scale), but a weak tradition of university–industry relations (as in Cambridge). Thus the major challenge in Lund was to create a new vision of a high-tech innovation system (frame breaking) and to bring actors from the university, industry and the political system into relationships with each other (relational entrepreneurs). These activities and roles could be related to the first step in Saxenian's model (1996, p.167), the creation of a community of interest in a new regional innovation system.

Our case study has specifically highlighted the importance of certain individuals in this first part of the process, that is the role of the relational entrepreneur. The county governor in the Ideon case embodied the interconnections of the Triple Helix throughout his career. The case is thus a striking illustration of prime movership in the innovation system creation process; the capacity to mobilize external actors, their mindsets and their competencies, relating these to the concrete building of a science park. He managed to mobilize the industry for the Ideon project, most importantly the first two tenants, Ericsson, representing the IT industry, and Perstorp, representing the chemistry/biotech industry. Industry, as financiers, was also mobilized: first the construction industry, then IKEA.

Relational entrepreneurs seem to be present in all three cases. In the Ideon case it was the county governor, in Cambridge the bursar at Trinity College and in Grenoble municipal politicians. Interestingly these individuals all seem to embody the Triple Helix; that is, they all had prior experience or good contact with all three types of actors of the Triple Helix: the university, industry and the political system.

The second step, according to Saxenian (ibid., pp.167–8) is to attract specialized service firms to the area in order to complement, develop and integrate the new regional innovation system. In the Ideon case this process took considerable time to develop. Similar tendencies could be found in the Cambridge and Grenoble cases (Druilhe and Garnsey, 2000; Saxenian, 1989). The science base and the industrial base in the region influenced the early development of the respective parks. In all three cases they specialized in electronics and IT. In Lund, there was also a stream of chemistry and biotechnology firms because of a strong science base and some firms in this sector. However the relations between the larger firms moving into the parks and new technology-based firms seemed to be limited and many new firms were dependent on a few important customers, that is the defence industry in Cambridge and large firms in Grenoble and Lund. Saxenian (ibid., p.454) asserts that Cambridge at the end of the 1980s suffered a crisis in which the new technology-based firms were not growing and the interactions between the small and large firms were very limited. The crisis at Ideon in the first half of the 1990s seems to some degree to have similar explanations.

An investigation of Ideon's companies at that time (Alexanderson 1993, p.14) concluded that the links between companies in the park and in the region were fewer and weaker when compared with other groups of small- and medium-sized companies. Thus the environment was differentiated and had not yet developed into a more integrated innovation system. More, and new, specialized companies both in terms of product and of service companies had to be developed and/or attracted to the area in order to develop a critical mass. While Saxenian (1996, pp.167–8) seems to focus on new service firms in this step, we believe that it also contains the development and inflow of new and specialized product firms to create a more integrated innovation system.

In 2003, a more integrated high-tech innovation system has developed at Ideon as well as in the region. The general boom in the IT sector as well as in biotechnology in the second half of the 1990s created room for many new technology-based companies and attracted specialized service companies, for example venture capital, patenting and licensing firms. A similar development seems to have been witnessed in Cambridge (Druilhe and Garnsey, 2000, p.174). In this phase new types of relational entrepreneurs have made their entry into Ideon. This time people with a background from working at the Ideon companies seem to have played a major role in funding new technology-based firms as well as creating linkages to established firms, not necessarily in the park but even in the region and elsewhere. The Ideon case shows that high-tech is only one area of innovation and entrepreneurship and that cross-fertilization between high-tech and other medium and low-tech companies is both possible and desirable.

A good example is the relations created between the regional food industry and biotech companies, relations that are otherwise seldom well-developed. Today regional politicians, university and industry in the county of Skåne are not only working for the establishment of new science parks, they have launched a campaign for a regional high-tech innovation system in the medical, pharmaceutical and biotechnology area, called Medicon Valley. The region has now been given a wider definition, that is, the whole of the Öresund region, comprising Skåne in Sweden and the Danish island of Zealand, including Copenhagen.

Our discussion could be summarized in a model of regional high-tech innovation system dynamics, where we see the science park as one important stepping stone in the development of a regional high-tech innovation system (Figure 4.1). The starting position is the government and university research labs with limited relations to a regional high-tech industry. The science park becomes a vision and a physical environment for the creation and development of relations between university and industry in order to bring about a new regional innovation system. However, while large firms are attracted to the area and new companies are established, the system is largely differentiated. The next phase is the creation of more tightly knit clusters with more specialized products and service spinoffs appearing both in the park and in the region. The model predicts that the last phase is a new development of differentiation in which new, specialized companies will be appearing between clusters, for example, cross-fertilization between different fields of knowledge. New companies appearing in the intersection between the food industry and biotechnology as well as biotechnology and IT are examples of this development. However, at this stage, the innovation focus is strong, creating a dynamic and self-reinforcing innovation system – a creative knowledge environment.

CONCLUSIONS

Ideon Science Park has played an important role in the development of a new regional high-tech innovation system in the south of Sweden. The role seems to be similar to that of the first science parks in France (Grenoble) and in

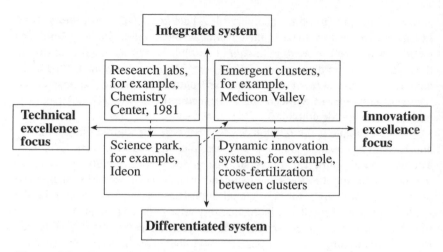

Figure 4.1   Four phases in the building of a new regional high-tech innovation system

Britain (Cambridge) (Druilhe and Garnsey, 2000). Initial conditions and key actors are important determinants of the way the process is going to start and how it will unfold subsequently. Accordingly we have highlighted the importance of frame breaking, that is the creation of new concepts and visions, and relational entrepreneurs in the starting as well as in later phases. The quality of the process tends to develop as an interaction between early concepts, prompting action leading to physical manifestations and in turn triggering new concepts. Creating development processes of high quality often implies two phases: the first in which seeds are sown, and the second where they are linked to each other so that a movement and a snowball effect can develop (cf. Normann, 2001).

The main contribution of this chapter is a more elaborated view of the process of creating a high-tech regional innovation system compared to Saxenian's (1996, pp.165–8) model. Even though each organization or firm is trying to solve its own problems and capitalize on opportunities in this process, we have also identified individuals and organizations that have shown institutional leadership in terms of envisioning a new innovation system in the region and have worked hard to create the right conditions for this process to unfold.

REFERENCES

Alexanderson, Ola (1993), *The Ideon Research Park – Functions and Effects*, Lund:

Ideon Center AB.

Bengtsson, Lars and Marie Löwegren (2002), 'Internationalisaticn in Nordic and Baltic Science Parks', in Peter van der Sijde, Birgit Wirsing, Rudi Cuyvers and Annemarie Ridder (eds), *New Concepts for Academic Entrepreneurship*, Twente: Twente University Press, pp.151–62.

Dahab, S. ard R. Cabral (1998), 'Services firms in the IDEON Science Park', *International Journal of Technology Management*, **16** (8), 740–51.

Druilhe, C. and E. Garnsey (2000), 'Emergence and growth of high-tech activity in Cambridge and Grenoble', *Entrepreneurship & Regional Development*, **12**, 163–77.

Edquist, Charles (1997), *Systems of Innovation: Technologies, Institutions and Organisations*, London: Pinter Publishers.

Etzkowitz, H. and L. Leyersdorff (2000), 'The dynamics of innovation: from National System and "Mode 2" to a Triple Helix of university–industry–government relations', *Research Policy*, **29** (2), 109–18.

Etzkowitz, H., A. Webster, C. Gebhardt, B. Regina and T. Cantisano (2000), 'The future of the university and the university of the future: evolution of ivory tower to entrepreneurial paradigm', *Research Policy*, **29** (2), 313–23.

Lind, Jan-Inge (2002), 'Regionala förändringsledare och produktiva växtkulturer–en teori om villkor för förnyelse i regionala ekonomier' (Regional change leaders and productive growth cultures – a theory about the conditions for renewal of regional economies), KEFU Skåne Skriftserie, 1, Lund Institute of Economic Research.

Normann, Richard (2001), *Reframing Business: When the Map Changes the Landscape*, Chichester: Wiley.

Porter, M.E. (1998), 'Clusters and the new economics of competition', *Harvard Business Review*, Nov.–Dec., 77–98.

Porter, Michael E. (1990), *Competitive Advantage of Nations*, New York: Free Press.

Saxenian, A. (1989), 'The Cheshire cat's grin: innovation, regional development and the Cambridge case', *Economy and Society*, **18**, 449–77.

Saxenian, AnnaLee (1996), *Regional Advantage*, Cambridge, MA: Harvard University Press.

Storey, D.J. and B.S. Tether (1998), 'Public policy measures to support new technology-based firms in the European Union', *Research Policy*, **26**, 1037–57.

Westling, Håkan (2001), 'Idén om Ideon – en forskningsby blir till' (The idea about Ideon – the creation of a science park), Årsbok 2001, Lunds universitetshistoriska sällskap.

5. The industry doctoral student: an educational challenge for academia and industry

Lillemor Wallgren and Sture Hägglund*

INTRODUCTION

The new knowledge society poses novel and changing requirements for knowledge and competence. The recent interest in the concept of 'the Triple Helix' as a model of the interplay between universities, industry and government to promote innovation and growth also emphasizes the entrepreneurial role of universities (Etzkowitz, 2002).

The observed importance of knowledge and competence development for individuals, organizations and the society as a whole leads to evolution and change in the educational system. Measures are sought to improve the educational process, making it more effective. One area of special concern is postgraduate education. In particular, there is a recognized need to increase the production of PhDs, especially for careers in industry. A general trend is to develop and strengthen the character of doctoral education as research schools, that is as integrated programmes with cooperating subject areas and professors. A specific issue is to develop doctoral study programmes arranged for PhD candidates affiliated with companies, not the least in engineering disciplines in general and in the area of information technology in particular.

In Sweden, as in other countries, major changes have taken place in higher education during the twentieth century. The traditional model of doctoral education based upon one-subject departments and a single professor supervising a group of doctoral students is gradually being superseded by integrated graduate schools with cooperating professors, emphasis on improved supervision and multidisciplinary course programmes. In Great

* The industry research school and the interview study reported in this article were funded by the Foundation for Advancement of Knowledge and Competence Development (KK Foundation). Professor Lars Owe Dahlgren supervised the interview study and made important contributions to the work. We also thank the editors for useful advice.

Britain, dramatic changes occurred during the 1980s, as described by Becher and Kogan (1992). Goodlad (1995) and Barnett (1992) emphasize the changing view on the role of higher education in society with an increased focus on the individual student and on the need for universities and the society outside to get closer to each other. Barnett, for instance, states that 'We're all Reflective Practitioners now', which can be understood as an argument for university education to strengthen its role as a provider of competence for industry needs.

A special interest has been taken in training PhDs aiming for a career outside universities. One way to approach this need has been to promote doctoral education in cooperation with industry. A major initiative in this direction in Sweden was seen when the Foundation for Advancement of Knowledge and Competence Development (KK Foundation) in the mid-1990s established a programme supporting industry research schools, where university departments sponsored by industry organized doctoral studies with a direct connection to companies. The goal was also to promote a build-up and exchange of knowledge for mutual benefit for involved parties. In practice this means that the doctoral students share their time between a university department and a company. The dissertation project is expected to have a strong connection with the company involved.

Thus the concept of doctoral studies arranged for PhD students affiliated with companies is becoming more and more important, yet this is a little understood area with respect to organizational matters and pedagogical issues involved in the doctoral education process. A number of questions with respect to the goals and prerequisites for such studies can be raised, for instance:

- Should the goals of a PhD education be formulated differently for industry-based doctoral students than for regular students?
- Should the studies be organized differently in order to reach the same result for industry-based and regular doctoral students respectively?
- Does the time needed in order to produce PhDs in industry differ from what is usually expected?
- Should the criteria for selecting and admitting PhD candidates differ when training together with industry is planned?
- To what degree is industry actually controlling and influencing the research topics selected and the results actually produced?
- To what degree and under what conditions can doctoral studies be located at the company and how important is the actual presence of the student in the academic research environment?

These questions are directly related to the educational process and its degree of flexibility. Today the framework and the goals of doctoral education are formulated without any reference to situations where non-traditional environments and partners for doctoral studies are involved. Specifically it is important to investigate and describe what are the special conditions and needs for such studies. Related questions also involve the attitudes and experience of the doctoral students with respect to different environments and situations for their studies.

In this chapter, we address these issues by relating our experience of running a research school for doctoral students performing part of their studies in industry. We summarize the findings from an in-depth interview study with 23 doctoral students belonging to an industry research school in applied information technology and software engineering. Experiences from this study and some conclusions are presented and discussed. The study analyses in particular the characteristics of the industrial environments involved in the doctoral education and how the situations of the doctoral students can be structured naturally according to a characterization of company environments as being research-intense, engineering-style or consultant-style respectively. Furthermore some general observations related to university–industry cooperation in rapidly developing areas, such as information technology, are presented.

DOCTORAL EDUCATION AND THE PROCESS OF DOCTORAL STUDIES IN SWEDEN

Doctoral education in Sweden is regulated to correspond to four years of full-time studies, assuming a bachelor degree as the minimal requirement for admission. However, in many subject areas, most candidates have a master's degree (or a half-way licentiate exam) before starting the studies for a PhD. Doctoral students are allowed to do a maximum of 20 per cent department service (teaching and so on) and in this case they have five years to complete their degree. Normally doctoral students are employed by the department, or by someone else (for instance a company) who has granted that they can use their time for the PhD studies. For doctoral students in engineering subject areas, the funding for their employment usually comes from external project grants even if they are hired by the department.

To get a general picture of such a doctoral education, it can be described as a four-year process with a number of milestones. The doctoral education process, illustrated in Figure 5.1, is supported by the supervision process, the examination process and the course study process (Bergman, 1997). The licentiate thesis is an optional degree, which can be planned as a step in the progress towards the PhD, or alternatively but more rarely, as a goal in its own

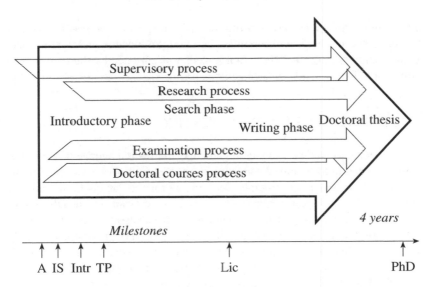

Supervisory process

Research process

Search phase

Introductory phase

Writing phase   Doctoral thesis

Examination process

Doctoral courses process

4 years

Milestones

A IS Intr TP   Lic   PhD

Note: The process is supported by subprocesses in which the doctoral student develops from a newly admitted doctoral student (A) to a PhD exam holder (PhD). After presentation of an individual study plan (IS) the introduction phase (Intr) is followed by a search phase aimed to result in a thesis proposal (TP). About halfway through the PhD process a 'licentiate' degree (Lic) is one possible milestone in Swedish doctoral education (and also a possible final exam in itself).

Figure 5.1   Overview of the four-year doctoral education process

right. The course programme may account for up to 50 per cent of the credits required for the PhD exam.

Although doctoral education is currently in a process of change, most of the studies undertaken in the area so far have been oriented towards the traditional professor-centred training of doctoral students (see, for instance, the study by Strömberg Sölveborn, 1983).

Through the increased interest in research schools during the last decade, the doctoral education environment was expanded and the number of involved researchers and doctoral students increased. Interdisciplinarity and inter-subject cooperation were promoted at the same time. Cooperation also includes joint activities between different universities in order to provide critical mass-size study programmes and more varied perspectives. With the organization of research schools, the possibility to influence and control doctoral education from faculties, external funding organizations and the government was improved.

The introduction of research schools also promoted the process of admitting and supporting doctoral students from industry. The expansion of the environment for doctoral studies to include both academia and companies created new challenges and opportunities with respect to the involvement of industrial partners with a different background, knowledge and competence. At the same time the education environment was enriched by the cooperation with people from outside the academic world.

DOCTORAL STUDIES IN INDUSTRY

Industry doctoral students may be regarded as innovation agents, both in their companies and in the doctoral education itself. By tradition we assume that the educational process is in principle the same as for regular doctoral students, while their thesis topic is expected to be at least relevant, but usually rather concerned with an issue of prime interest, to the company. The supervision and in particular informal advising will often be shared between the university and the company. However this situation may create uncertainties with respect to the allocation of responsibility to handle research questions, problems and general advice for the individual doctoral student.

The industry doctoral student may be envisioned as a bridge builder between two separate worlds with different cultures and values. Sometimes the contrast is huge between a university department with its focus on science and the search for knowledge and understanding on the one hand, and the goals of finding practical solutions and engineering efficiency in a company on the other.

Research about Doctoral Education

The literature about doctoral education is primarily concerned with studies taking place in a pure academic environment. However a general interest in cooperation between academia and industry, the 'third mission' of the university (to interact with the society and inform the public) is rapidly growing and was also formalized as a main assignment for Swedish universities in the 1990s. In this context, relevant knowledge creation also relating to doctoral education in cooperation with industry is beginning to appear; see, for instance, Jacob and Hellström (2000) and Slaughter *et al.* (2002).

According to Säljö (2000) many pedagogues believe that the environment and the culture a person inhabits is of major importance for their way of learning and developing. However it is not just in school or through education that a person learns, but also in other experiences, situations and environments that are not primarily intended to mediate knowledge, such as friends, colleagues and places of work. Learning is a possible result of all human activity. Säljö refers to John Dewey ([1916]1966, p.13) who says, 'The very process of living together educates.' Learning basically involves what individuals and the collective extract from social situations. How we learn is not just a matter of an individual's capacity for learning but also of the way the environment is shaped. We are cultural creatures who interact and think together with others in daily life.

Gibbons *et al.* (1994) describe knowledge as something developed both within traditional scientific disciplines and within broader multidisciplinary social and economic environments (Mode 1 and Mode 2, respectively) which jointly contribute to a common understanding. Etzkowitz *et al.* (2001) extend this view by emphasizing the shift in attitude and behaviour from viewing research resources as divided into two different categories, one dedicated to theory and the other to practice, to a synthetic view of research objectives and outcomes which sees the possibility of attaining both simultaneously (Mode 3). This unified mode can be seen as the knowledge foundation for industry research schools, which try to implement creative and innovative environments where industry and academia both benefit and with the doctoral students acting as bridge builders and innovation agents.

The Industry Research School in Applied IT and Software Engineering

At Linköping University, a special industry research school in the area of applied information technology and software engineering within the Graduate School of Computer Science was started in 1997, sponsored by the KK Foundation and a number of companies. The industry research school attempts to offer (a) an industry-related, high-quality doctoral programme which is based on and utilizes the special IT competence at Linköping University, (b) an effective organization coordinated with the regular doctoral study programme and other strategic research efforts, and (c) a market-oriented and individually designed doctoral education with extensive advisor capacity, leading to an exam as PhD or licentiate.

The programme has the capacity to train at least 20 industry doctoral students each year in various areas of computer science and applied information technology. Doctoral students are admitted continuously. Areas studied include software architecture and support environments for software development, IT management, information system development, electronic commerce, multimodal user interfaces, usability engineering, requirements engineering, database technology and intelligent agents. Companies active in the industry research school include major multinationals such as Ericsson, Nokia, SKF and IKEA, as well as small and medium-size enterprises.

The doctoral students are admitted to six different academic subject areas, all of which cooperate within an integrated doctoral education organization. Thesis projects, in addition to the company connection, also belong to research groups including regular doctoral students as well. Supervisors typically have their main occupation with regular students, with the exception of some part-time adjunct research professors who predominantly work with industry doctoral students.

The course programme offers about 30 general courses each year in various areas of computer and information science, but there are also some courses arranged especially for the industry doctoral students, for example a course in industrial project management. PhD students are recruited both directly from undergraduate education and from industry. Ideally students in the industry research school should spend the initial part of their studies mainly in the university environment where they get their scientific training, while the thesis project can be carried out inside the company.

By the end of 2002, the industry research school in applied information technology and software engineering had enroled a total of 23 doctoral (and licentiate) students. About half of the students were already employed in companies when they applied as PhD candidates, while the rest were either recruited directly from undergraduate education or had previous experience as regular doctoral students. The age of the industry doctoral students varies a lot, and in general they are older than the regular students in the participating research groups. A few even had more than 20 years of industry experience before joining the doctoral programme. The doctoral students sometimes work locally or at a considerable distance, with several of the participating companies having their business in other cities than Linköping. This poses special challenges also in terms of mechanisms for the management of distributed PhD study programmes (Hägglund, 2000).

Nine doctoral dissertations and ten licentiate theses have been presented so far. Very few doctoral students have left the school without finishing an exam. Actually it appears that the industry doctoral students probably have a higher or at least as high a success rate in their studies as the regular doctoral students in corresponding subject areas, although it is difficult as yet to produce reliable figures supporting this observation.

Subsequently a number of industry research schools have been created with funding from the KK Foundation and at present about 15 such schools are in operation. An overview of experiences from the programme itself is presented in a mid-term evaluation report (Hanberger *et al.*, 2001). The research schools cover a broad spectrum of subject areas and differ in an number of dimensions; for instance:

- the degree of interdisciplinarity and the number of different universities, departments and subject areas engaged;
- organizational form, which may be as a separate independent unit or

with industry doctoral students integrated with regular doctoral students in existing research groups;

- whether admission of doctoral students takes place at one time for a larger group of students, who are trained together, or if each doctoral student may follow an individual study path;
- the type of industry involvement in the definition of research topics, varying from companies defining thesis projects in advance and before committing themselves to participate in the research school to companies joining the school with an identified doctoral student candidate with an open thesis proposal;
- requirements for presence in the academic and industrial environment respectively, varying between schools where most of the training is done in industry and schools where the students spend the main part of their time at the university or in a research institute.

The industry research school in applied information technology and software engineering can be described as integrated into a regular graduate school, with groups of about five industry doctoral students belonging to each participating research laboratory. Students are admitted twice a year and in competition with other doctoral student candidates. Companies typically join the school in connection with admission of a suitable PhD candidate. Studies are organized with an individual study plan, observing the requirements for the particular graduate study subject area chosen, but with few mandatory requirements defined by the industry research school. Considerable flexibility with respect to where to perform studies and the selection of thesis project is allowed for the industry doctoral students.

As an example of an industry research school with a quite different organization within the programme sponsored by the KK Foundation, FENIX, working in the area of economy and management, in particular management of innovation and technology, may be mentioned (Adler *et al.*, 2000). Thus FENIX organizes a tightly integrated group of industry doctoral students with the ambition also to manage a joint research programme.

THE INTERVIEW STUDY

Twenty-three doctoral students enroled at the industry research school in applied IT and software engineering at Linköping University were interviewed during the spring and summer of 2001. There were 19 men and four women, affiliated with about 15 companies (some doctoral students switched from one company to another during their studies). The majority of the students were already employed in companies when they were recruited onto the PhD programme or had previously undertaken some sort of doctoral studies. A minority came directly from undergraduate education. This study was performed using an interview template based both on literature in the area and on one of the present authors' personal experience of doctoral education since 1975 as a doctoral education organizer. The interviews were performed for the most part at the students' places of work as a complement to our more in-depth knowledge of their academic study environment. The interviews were recorded on tape, each taking between one and one and a half hours.

This study aims to cast light on the conditions for a continued collaboration between university and industry in terms of industry doctoral students. Another aim is to clarify how industry doctoral students view their education in relation to views held by government, university officials, the KK Foundation and researchers concerned with joint doctoral education in industry and university. We describe the views, needs and expectations industry doctoral students have and how the collaboration between industry and university was experienced by the doctoral students during their period of study. The overall aim of the investigation is to provide insight into the situation of the industry doctoral student in order to develop further an efficient and high-quality study programme in a collaboration between university and industry. The complete study is reported in the form of a licentiate thesis in pedagogy (Wallgren, 2003).

Analysis and Description of the Industry Work Environment

For the purpose of this chapter, the focus here will be on how the doctoral students describe their company environment and how the interaction between this and their doctoral education works. The analysis of the responses, presented below, emphasized the company's (or rather the work unit's) business, since during the interviews it became clear that this had a major influence on the student's study situation. Also the analysis identified to what extent research/doctoral education took place in the company environment. The next step was to study similarities and differences in their descriptions of the company environment in general by finding out what they found most characteristic of the company environment in question. These characteristics were then further categorized and the specific factors in this categorization related to the research process to see how well they match.

The business of the company and in particular of the work unit seem to have a major influence on the situation of being a doctoral student. This is clear from the analysis of the responses to the following questions, which were part of the interview:

- What do you do at your company?

- How do you feel that your company views research?
- What role have you had in the projects that your research project involves?
- Who do you discuss your research with?
- How much time do you spend discussing research per week?
- How has your company influenced your research?
- In which situations do you feel your company has influenced your research?
- If you have felt hindered in your research / doctoral education, what is the cause?

A deeper analysis of the answers to the questions shows that three different kinds of company environments can be identified based on the extent to which research/doctoral education occurs or is recognized in the environment. Depending on this classification, three categories of work cultures can be described: research-intense environment, engineering environment, and consultant environment. The different types of environments are also related to a number of recurring factors that can be identified in the interview material:

- the type of business activities taking place in the close work environment;
- how common is previous experience of academic research doctoral education in the organization;
- the degree to which there are other employees, in particular management, in the place of work with a PhD degree or at least experience of postgraduate education;
- how organizations envisage the time perspective of project activities,
- the character of the doctoral students' research projects.

This is described in Table 5.1. As the students' descriptions of their company environments vary among the given categories, the environments can be viewed as representing a clustering of similar situations. Typically there are a significant number of employees with doctoral education and doctoral students in research-intense environments, while in the consultant environment there is hardly anyone who knows what doctoral education involves. The time perspective typically varies from very short in the consultant environment to rather long in the research-intense environment. Research projects in the engineering environment are often rather tightly connected to product development, while in the consultant environment they may only indirectly relate to the company's operations. In the research-intense environment, projects are more concerned with future than with current

Table 5.1   Characteristics of the different environments

Categories/ factors	Research-intense environment	Engineering environment	Consultant environment
Type of activity	This type of environment is most commonly found at companies with special departments for research and development. The companies make a product, but the doctoral students are not involved in production as there are special departments for research and development. These departments are moreover most often separate from each other	In this environment products are produced and the product is highly central. The doctoral students are located in the organization and closer to production than research-intense environment. The company is often found to be interested in the doctoral students' research being used to develop the product	No actual production, but services are sold. The workplace is sometimes at the company and sometimes at the client's. Interest in industry doctoral students is found to be to show externally that they have the competence; also for marketing purposes
Employees	Many of the employees have postgraduate degrees and there are several doctoral students in the group. Most often, however, the supervisor is located at the university. There is little cooperation with others especially outside the group	In this environment there are significantly fewer with post-graduate education and fewer doctoral students than in the research-intense environment. The supervisor is most often employed at the company. There is often much contact and collaboration with other employees	There is a lack of employees with postdoctoral education and of other doctoral students. The doctoral student is often the only one familiar with doctoral education. Only occasionally is there an assistant supervisor at the company. There is little collaboration with other employees on the whole
Time perspective	The time perspective is often long-term	Shorter than the research–intense	Short time perspective,

Table 5.1 Continued

	and there is an understanding of how long research takes	environment and highly related to the product and on what phase production is in or when it will be delivered	significantly shorter than both the research-intense environment and the engineering environment. Time is measured more in hours than in years. Time is directly related to cost, as charges are paid by the customer
Research project	The research project is usually independent of and well separated from production	Usually near the product, so that usability of the result which is dependent on the production process can be high	Empirical findings for the thesis are gathered outside the company and usually from a customer's business operations

production. Generally the situation for doctoral students in research-intense environments differs more from what is the case in consultant-type environments than from engineering environments, which fall somewhat in between. However there are also sometimes interesting similarities between research-intense and consultant environments, for instance when the consultant sells competence based on PhD-level skills, though typically they differ more than the other two combinations.

Table 5.1 shows in more detail that the variation between the three identified environments is large, at least when applying the four chosen factors. But within one and the same company all three environments can be found. This applies especially to companies which are research-intense, or where there are different units of operation dealing with the various types of activities.

Implications of the Environment for the Doctoral Education Process

An issue of special interest is the relationship between the characteristics of these environments and the doctoral education process, as presented in Figure 5.1. In the following we state what is relevant and most typical of each of the environments, based on the outcome of the interviews conducted with the doctoral students in the industry research school in applied IT and software engineering.

Research-intense environment

The organization in these company environments focuses on research and advanced development. This is positive from a doctoral education perspective as doctoral students can participate in research where they work at the company. There are good opportunities for doctoral students to write articles both in their daily work and in their doctoral projects and in this way to participate continuously in the examination process and follow routines for research such as how to go about publishing research results. However there can be a limiting factor in the organization where a doctoral student might feel isolated from important business operations.

The fact that there may be several employees with research degrees means that there is a wealth of knowledge on the doctoral education process which can provide support in many ways for the research process, an understanding of the student's situation and, not least, proximity to the researchers' contacts. In such cases the prerequisites are available for creating research environments within a group similar to that at the university. But because of the organization there is often no dialogue or meeting with people such as other doctoral students outside their own work unit. There is also a risk, when such good opportunities are available within one's own local environment, that collaboration with the university will be reduced unless common arenas and meeting places are created.

Although the time perspective in the environment is long-term and knowledge about the research process is available, four years is a long time for all company activities that are eventually dependent on market forces. This involves a risk of reorganization or shut-downs. There are good conditions for the doctoral student to find a suitable doctoral project at the company, but this is often separate from business operations.

Engineering environment

In this environment the doctoral student will come into close contact with business operations in a different way than in a research-intense environment. This means that he or she will participate in various projects and activities, but at the same time attention may be split among several competing interests. As a result of this proximity, the production process has a high impact on the doctoral education process. This means that it can be difficult to find sufficient support for the various phases of the doctoral education process (the introduction phase, search phase and the writing phase in thesis writing) if there is a lack of synchronization with the production process. In this type of environment it is the product and its development and marketing that have a high impact on steering business operations and what employees are busy with. The doctoral student often lacks the built-in support for the doctoral education process through the business organization, competence in doctoral education among other employees and routines for research to be found in research-intense environments.

Among the employees there are people with varying competence and significantly fewer with research or doctoral study experience than in the research-intense environment, but the supervisors are usually closely connected to the company environment. Sometimes the doctoral student introduces other employees to his university environment through the graduate course process. There is often a close dialogue between the doctoral student and other employees at the company. This means that professional skills and theoretical knowledge are confronted in this meeting, creating interesting challenges, not least for the supervisor.

The time perspective is significantly shorter than in a research-intense environment, which is dependent on which stage production is in. Here a four-year education process means a time period that is difficult to control. Market forces have a significant impact on the time perspective of the company, with consequences for all employees, including the doctoral student.

The thesis project is often closely tied to the product. There is a risk of its being so close to the product that completing the thesis depends on the production process. One advantage with this is that the doctoral student experiences the importance of the result of his or her research as they know that the results obtained in the thesis project can be used in the development of the company's product. Usefulness in this type of environment becomes a success criterion.

Consultant environment
Here there is no actual production, but rather the services that are offered. Sometimes there is no fixed place of work as some assignments from clients require the doctoral student to be in place at their premises, often for a relatively long period of time. Interest in doctoral studies in such companies is often based on the need for the competence they can offer their clients and for marketing themselves. In this type of environment it is difficult to anchor doctoral education, which means that the doctoral student sometimes lives an anonymous life in the role.

People with research competence are usually rare in the consultant environment. In our interviews there is only one case where the situation is different, with a consultant environment with high scientific competence. In general only the doctoral students know what a doctoral education involves and there is no research environment at the place of work. This means that there is no dialogue on research with other employees. Furthermore doctoral students sometimes live a lonely life. Common arenas and meeting places are often lacking as the employees are often located at places other than the company. In such cases the doctoral education process is totally in the hands of the doctoral student and the supervisor and the connection between the company and the university may be rather weak.

The time perspective is very short and, instead of talking about years, as when discussing the research programme process, the talk is often of hours, as reimbursement for services offered are often measured in hours. This puts the doctoral student in an extreme situation in comparison with other employees, especially if an assignment has been given to a team of employees. Employees in this environment are highly dependent on fast changes in the market.

As far as the work on the thesis is concerned, empirical results come almost always from a client. This creates a dependence on the client where the work on the doctoral project is not part of the common knowledge-creating process with employees at the company, with other doctoral students at the university or with the company or university.

The Experience of the Doctoral Students

All doctoral student participants in the study, regardless of type of company environment, have difficulties as regards time with balancing doctoral education, including work on the thesis, and work at the company. How they attempt to solve this varies widely from individual to individual, but all try actively to secure sufficient time. For example, some doctoral students choose to create a work environment also at home to avoid being disturbed, while being electronically connected to the global scientific community. Others try to reach a balance by being at the company on certain days of the week and at the university on other days. Some choose to work longer periods at the company and other periods in the university environment. This issue is often dependent on the stage which the student has reached in his or her studies, or the phase in which their duties at the company are carried out.

Another common experience is that doctoral students do not report any strong form of control from their companies as far as their degree projects are concerned, other than that they should be beneficial to the company. This lack of active control may be explained by a fear in companies of disturbing academic freedom, but also in some cases as an expression of indifference with respect to the research project. The company may thus be more concerned with the competence development of the doctoral student himself or herself, than with the outcome of the particular research project.

A similar experience is reported with respect to the freedom to publish the results of the research. Typically the individual agreement with the company states that the company has the right to delay publication of a paper for up to one month, in order to make sure that no confidential information is disclosed. The motivation for secrecy may be both technical results, for instance the need to take out a patent, and indirect information such as data about the company's operations. The impressions from the interviews are, however, that delayed or halted publication has rarely posed a problem for the interviewed doctoral students.

Another aspect of a company's commitment arises, though this is not always explicitly stated, when the doctoral student is uncertain of how far up the hierarchy support for the research is anchored. How and when a doctoral student thesis project is identified and whether it is to be a separate project, or a part of a larger industry project, has a significant impact on the doctoral student's general situation. Like other doctoral students, those who for various reasons were forced to change the topic of their thesis project during the study period experience this as a major obstacle in the research process, not least as far as time is concerned.

Supervision is a particulary important activity in research education. Lindén (1998) argued that the focus of supervision is on the relation between the people involved. Her investigation highlights the importance of the interaction between persons playing different roles in supervisior, and the problems that may arise when trying to separate or combine roles. For instance, the combination of roles as manager with economic responsibility and as academic supervisor may create intricate decision situations.

It is also obvious from the interviews that new dimensions of supervision are introduced in industry research schools when compared with traditional doctoral education. The background for industry doctoral students is often quite different from that of regular doctoral students with respect to experience, age, theoretical background and motivation for entering the research school. The difference in work situation is another factor that may account for the fact that the industry doctoral students more often report communication problems with their supervisors than comparable groups of regular doctoral students do, for instance as reported by Wallgren (1994, 1997). Some doctoral students interviewed characterized the situation as 'two lost souls meeting'. The difference in Mode 1 and Mode 2 knowledge (Gibbons *et al.*, 1994) is also highlighted by doctoral students advocating a different view of knowledge than the traditional academic disciplines presumed by some supervisors. Communication problems were also reported with respect to contacts between academic supervisors and industry representatives.

Despite the fact that the industry doctoral students interviewed find the studies difficult and that they have to walk a tightrope, all these innovators in doctoral studies say that it is fun and something special to be an industry doctoral student. Many say that they feel useful at the same time that they are educating themselves as they attack real-world research problems. Others feel that it is a dream come true and that it is the best thing in life they have ever done.

However, in the interviews the doctoral students have highly varying views on their situation; that is, how they experience being a doctoral student and how they feel that the doctoral student process works. Some of them particularly stress the need to find a balance among their various duties at work. Even if regular doctoral students usually share their time between research and teaching, the dichotomy between research studies and other duties in the company is especially pronounced for the industry doctoral students. The results of the study also show that they feel that both their situation and success are heavily dependent on whether they have previously participated in postgraduate research, or been employed at the company before their studies as doctoral students commenced, or whether they have come directly from undergraduate studies.

However what is decisive is who the industry doctoral students themselves are, what relationships they create and what capacity they have for handling and finding a balance in their work and studies. They carry a heavy responsibility for ensuring that the doctoral student process works, that they develop as individuals and as researchers in this process and that they can contribute to knowledge creation and dissemination. They have a clear opinion themselves about the characteristics that are essential for industry doctoral students and why they have decided to choose this particular way of developing. Finding a balance also includes their private lives, as their involvement as industry doctoral students is high.

CONCLUSIONS

Using experience from an industry research school in applied information technology, we have in this chapter analysed the experiences of 23 industry doctoral students as contributors to the enhancement of industry–academia cooperation. The role taken by the research school is not only to prepare doctoral students for a career in industry, but also actively to build bridges between the university and companies and to promote the formation of creative environments and industrial growth. Especially in the area of information technology and software-related research, the role of people commuting between the different environments rather than just delivering reports and product concepts is crucial. Thus industry doctoral students play an important role as intermediaries and change agents, promoting both innovation in industry and renewal of research education itself.

Discussion of the Interview Study

In our study, with the companies involved ranging from large R&D-intensive firms to consulting companies without any in-house research activities, a wide spectrum of industrial environments was covered. Not surprisingly, there were major differences between the situations for doctoral students working in research departments or research-intensive companies and in service or consulting companies, respectively. Furthermore, during the period of study for the doctoral students interviewed, we have experienced an extreme IT boom and a later recession, affecting many of the companies involved. Still the correspondence between type of company environment and educational situation seems to be valid, independently of such fluctuations.

Some observations from the interviews are notable. It appears that the companies involved have actually influenced the selection of research topics and controlled the research process much less than expected. As a matter of fact, there were more complaints about lack of active engagement and interest than about excessive control from the company.

The process of choosing a thesis topic in itself appears to be of crucial importance for industry doctoral students, more so than for regular doctoral students, for whom it is usually less dramatic to change or adapt the subject of study. Another significant factor influencing the study process and situation is the students' background at the time of admission to doctoral studies. This varies much more than for regular doctoral students, especially with respect to age and work experience.

The opportunity to publish results freely and without undue delay was a great concern when organizing the industry research school. So far the experience has been very promising. It appears that supervisors have been attentive to potential secrecy conflicts and that companies have been effective in reviewing manuscripts before publication. No problems in this respect were reported in our study.

Supervision is a crucial factor for successful doctoral education in general and for industry doctoral students in particular. The need for the academic advisor to understand the special conditions for industry doctoral students and to adapt the supervision process is emphasized by the study. The special role of the contact person or local supervisor in industry is also of prime importance for a successful education process. In particular the cooperation and division of roles and responsibility between advisors involved is a topic that needs a deeper understanding and further study.

An overall impression from the interview study is the great diversity of situations and experiences accounted for. This means that, even in the studied research school with a comparatively homogeneous subject area background, measures to support the doctoral students must be very flexible and account for a variety of needs.

The difference between the conditions of the thesis work for traditional doctoral students and for industry doctoral students can be related to the work of Gibbons *et al.* (1994), who write about the contrast between problem solving in a context which is defined in relation to the cognitive and social norms that govern basic research or academic science (Mode 1) and knowledge production from a broader range of considerations which is intended to be more immediately useful for industry, government or society more generally, in which supply and demand factors are operating (Mode 2). Our study supports the view of Gibbons *et al.*, in that it illustrates how the expansion of higher education has involved new types of sites where research education is taking place and also that new kinds of people with a different background are engaged in activities together with the industry doctoral students and their supervisors.

Consequences for Industry Research Schools

Returning to the open questions, stated in the introduction, about what may be special for doctoral education carried out together with industry, we can make the following observations:

- So far, we regard it as an open question whether the goals of a PhD education should be formulated differently for industry-based doctoral students than for regular students.
- There seems to be a need to follow up the support processes for the studies for industry-based students, at least for students in company environments with limited research tradition.
- Surprisingly enough, there is no indication in our material that the time needed in order to produce PhDs in industry differs from what is usually expected.
- Without any particular evidence in the interview material, we still feel that there is reason to investigate further whether and how the criteria for selecting and admitting PhD candidates might differ when training together with industry is planned.
- In our investigation, industry was not reported to execute any undue control or influence on the research topics selected and the results sought.
- More studies need to be performed in order to investigate to what degree and under what conditions doctoral studies should be located in the company and how important actual presence in the academic research environment is for the doctoral student.

A general experience is that companies active in the IT area can rarely provide an environment stable enough to sustain a complete PhD study period of about four to five years. Even in large R&D-intensive companies organizational changes were frequent, not to mention the situation in small and medium-size enterprises. Thus the doctoral students experienced several reorganizations and structural changes, with some of the companies involved disappearing or being bought by others. Even if the doctoral student was allowed to continue the studies in such a case, major obstacles with serious consequences for the doctoral education were usually created by these organization al changes.

On the evidence of these experiences, there are reasons to consider changes in the doctoral education for industry doctoral students in the future, with an increased focus on an organization providing closure after shorter periods of study, including for instance the following:

- an independent preparatory programme with doctoral courses;
- a special study plan for an industry licentiate preparing for a career in industry;
- an organization with two-phase doctoral studies with distinct periods at the university and in industry, respectively;
- a 'rapid' industry doctoral programme requiring licentiate-level qualifications for admission, where the doctoral student may have a traditional scientific training before undertaking a dissertation project in industry.

To summarize, the in-depth interview study of the experiences of the doctoral students in the industry research school in applied IT and software engineering indicates that, even within a single research school, there is a huge variation in conditions, depending on the type of work environment provided by the company. By discriminating between research-intensive, engineering and consultant environments, we can identify important descriptive factors for understanding the situation of the individual student. In general, the study casts light on the hard conditions for industry doctoral students to comply with the demands from the two worlds or cultures involved. while at the same time they expressed their appreciation of the personal satisfaction, not to say joy, resulting from the studies. For the future, many open questions about how to organize doctoral education for PhD students affiliated with companies, as exemplified at the beginning of this chapter, still remain to be settled. More research is needed in order to create an understanding of the ways in which the open education process with doctoral students at companies can be improved.

REFERENCES

Adler, N., T. Hellström, M. Jacob and F. Norrgren, (2000), 'A model for the institutionalization of university–industry partnerships: the FENIX research programme', in M. Jacob and T. Hellström (eds), *The Future of Knowledge Production in the Academy*, Buckingham: Open University Press.

Barnett, R. (1992), *Improving Higher Education – Total Quality Care*, Buckingham: Open University Press.

Becher, T. and M. Kogan (1992), *Process and Structure in Higher Education*, London: Routledge.

Bergman, B. (1997), 'Forskarutbildningsprocessen' (The postgraduate education process), unpublished manuscript, Department of Mechanical Engineering, Quality Technology and Management, Linköpings University.

Dewey, J. ([1916] 1966), *Democracy and Education: An Introduction to the Philosophy of Education*, New York: Free Press.

Etzkowitz, H. (2002), *MIT and the Rise of Entrepreneurial Science*, London: Routledge.

Etzkowitz, H., P. Asplund and N. Nordman (2001), 'Beyond Humboldt: emergence of academic entrepreneurship in the U.S. and Sweden', Cerum working paper no 27, Centre for Regional Science, Umeå University.

Gibbons, M., C. Limoges, H. Novotny, S. Schwarzman, P. Scott and M. Throw (1994), *The New Production of Knowledge: The Dynamics of Science and Research in Contemporary Society*, London: Sage.

Goodlad, S. (1995), *The Quest for Quality: Sixteen Forms of Heresy in Higher Education*, Buckingham: Open University Press.

Hanberger, A., I. Schild and D. Hamilton (2001), 'Academy–industry collaboration. Mid-term evaluation of the knowledge foundation's knowledge exchange programme', Umeå Center for Evaluation Research, Umeå University.

Hägglund, S. (2000), 'IT and the management of distributed PhD study programs', proceedings of the 5th Peder Sather Symposium, Higher Education in the Digital World, University of California at Berkeley, March.

Jacob, M. and T. Hellström (eds) (2000), *The Future of Knowledge Production in the Academy*, Buckingham: Open University Press.

Lindén, J. (1998), *Handledning av doktorander* (Supervision of doctoral students), Nora: Nya Doxa.

Säljö, R. (2000), *Lärande i praktiken – Ett sociokulturellt perspektiv* (Learning in practice – a sociocultural perspective), Stockholm: Bokförlaget Prisma.

Slaughter, S., T. Campbell, M. Holleman and E. Morgan (2002), 'The "traffic" in graduate students: graduate students as tokens of exchange between academe and industry', *Science, Technology, and Human Values*, **27**, 282–312.

Strömberg Sölveborn, L. (1983), 'Doktoranders studiesituation – en undersökning vid samhällsvetenskapliga fakulteten' (Doctoral students' study situation – an investigation at the faculty of social science), PhD dissertation, Uppsala: University.

Wallgren, L. (1994), 'Handledningens roll för genomströmningen' (The role of supervision in throughput), bachelors's thesis, Department of Behavioural Sciences, Linköping University.

Wallgren, L. (1997), 'Forskarutbildningens två arenor – Doktoranders syn på sin situation'. (The two arenas of postgraduate education – doctoral students' view of their situation), master's thesis, Department of Behavioural Sciences, Linköping

University.
Wallgren, L. (2003), 'Skilda världar – Företagsdoktoranders upplevelser av forskarutbildning' (Different worlds – industrial doctoral students' experiences of postgraduate education), Licentiate thesis 64/03, LiU-PEK-R-232, Department of Behavioural Sciences, Linköping University.

6. Cross-national variation in knowledge search and exchange activities: optoelectronics suppliers in Britain and France

Geoff Mason, Jean-Paul Beltramo and Jean-Jacques Paul

INTRODUCTION[1]

In recent years corporate managers have paid increasing attention to ways in which the creativity of their organizations might be enhanced as a means of responding to more intense competitive pressures in international product markets and the speeding up of innovation cycles. In particular, it is recognized that expansion of creativity and innovative potential at enterprise level depends greatly on the ways in which highly-qualified engineers and scientists are recruited, trained and deployed. Yet employers hardly have a free hand in making such choices. On the contrary, cross-country comparisons suggest that, wherever they are based, enterprises typically adjust to country-specific characteristics of higher education structures and high-level labour markets in developing strategies for recruitment and deployment of highly-qualified personnel.

For example, in comparisons of matched samples of production and research establishments in the British and German chemicals, mechanical engineering and electronics industries, Mason and Wagner (1994, 1999, 2000) found that the very different predominant criteria for recruitment of engineers and scientists in each country reflected marked differences in national–institutional arrangements for higher education. Thus in Germany nearly all employers emphasized their preference for the higher level of theoretical knowledge signified by MSc- and PhD-level qualifications which constitute a much larger proportion of higher education qualifications in Germany than in Britain. Conversely in Britain the great majority of engineers and scientists enter employment after completion of first (bachelor-level) degrees and British employers typically placed a high value on the work experience which first degree graduates could accumulate while postgraduates of the same age were still involved in full-time education.

The great majority of highly-qualified scientists and engineers in German establishments had been recruited directly from their universities. In some cases they were already known beforehand to their employers through previous industry-based project work or periods of industrial experience associated with their degree studies. Most of them were expected to remain with their companies, often spreading out from research, design and development to other departments. By contrast, in British establishments labour turnover was generally higher than in Germany and two-thirds of recently-recruited scientists and engineers had previous experience of full-time employment in other companies. British managers stressed that recruiting experienced personnel was not just a means of reducing training requirements but also helped to bring 'new ideas' and new approaches to technical problem solving into their firms. 'British–German' differences of this kind were apparent even within third-country multinational enterprises operating in both countries which appeared well capable of adapting to host country labour market settings and higher education structures (Mason and Wagner, 2000).

The present chapter reports on an extension of the matched-sample comparative method to the British and French electronics industries, based on a rapidly changing product area where the creative potential of organizations greatly depends on the capability of their highly-qualified employees to stay up-to-date with, and make effective use of, advances in knowledge generated elsewhere, as well as on their own collective ability to create and make use of new knowledge.

As indicators of the capacity of electronics establishments to develop creative knowledge environments, we focus on measures of research interactions and collaboration with other establishments engaged in new product development and with external organizations such as universities and research institutes. This emphasis on openness to knowledge sources external to each establishment reflects the increasing extent to which enterprises need to diversify into areas of knowledge which lie beyond their traditional competences, for example to assimilate new technical advances which depend on the combination of previously distinct technologies (such as the use of new materials in electronics).

From a different but related perspective Camagni (1991) stresses the role which network relations between different organizations play in reducing technical and market uncertainty for network participants. In developing networks of this kind, it is a great asset to establishments if individual engineers and scientists in their employ are themselves well plugged into personal networks. The origins of networks embracing firms, universities and specialist research organizations often lie in informal information trading and reciprocal favours between individual researchers which subsequently serve as a foundation for formal research collaboration between the organizations in which they are employed (Von Hippel, 1987; Krainer and Schultz, 1993).

Given the potential for individual engineers and scientists to carry personal contacts and networks with them when transferring between employers, it seems likely that inter-country differences in highly-qualified labour mobility may contribute to very different patterns of interorganizational network formation and knowledge transfer in different national economies. In this context, the first hypothesis we wish to explore is as follows.

H1   That the incidence of external knowledge search and exchange activities and research linkages at establishment level will be positively associated with individual mobility in national labour markets for engineers and scientists.

Secondly, given the advantages enjoyed by postgraduate engineers and scientists, particularly PhDs, in developing mutually beneficial collaborative relationships with academic researchers, we also examine the evidence for a more narrowly-defined hypothesis:

H2   That enterprise research linkages with universities and public or private, non-profit research institutes will be positively associated with the orientation of national higher education systems towards production of postgraduates in engineering and science subjects.

The chapter is organized as follows. The second section provides details of sample selection and methodology. The third section examines how British–French differences in higher education systems and highly-qualified labour markets manifested themselves in the two samples of establishments. The fourth section reports on quantitative measures of external research linkages and knowledge search and exchange in each sample, while the fifth presents qualitative research findings on the extent and nature of establishments' external research interactions and knowledge sourcing activities. The sixth section concludes.

THE MATCHED SAMPLES OF ESTABLISHMENTS

The specific product area chosen for investigation was optoelectronic components which have a range of potential applications in industries as diverse as telecommunications equipment, machinery manufacturing and defence systems.[2] In this sector the term 'components' typically refers to both physical devices and subassemblies which incorporate new software developments and is by no means confined to hardware.

In total, visits were made to 26 British and 22 French establishments during 1996–97. As shown in Table 6.1, some 31 of these visits were to corporate establishments (either production sites, detached research centres within larger enterprises or smaller establishments which were principally engaged in R&D and prototyping activities at the time of our visits). The remaining visits were to private, non-profit or public research institutes, university departments or other organizations such as regional development agencies. Given the relatively small size of samples involved in labour-intensive research of this kind, care was taken to ensure that the two samples of establishments were not only well-matched for product area but also comprised a mix of establishment employment sizes which broadly reflected the population size distributions for

Table 6.1   Number of establishments visited, by type and employment size group

	Britain	France
Corporate establishments		
Production[a]	10	8
R&D, prototyping[b]	4	5
Detached R&D centres[c]	3	1
Private non-profit research organizations/institutes	4	0
Public research institutes	0	4
Universities	2	1
Other organizations	3	3
Total	26	22
Employment size group (corporate establishments only)		
Under 100	6	5
100–499	6	8
500–999	2	0
1000 plus	3	1
Total	17	14

Notes:
[a] Production establishments including on-site research, design and development departments.
[b] Establishments where R&D expenditures represented more than 50% of annual turnover.
[c] Detached research centres within larger enterprises.

the wider electronic component industries in each case (Table 6.2).[3] In both countries the corporate establishments comprised a mix of largely 'domestic' small and medium-sized enterprises and larger sites owned by multinational enterprises. Thus both samples included establishments owned by large domestically owned enterprises which are among the largest R&D spenders and producers of electronics patents in each country. At the same time the British sample included a higher proportion of foreign-owned enterprises in order to reflect the greater importance of such enterprises in the wider British industry. The visits were geographically clustered in the following regions: southern England, Scotland, Brittany, Ile de France and the Rhône-Alpes.

The establishments visited were initially identified through trade directories and listings of research organizations. Detailed information about employment and principal activities was sought by telephone before formal requests for visits were made. In Britain two-thirds of corporate establishments which were formally approached for a visit agreed to participate. In France the response rate was just over 90 per cent. The principal form of information gathering during the visits was extensive semi-structured interviews with senior technical directors or managers. Nearly all visits included direct observation of production and/or research facilities. The visits lasted between half a day and a day and, if necessary, were followed up with further detailed enquiries by telephone or letter. The main characteristics of sample establishments are summarized in Table 6.2, together with code numbers used to refer to extracts from managerial interviews in subsequent sections.

HIGHER EDUCATION STRUCTURES AND HIGHLY-QUALIFIED LABOUR MARKETS IN BRITAIN AND FRANCE

There are several longstanding differences between Britain and France in higher education structures and the operations of high-level labour markets which might be expected to have a bearing on knowledge search and exchange activities at establishment level.

As in Germany, the great majority of higher education diplomas in engineering and science subjects in France have long required five years of study (including several months' industrial training inside a company). This contrasts with first (bachelor) degrees (such as BSc awards) in engineering and science subjects in Britain, which typically require only three or four years of study. In length and breadth, therefore, French university courses effectively correspond to the British postgraduate masters degrees.

In recent years the annual output of new engineers per head of population from French engineering schools has been much the same as the annual output

Table 6.2 *Main characteristics of samples of establishments*

Code	Establishment size group (no. of employees)	Principal activity[a]	Main end-user market[b]	Region[c]	Ownership and geographical orientation[d]
Britain					
B1	1000 plus	Production	Telecoms	SE	FMNC
B2	1000 plus	Production	Defence	Scot	DMNC
B3	500–999	Production	Telecoms	SE	FMNC
B4	500–999	Production	Defence	Scot	DMNC
B5	100–499	Production	Telecoms/Defence	Scot	DMNC
B6	100–499	Production	Diverse industries	SE	Domestic
B7	100–499	Production	Diverse industries	Scot	FMNC
B8	100–499	Production	Diverse industries	Scot	FMNC
B9	Under 100	R&D/prototyping	Telecoms	SE	Domestic
B10	Under 100	Production	Telecoms	SE	Domestic
B11	Under 100	Production	Defence	SE	Domestic
B12	Under 100	R&D/prototyping	Diverse industries	Scot	Domestic
B13	1000 plus	Detached R&D centre	Telecoms	SE	FMNC
B14	500–999	Detached R&D centre	Telecoms	SE	FMNC
B15	100–499	Detached R&D centre	Defence	SE	DMNC
B16	Under 100	R&D/prototyping	Diverse industries	Scot	Domestic
B17	Under 100	R&D/prototyping	Diverse industries	Scot	Domestic

131

Table 6.2   Continued

Code	Establishment size group (no. of employees)	Principal activity[a]	Main end-user market[b]	Region[c]	Ownership and geographical orientation[d]
France					
F1	1000 plus	Production	Defence	Ile de F	DMNC
F2	100–499	Production	Defence/Diverse industries	R-A	DMNC
F3	100–499	Production	Telecoms	Ile de F	DMNC
F4	100–499	Production	Telecoms	Brit	FMNC
F5	100–499	Production	Telecoms	Other	DMNC
F6	100–499	Production	Defence	Other	DMNC
F7	100–499	Production	Telecoms	R-A	DMNC
F8	100–499	R&D/prototyping	Defence	R-A	Domestic
F9	Under 100	Production	Diverse industries	R-A	DMNC
F10	Under 100	R&D/prototyping	Diverse industries	R-A	Domestic
F11	Under 100	R&D/prototyping	Diverse industries	R-A	Domestic
F12	100–499	Detached R&D centre	Telecoms	Brit	FMNC
F13	Under 100	R&D/prototyping	Diverse industries	Ile de F	Domestic
F14	Under 100	R&D/prototyping	Diverse industries	Brit	Domestic

Notes:

[a] See notes to Table 1.

[b] Establishments are classified as serving particular end-user markets if those markets account for in excess of 50% of total sales.

[v] SE = Southern England & East Anglia; Scot = Scotland; Ile de F = Ile de France; R-A = Rhône-Alpes, Brit = Brittany; Other = Other French regions.

[d] Codes refer to parent companies as follows: FMNC = Foreign-owned multi-national; DMNC = Domestically owned multinational; Domestic = Other domestically owned enterprises.

of new graduates in engineering and technology subjects in the UK. However, for the reason just noted, this represents a substantially larger annual output of postgraduates in these disciplines in France than in Britain and this is reinforced by an annual output of new doctorates in exact and natural sciences (including engineering) in France which is almost a third higher than the total number of doctorates in engineering and science awarded annually in Britain.[4]

In engineering and science subjects the tradition of obligatory training placements as part of French university courses is also in harmony with the prevalence of internal labour markets (ILMs) in large French enterprises; that is, a longstanding preference for external recruitment to be confined to a range of 'entry-level' jobs and for the bulk of more senior positions to be filled through internal promotion (Eyraud *et al.*, 1990). In recent years there have been some signs of French ILMs being 'destabilized' but Beret (2000) reports their continued dominance in engineering sectors (if not in service sectors). Since the majority of French engineers are expected to stay with their initial employers throughout their careers, industrial training placements during higher education studies have traditionally played a key role in enabling enterprises to evaluate prospective employees in some depth before making job offers.

By contrast, in Britain, highly-qualified engineers and scientists tend to operate in occupational labour markets (OLMs) which are characterized by a much higher degree of individual mobility between enterprises than is found in France. The proportionately greater availability of experienced engineers and scientists on the open market encourages many British employers to recruit sizeable proportions of experienced engineers and scientists at the same time as taking on brand new graduates in these subjects who are less likely than their French counterparts to have had any serious prior exposure to industrial workplaces.

In our two samples of establishments the mix of qualifications held by research engineers and scientists broadly mirrored the British–French differences in higher education structures described above. In British establishments roughly 12 per cent of graduate employees in R&D departments held PhDs, another 12 per cent held masters degrees and the remaining 76 per cent were qualified to bachelor degree level. In the French sample some 16 per cent of graduate employees were PhD-qualified and the remainder all held engineering diplomas corresponding to British masters degrees.

External recruitment patterns in the two samples also reflected the national characteristics described above. For example, in French production and R&D/prototyping establishments about 64 per cent of externally recruited graduate engineers and scientists engaged in R&D activity had been taken on direct from engineering school or university in the three years prior to visits, a considerably higher proportion than in Britain (41 per cent).[5]

This reflected a common preference among French managers for recruitment of relatively young graduates in order to 'form' (train and develop) them in 'enterprise culture' (F8) and in order to benefit from their up-to-date academic knowledge and training (F5). Other advantages cited were their youthful enthusiasm and their close personal contacts with the institutions from which they had graduated. Some French-based companies did show signs of increased willingness to recruit engineers who had some post-university employment experience with other companies, but even in these cases recruitment of experienced engineers was still largely confined to relatively young people (usually with about two years' experience in smaller electronics companies, not always specifically engaged in optoelectronics).

In the British sample the recruitment practices of large defence electronics companies resembled those of their French counterparts, with strong preferences for taking on new graduates direct from university who could be 'moulded into [company] ways' and for relying on internal promotion to fill senior jobs. However the majority of British companies operating in civilian product markets were keen to recruit large numbers of graduates who had previous experience of full-time employment, alongside a proportion of new young graduates. Individuals with long histories of work experience and mobility between companies were sought after, not just to help reduce the time and resources needed to train new graduates but also in a desire to bring new ideas and 'ways of thinking' into their companies, to help 'see problems from a different perspective' (B1) or as 'a good way to absorb new technologies' (B5).

Taken together these findings confirm that the two samples of establishments were indeed operating in distinctively national labour markets with close links to domestic higher education structures. We now go on to test the two hypotheses outlined in the first section by examining the quantitative and qualitative evidence on the different patterns of external knowledge sourcing and research collaboration in each sample of establishments.

RESEARCH LINKAGES WITH EXTERNAL ORGANIZATIONS: QUANTITATIVE EVIDENCE

Table 6.3 compares the incidence of formal (contractual) research links between sample establishments and other organizations such as customer enterprises and university departments. The simple binary measure used cannot do justice to informal research contacts involving individuals employed in the different organizations. However interviews with managers and researchers in the two countries highlighted the many ways in which informal and contractually based linkages tend to overlap: in some cases informal discussions and contacts between individual engineers and scientists in different organizations had led to the development of formal relationships and the level of informal interactions had subsequently been intensified in the course of implementing formal arrangements for collaboration. In other cases it was the formalized linkages which had come first, for example companies coming together with other companies or university departments to apply for funding for joint research projects supported by national or European funding bodies. Subsequently this had provided a basis for individual researchers to develop a range of informal modes of communication with counterparts in other organizations.

The most striking inter-country difference in formal research linkages was the fact that all but one of the French sample establishments had collaborative research relationships with public sector research institutes and laboratories which are still largely financed by public funds and have thus been able to remain deeply involved in strategic research with time horizons of three years or more before any prospect of industrial commercialization (Lawton Smith, 1997). By contrast, in Britain the great majority of formerly publicly owned laboratories have been privatized and are now obliged to generate a large proportion of their annual income through short-term industrial consultancy activities. As a result the nearest equivalent to French establishments' links with public labs relationships in the British sample was the much smaller proportion (one in five) of British establishments involved with private non-profit research and technology organizations (RTOs).[6]

By contrast there were much smaller inter-country differences in the extent of establishments' research interactions with supply-chain partners. 'Research interactions/linkages' are here defined as occurring only when establishments' contacts with technical staff from customer or supplier companies go beyond discussions about clients' requirements and periodic progress reports on new product development to include two-way knowledge sharing and exchange. The unweighted measure of R&D interactions with customers shows that roughly three-quarters of British establishments had collaborative links of this kind with customers, as did almost two-thirds of their French counterparts. The unweighted incidence of formal technical alliances along the supply chain was also greater in Britain than in France. Against this the employment-weighted measures of customer interactions in the French sample are slightly above British levels, reflecting the fact that in France, to a greater extent than in Britain, it was the larger companies (rather than SMEs) which were working closely with customers (Table 6.3, rows 1 and 2). Given the small size of the samples concerned, no statistical significance can be attached to these British–French differences in measures of R&D involvement with customers, and the same applies to R&D links with suppliers (which were generally less intensive than interactions with customers in both countries).

Table 6.3 Incidence of research linkages with external organizations in national samples of corporate establishments (yes = 1, no = 0 for each establishment)

	Britain		France		Tests for equality of respective sample means (p-values)	
	Unweighted average	Employment-weighted average[a]	Unweighted average	Employment-weighted average[a]	(unweighted)	(weighted)
Supply-chain interactions						
Customers						
regular knowledge exchange[b]	0.76	0.73	0.64	0.80	0.4637	0.6657
full technical partnership[c]	0.53	0.59	0.36	0.73	0.3541	0.4523
Suppliers						
regular knowledge exchange[b]	0.35	0.47	0.23	0.15	0.4865	0.1462
full technical partnership[c]	0.18	0.32	0.08	0.18	0.4442	0.1234
Other external research linkages[d]						
Other firms (including competitors)[e]	0.12*	0.28	0.38	0.43	0.0924	0.4781
Public research institutes/ organizations[e]	0.00***	0.00***	0.92	0.98	0.0000	0.0000
Private non-profit research institutes/organizations[f]	0.18	0.30	0.00	0.00	0.1181	0.1119
Universities[g]	0.88	0.89**	0.77	0.50	0.4276	0.0230
No. of establishments	n=17	n=17	n=13	n=13		

Notes:

F-tests of equality of respective country averages (one-way analysis of variance);*** = British–French differences statistically significant at the 1% level or better, ** = 5% level, * = 10% level.

a Establishments weighted for shares of total R&D employment in national samples. Detached research centres accounted for 30% of total R&D employment in the British sample as compared to 35% in the French case. (Calculations exclude one French production establishment (F1) for which data could not be obtained.)

b Refers to contacts/meetings with customers/suppliers in course of product development process that often involve exchanges of technical knowledge and ideas which go beyond simply clarifying the details of customer/supply contract specifications. In addition to periodic technical discussions, customers/suppliers may also be involved with prototyping and/or testing.

c Refers to close technical partnerships with customers/suppliers that involve regular scheduled meetings of key personnel plus multiple layers of informal communication to discuss details of product specification and problems encountered in the course of projects; full involvement in prototyping and testing; projects may even have been initiated by customers/suppliers. Establishments classified to this category are also included under the heading 'regular knowledge exchange' with customers/suppliers in Row 2.

d Refers to formal (contractual) research linkages with firms outside the supply chain, specialist research institutions and universities.

e 'Public' here refers to non-university research institutions which typically receive core funding from governments in excess of 50% of their financial resources.

f 'Private, non-profit' here refers to research institutions which typically receive some core funding from governments but not in excess of 50% of their financial resources, and are not classifiable to either the university sector or the business enterprise sector according to guidelines laid down in the OECD's 'Frascati Manual' (OECD, 1994).

g Includes the Centre National de Recherche Scientifique (CNRS) in France.

137

However the incidence of 'pre-competitive' joint research projects and other forms of collaboration with enterprises outside the supply chain was markedly higher in France than in Britain (Table 6.3, row 5). Only two of the 17 British sample establishments had formal research links with firms outside the supply chain, compared with five of the 13 French establishments. In both British cases this involved pre-competitive collaboration with European rivals in the context of European Commission (EC) programmes, while most of the French partnerships between rival firms had been funded through the government Fonds de recherche technologique (FRT) or through joint projects supported by public sector agencies for telecoms and defence procurement, respectively, CNET (Centre National d'Etudes Télécommunications)/France Télécom; and the DGA (Direction générale pour l'armement) and DRET (Direction de la recherche et des études techniques du ministère de la défense).

Just under 90 per cent of British sample establishments and three-quarters of French establishments had formal research links with universities (Table 6.3, row 8). However, whereas four in five of the British establishments either employed university-based technical consultants or hired specialist equipment from universities or purchased both these types of service, only about half the French establishments purchased similar technical services from universities; this difference is statistically significant at a 97 per cent level of confidence (Table 6.4, row 2). Many French firms had no need of university contacts of this kind because of their continuing close involvement with public research laboratories, which tended to preclude the need for using university-based consultants and equipment.

The British sample was also characterized by a relatively high level of industrial support for PhD students (Table 6.4, row 6). British–French differences in industrial support for PhD research were statistically significant at the 96 per cent level. This gap occurred even though the proportions of sample establishments receiving government subsidies for such involvement were much the same. About 30 per cent of British sample establishments were involved with PhD training through the CASE programme, whereby doctoral students are jointly funded by government research council and industrial partners. In France a similar proportion of sample establishments were involved with the CIFRE scheme through which doctoral students are taken on as employees by sponsoring companies for three-year periods.

Taken together, the patterns of external research collaboration and knowledge sourcing shown in Tables 6.3 and 6.4 provide little support for the two main hypotheses under investigation. In respect of H1, the overall incidence of interorganizational research linkages is much the same in France (where the mobility of engineers and scientists is relatively low) as it is in Britain. Reported links with supply-chain partners do not differ significantly in the two samples and the British lead in establishment relationships with

Table 6.4   Research interactions with universities (yes = 1, no = 0 for each establishment)

	Britain		France		Tests for equality of respective sample means (p-values)	
	Unweighted average	Employment-weighted average[a]	Unweighted average	Employment-weighted average[a]	(unweighted)	(weighted)
Informal contacts with universities	1.00	1.00	0.86	0.93	0.1143	0.2570
Purchase of university services technical expertise and use of						
specialist equipment	0.65	0.78**	0.38	0.31	0.1641	0.0203
use of equipment only	0.18	0.05	0.08	0.03	0.4442	0.9030
no purchase of university technical services	0.18**	0.17**	0.54	0.65	0.0380	0.0126
Total	1.00	1.00	1.00	1.00		
Formal research contracts						
PhD	0.59	0.72**	0.38	0.28	0.2849	0.0385
other research contracts	0.53	0.66	0.46	0.32	0.7240	0.1232
No. of establishments	n=17	n=13	n=13	n=13		

Notes:
F-tests of equality of employment-weighted averages (one-way analysis of variance):
**=British–French differences statistically significant at the 5% level or better, *=10% level.
[a] See Table 6.3, note a.

universities is offset by the French establishments' close links with public laboratories. Furthermore the strength of British establishments' relationships with university-based researchers is at variance with H2 that postulated a positive link between such relationships and the orientation of national higher education systems towards postgraduate education and training in engineering and science subjects.

However, as we will now go on to describe, the *qualitative* evidence gathered during our research visits proved more fruitful in identifying the effects of different national higher education systems and labour market mobility patterns on network formation and knowledge search and exchange.

RESEARCH LINKAGES WITH EXTERNAL ORGANIZATIONS: QUALITATIVE EVIDENCE

In Britain several of the smaller sample establishments reported very close links with their main customers which involved multiple layers of informal communication between technical staff on both sides as well as regular scheduled meetings of key personnel to discuss changes to product specifications and ways to tackle technical problems which had arisen in the course of product development projects. However these relationships were frequently in a state of flux.

For example, a manager at B6 described a process whereby prospective new customers would approach several small firms like themselves to discuss their product requirements and might even commission prototypes from more than one supplier. Relationships were only likely to deepen if engineers from both the customer and the supplier firm worked well together while maintaining a mutually beneficial balance between knowledge sharing and retention: 'We learn a lot from customers and vice versa.... but we don't want to give too much knowhow away.' Another small firm (B11) regularly participated in technical meetings involving not just its own customers but its customers' customers as well and the information exchanged at these meetings often led to the development of new relationships with subcontractors for various specialist services.

In this kind of rapidly changing creative knowledge environment rival companies are well positioned to monitor each other's progress through customer and supplier contacts as well as through a general 'grapevine' in the industry based on personal contacts. Although, as noted above, each company is aware of disadvantages of giving away 'too much' information, they also have experience of the positive advantages of two-way knowledge sharing which provides incentives to stay active in new relationship building.

As might be expected, the proportionate importance of newly formed relationships with customers and suppliers – with their attendant risks and uncertainties – was less for larger British-based companies than for SMEs. This was particularly true of large defence equipment suppliers such as B2 and B4, which tended to work within the context of long established relationships with customers and suppliers. As noted in the third section, these were also the most likely of the British establishments to rely on recruitment of new young graduates rather than bring in older, experienced engineers or scientists.

But in most other British establishments a steady flow of individual engineers and scientists moving from jobs in one company to another, and bringing new personal networks of contacts with them, helped to maintain the momentum of relationship building between companies. As a result of the relatively high level of foreign investment in the British optoelectronics sector, these personal networks had often been expanded beyond the UK by working in US-owned R&D facilities in Britain (such as B1, B3, B13 and B14) where individual scientists and engineers engaged in intensive, daily communication by telephone, e-mail and video-conferencing with researchers based in other countries and also regularly crossed the Atlantic for face-to-face meetings and discussions.[7]

In the French sample the most intensive collaborative relationships between firms all seemed to hinge on a small number of large domestically owned companies, particularly the leading customers and suppliers in defence and telecoms equipment sectors. Not only did these large firms have long-established relationships with each other but SMEs also looked to them as sources of both research funding and expertise. Examples of research interactions which had been fostered in this context included a newly established small defence equipment supplier (F8) whose initial product development had been heavily subsidized by the state armaments authority (DGA). Its R&D projects had been largely motivated by two large customer enterprises which had specific applications in mind and the small firm concerned had been able to draw on the knowledge and expertise of technical staff at these large companies' own research centres throughout the projects. In another case, a small firm (F14) offering design and development services to telecoms equipment producers had benefited from access to specialist equipment belonging to France Télécom (its main customer) and from regular technical discussions with other customers in the same region where a majority of R&D personnel in each organization had over many years built up personal contacts through interactions with France Télécom's national research centre (CNET).

With the aid of government procurement agencies and (until recently) state-owned enterprises, therefore, these patterns of knowledge search and exchange among supply-chain partners were if anything more structured and well entrenched in France than in Britain. This reflects a long heritage of

French industrial planning based on the supply chain, with state agencies initially involved in constructing networks of subcontractors rather than leaving such decisions up to prime contractors (Storper, 1993). As recently pointed out by Mustar and Larédo (2002), the large civil research programmes underlying this model of state intervention largely disappeared during the 1990s and French defence research programmes have been subject to cuts in public spending. However our findings (during 1996–97) highlight the lingering effects of the large state-directed research programmes which may take some time to dissipate.

In particular there was less evidence of French companies engaging in the more risky type of relationship building found in Britain where (as described above) many of the interactions between sample establishments and their customers were based on relatively new relationships which both sides had initially entered into in a fairly speculative manner (often involving partners from other regions or other countries). For example, two of the smaller companies in the French sample which had been set up in order to commercialize scientific discoveries in public research institutes had maintained exceptionally close working relationships with those research institutes but their relationships with customers had not developed beyond discussions of those customers' specific requirements (F9, F10).

In other cases where supply-chain interactions did involve two-way knowledge sharing this tended to be confined to well established relationships with large clients. One medium-sized French-owned company (F7) had gradually reduced its dependence on defence-related markets in recent years but had not developed close collaborative research relationships with civilian clients to match those it had earlier built up with large defence equipment producers. At another medium-sized company (F5) attempting to make a similar transition away from defence and aerospace markets, a manager said that, in the event of technical problems, they were still most likely to turn to their long standing '*grands clients*' for assistance and advice.

As with research interactions along the supply chain, the two samples turned out to differ markedly in the degree of stability in establishment relationships with universities. The qualitative evidence on this score suggests that relationships between many French companies and universities, once formed, are rarely subject to change and re-formation. One large domestically owned multinational (F3) had long relied on certain universities and CNRS labs (based in universities) for scientific advice, tests and analysis and it was increasing its involvement in medium-term research programmes in conjunction with these same universities in order to meet the requirements of various government and EU funding programmes. It was taken for granted that they 'had to avoid certain [other] universities because of their close relationships with competitors'. At another French-owned multinational (F7) it was even said that they preferred to work with university and CNRS research teams that they already knew (described as '*équipes privilégiées*') rather than with unknown teams, even if the unknown teams were identified as specialists in the problems needing to be resolved.

This tendency towards stability in enterprise–university research links in the French sample was reinforced by some SMEs (F5, F14) whose university contacts were confined to their immediate region and the fact that firms often relied on individual staff members for personal contacts with universities. Since so many French firms confine new recruitment to newly qualified graduates or to people with small amounts of work experience (and, in particular, the large companies refrain from recruiting from each other) this means that very few French engineers and scientists have been able to expand their personal contacts to cover a range of different universities by working with a series of different employers.

In Britain there were also several examples of longstanding relationships between particular companies and universities which resembled those found in France and there were similar concerns about confidentiality. However these factors did not prevent the majority of British sample enterprises from actively pursuing opportunities to develop new collaborations which could prove advantageous. Indeed the relatively high mobility of experienced engineers and scientists in Britain contributed to substantial fluidity and change in research relationships with universities. For example, at the large telecoms equipment producer B1, the basic approach was described as 'defining unmet research needs and looking for the best university to carry them out'. These choices were often guided by suggestions from individual researchers who had developed extensive networks of university contacts prior to joining B1. Another foreign-owned multinational (B3) had initially taken proximity to certain universities into account in choosing its British R&D locations but was still ready to develop new relationships with other British universities in order to gain access to specific expertise and equipment. To some extent the faster rate of new relationship building in British enterprise–university links reflected the considerable financial pressures on universities to generate contract income and thus to take a proactive approach to identifying prospective industrial research partners.[8]

SUMMARY AND ASSESSMENT

It is now widely recognized that expansion of creativity and innovative potential at enterprise level depends greatly on the ways in which highly qualified engineers and scientists are recruited, trained and deployed. Yet, in developing strategies for recruitment and deployment of highly qualified personnel, previous cross-country comparisons have suggested that employers need to adjust to country-specific characteristics of higher education structures and high-level labour markets.

This chapter reports on a comparison of high-level skills, labour mobility and knowledge search and exchange and external research linkages in matched samples of production and research establishments in the British and French electronics industries. As indicators of the capacity of electronics establishments to develop creative knowledge environments, we focus on measures of openness to external sources of technical and market knowledge and organizational capacity to develop network relations with other firms, universities and specialist research organizations.

Two main hypotheses were investigated:

H1   That the incidence of external knowledge search and exchange activities and research linkages at establishment level will be positively associated with individual mobility in national labour markets for engineers and scientists.

H2: That enterprise research linkages with universities and public or private, non-profit research institutes will be positively associated with the orientation of national higher education systems towards production of postgraduates in engineering and science subjects.

The two samples of establishments were found to be operating in distinctively different national labour markets for engineers and scientists, reflecting structural differences in national higher education systems (with a greater orientation towards production of PhDs and other postgraduates in France than in Britain) and a far higher level of individual mobility between enterprises in Britain than is found in France.

However quantitative measures of establishments' external knowledge sourcing and research interactions did not support either of our two main hypotheses. In respect of H1, the overall incidence of interorganizational research linkages was found to be much the same in Britain (where the mobility of engineers and scientists is relatively high) as it was in France. In particular the proportions of establishments collaborating with customers or suppliers on new product development were found to be broadly similar in the two countries. Secondly, in relation to H2, it was actually in Britain, where higher education structures are much less geared to postgraduate education and training than in France, that the strongest relationships between establishments and universities were identified, especially links involving PhD training or purchase of university-based technical services.

One factor driving the relatively high level of enterprise–university interactions in the British sample was the severe financial constraints on UK universities which had induced many academic departments to take a highly proactive approach to identifying potential new sources of income in the form of industrial research partners. By contrast some French establishments saw little need to develop relationships with universities because of their close research links with public laboratories.

The *qualitative* evidence gathered during our research visits proved much more fruitful in identifying the effects of different national higher education systems and labour market mobility patterns on network formation and knowledge search and exchange. In the case of supply-chain research linkages, there was a faster rate of *new* external relationship building in Britain which was stimulated to a considerable extent by steady flows of individual engineers and scientists moving from jobs in one company to another and bringing new personal networks of external contacts with them. These individual-level connections provided the basis for British-based establishments to widen the range of external knowledge sources available to them and to embark regularly on new collaborative relationships with current or prospective supply-chain partners while disengaging from some of their other relationships. At the same time the majority of British establishments actively sought to diversify their relationships with universities as well in order to gain access to a range of expertise, and this tendency was encouraged by the establishments being regularly approached by different university departments in search of industrial funding.

By contrast external research relationships and knowledge sourcing patterns in the French sample of establishments were characterized by a high degree of stability. In the case of inter-enterprise interactions, this partly reflected the lingering effects of previous French state involvement in supply-chain planning. However relationships with public laboratories and universities were also remarkably stable, in part because of the French establishments' limited recruitment of experienced engineers and scientists who might bring with them the personal contacts needed to cultivate new knowledge sources and potential new collaborators outside the firms' existing relationships.

These findings suggest that British–French differences in higher education structures and highly qualified labour markets contribute to very different patterns of comparative advantage in the development of creative knowledge environments. Many researchers have highlighted the time, effort and resources that are needed to develop innovation networks involving industrial establishments and supply-chain partners, universities and research institutes, typically requiring a progressive build-up of trust and recognition of mutual self-interest on the part of key technical personnel on all sides (Powell, 1990; Grandori and Soda, 1995; Lazaric and Lorenz, 1998). In this respect French establishments may well derive benefits from the relative stability of their external research relationships.

However, in a rapidly-changing industry, constituent members of networks also need to be open to new sources of knowledge and ideas which lie outside those networks (Granovetter, 1983, 1985; Cooke and Wills, 1999). Here our qualitative findings point to clear advantages to British establishments in their efforts to enhance organizational creativity and innovative potential. Firstly, the greater fluidity of their collaborative relationships, often in the process of change and re-formation, helps to expand the scope of their employees' knowledge search and exchange activities. Secondly, the higher level of highly qualified labour mobility in Britain contributes directly to enterprise knowledge bases and capacity for network building through the new ideas and personal contacts which experienced engineers and scientists carry with them when they move between employers.

The implications of these findings for policy designed to promote network formation and knowledge transfer are rather different in each country. In Britain a case can be made for policies aimed at encouraging innovation partnerships between enterprises and other organizations to include incentives for the various partners to pursue more research projects of a medium-term strategic nature than they might otherwise be inclined to do. Conversely, in France, greater priority arguably needs to be given to incentives for enterprises to seek new partners outside their existing networks.

NOTES

1. This chapter is based on research which was supported by the UK Economic and Social Research Council (Grant No. L323253028). It draws on similar material to that contained in a longer and more detailed paper published in *Research Policy* (January 2004) which focuses on external knowledge sourcing in different national settings. We are grateful to the ESRC and to the companies, research institutes and other organizations which participated in the research. Responsibility for any errors is, of course, ours alone.
2. More precise details about the selected product area are withheld to ensure the confidentiality of participating companies and research organizations.
3. Estimated medians and quartiles of enterprise size distributions in the electronics components industries are as follows: Britain median 350 employees; lower quartile 85; upper quartile 1850; France 375, 60, 1600 (Sources: CSO, *Annual Census of Production*, 1993; SESSI, *Enquête Annuelle d'Entreprise*, 1995).
4. Sources: *Repères et Références Statistiques sur les enseignements et la formation*, 1997 edn; Ministère de l'Education, de l'Enseignement Supérieur et de la Recherche; Rapport sur les études doctorales, DGRT, Ministère de l'Education nationale, de la recherche et de la technologie (MENRT), December 1997; DfEE, Education and Training Statistics for the United Kingdom, 1997.
5. This difference in recruiting practices is statistically significant at a 95 per cent confidence level.
6. 'Public labs' here refers to non-university research institutions which typically receive core funding from governments in excess of 50 per cent of their financial resources. This category does not include the Centre National de Recherche Scientifique (CNRS) in France because of its assimilation into university research.
7. The rates of inward investment by foreign-owned electronics producers into Britain and

France have differed greatly over the last two decades. Estimated values of the US foreign direct investment position abroad in electric and electronic equipment in 1996 were US$3256 million (Britain) and US$652 million (France). (Source: Economics and Statistics Administration / Bureau of Economic Analysis, US Department of Commerce.) This position is measured as the year end value of US parents' equity (including retained earnings) in, and net outstanding loans to, their foreign affiliates.

8. In a survey of higher education institutions in the UK, Howells *et al.* (1998) found that 'access to industrial funding' ranked far higher than any other motive for universities to establish research contract and consultancy links with enterprises.

REFERENCES

Beret, P. (2000), *Les Transformations de l'Espace de Qualification des Chercheurs des Entreprises*, Paris : Service du Développement Technologique et Industriel.

Camagni, R. (1991), 'Local "milieu", uncertainty and innovation networks: towards a new dynamic theory of economic space', in R. Camagni (ed.), *Innovation Networks: Spatial Perspectives*, London: Belhaven Press.

Cooke, P. and D. Wills (1999), 'Small firms, social capital and the enhancement of business performance through innovation programmes', *Small Business Economics*, **1**, 1–16.

Eyraud, F., D. Marsden and J-J. Silvestre (1990), 'Marché professionnel et marché interne du travail en Grande-Bretagne et en France', *Revue Internationale du Travail*, **129** (4).

Grandori, A. and G. Soda (1995), 'Inter-firm networks: antecedents, mechanisms and forms', *Organization Studies*, **16**(2), 183–214.

Granovetter, M. (1983), 'The strength of weak ties', *American Journal of Sociology*, **87**(1), 1360–80.

Granovetter, M. (1985), 'Economic action and social structure: the problem of embeddedness', *American Journal of Sociology*, **91**(3), 481–510.

Howells, J., M. Nedeva and L. Georghiou (1998), '*Industry-Academic Links in the UK*', HEFCE ref. 98/70, Higher Education Funding Council for England, Bristol.

Krainer, K. and M. Schultz (1993), 'Informal collaboration in R&D. The formation of networks across organizations, *Organization Studies'*, **14**(2), 189–209.

Lawton Smith, H. (1997), 'Adjusting the roles of national laboratories: some comparisons between UK, French and Belgian institutions', *R&D Management*, **27**(4), 319–31.

Lazaric, N. and E. Lorenz (1998), 'Trust and organisational learning during inter-firm cooperation', in N. Lazaric and E. Lorenz (eds), *Trust and Economic Learning*, Cheltenham, UK and Lynne. USA: Edward Elgar.

Mason, G. and K. Wagner (1994), 'Innovation and the skill mix: chemicals and engineering in Britain and Germany', *National Institute Economic Review*, **148**, 61–72.

Mason, G. and K. Wagner (1999), 'Knowledge transfer and innovation in Britain and Germany: "Intermediate institution" models of knowledge transfer under strain?, *Industry and Innovation*, **6**(1), 85–109.

Mason, G. and K. Wagner (2000), *High-Level Skills, Knowledge Transfer and Industrial Performance: Electronics in Britain and Germany*, London: Anglo-German Foundation.

Mustar, P. and P. Larédo (2002), 'Innovation and research policy in France

(1980–2000) or the disappearance of the Colbertist state', *Research Policy*, **31**, 55–72.

OECD (1994), 'Proposed standard practice for surveys of research and experimental development – Frascati manual', Paris.

Powell, W. (1990), 'Neither market nor hierarchy: network forms of organization', *Research in Organizational Behaviour*, Greenwich, CT: JAI Press, pp. 295–336.

Storper, M. (1993), 'Regional "worlds" of production: learning and innovation in the technology districts of France, Italy and the USA', *Regional Studies*, **27**(5), 433–55.

Von Hippel, E. (1987), 'Cooperation between rivals: informal knowhow trading', *Research Policy*, **16**(6), 291–302.

7. Technological paradigm shifts and new modes of coordination in science-based industries

Robert Kaiser

INTRODUCTION

Technological paradigm shifts have occurred in recent years especially in industries that have commonly been characterized as science-based. In science-based industries, firms are intensively engaged in cooperation with universities and non-university research institutes as they rely heavily on the exchange of knowledge with the domestic or international science base. The dependence on scientific knowledge is mainly due to four distinct features that characterize those industries: drastically increasing costs of innovation, the growing significance of interdisciplinarity, an increasingly close relationship between basic research and industrial application, and a tighter meshing of research and demand (cf. Meyer-Krahmer, 1997, p.298). In order to measure the extent to which a specific industry is dependent on scientific knowledge, Grupp and Schmoch (1992), among others, used citations of scientific publications in patents as a quantitative operationalization of science-based technologies and applied this indicator to 30 technical fields. Their results confirm that both fields that are under consideration for this analysis, telecommunication equipment and pharmaceutical biotechnology, belong to the group of science-based technologies. Biotechnology and pharmaceuticals showed the strongest relationship to science, while telecommunications followed some distance behind (cf. Meyer-Krahmer and Schmoch, 1998).

This chapter analyses new modes of coordination within the German telecommunication equipment and the pharmaceutical biotechnology industries that have emerged primarily as a result of technological paradigm shifts.[1] Modes of coordination have changed not only in the relationship of firms with external knowledge providers, such as universities and non-university research institutes, but also concerning linkages with customers or competitors. However this chapter focuses on changes in science–industry relations within the process of innovation as well as on the role of public policies which promoted those changes. It will be argued that, in the case of telecommunications, universities and specialized non-university research organizations became an integral part of the firms' R&D system, whereas in biotechnology the technological paradigm shift created totally new phases at the beginning of the innovation process. Specialist small and medium-sized research companies, which often have been established out of publicly funded research organizations, did not only become involved in those early phases, but they were able to monopolize related activities. Public innovation policies at different territorial levels have reacted to and supported these changes. In telecommunications, for example, public funding for basic research has been increased in order to compensate for decreasing investments on the corporate side. Moreover the state put financial pressure especially on universities and non-university research institutes and thus increased dependence on private sector funds. In biotechnology, public policies have focused on various measures that were aimed at facilitating the commercialization of biotechnological research, either through the provision of venture capital or by initiating innovative programmes which supported the creation of network-based clusters.

The chapter is organized as follows. Subsequent to this introduction, the second section will refer to the theoretical literature on different modes of economic coordination as far as the governance of innovation processes is concerned. The third section provides a short overview of the technological paradigm shifts that have occurred in the telecommunication equipment and the pharmaceutical biotechnology sector. The fourth section analyses to what extent organizational reforms within Germany's leading telecommunication equipment manufacturers and public research organizations supported the emergence of new modes of coordination, whereas the fifth section focuses on the pharmaceutical biotechnology industry which has emerged in Germany only since the mid-1990s after reforms of certain institutional framework conditions that were aimed at facilitating the commercialization of knowledge in this field. The sixth section deals with the institutional level, showing that public policies at different territorial levels have promoted these changes in both industries. A final section summarizes the major findings.

The study is based on systemic analytical concepts of innovation in so far as firms, universities and non-university research laboratories are considered as innovative organizations that interact with each other under conditions set by an institutional environment in which these organizations are embedded (cf. Braczyk *et al.*, 1998; Cooke, 2001; Dosi *et al.*, 1988; Edquist, 1997; Freeman, 1987, 1995; Lundvall, 1992; Nelson, 1987, 1993; OECD, 1999a, 1999b, 2001; Porter, 1990). Analysing innovation processes under a systemic approach provides the advantage that differentiations in institutional, infrastructural or cultural conditions for innovation, which exist among countries, regions or sectors, become visible. These conditions determine the relationships among private industrial actors, public administrations and the science and education systems, as well as the forms and intensity of their interactions. Therefore, a systemic approach towards innovation allows us to look more deeply into recent changes that have occurred within university–industry–government relationships which are certainly crucial for science-based industries.

These relations, along with the internal transformations within each of these spheres, have been stressed especially by the so-called 'Triple Helix' thesis (Benner and Sandström, 2000; Etzkowitz and Leydesdorff, 2000; Leydesdorff and Etzkowitz, 1996; Leydesdorff, 2000). From this literature the chapter borrows the ideas that relations within a triple helix configuration cannot be expected to be stable and that the systems of innovation, in which such relations exist, remain in transition (Etzkowitz and Leydesdorff, 2000, pp.112–13).

Finally it seems obvious that new modes of coordination between and within organizations have an impact on the specific characteristics creative knowledge environments (CKE) develop. This chapter primarily deals with those environments at the macro and meso levels where organizational relationships changed significantly at the sectoral and national level. However, as this volume shows, there are many interactions between environments at different levels. With respect to the two industries which have been analysed for this chapter, it can be said that changes in interorganizational relations have certainly altered the conditions under which employees or corporate units perform creative work.

THE THEORETICAL BACKGROUND: DIFFERENT MODES OF ECONOMIC COORDINATION FOR THE GOVERNANCE OF INNOVATION PROCESSES

Innovative actors engage in institutional arrangements in order to coordinate economic activities related to research and development. They thus aim at reducing uncertainty which is inescapably linked to the innovation process. Institutional arrangements are central for the study of the way in which innovation processes are governed. As an analytical approach, the governance concept differentiates between various modes of coordination as well as between different types of actors and actor constellations. Scholars from various disciplines, such as economics, sociology, political science and even anthropology, have been concerned, from many points of view, with the question of the way different actors coordinate their (economic) activities. However it seems to be widely accepted that there are at least five different kinds of institutional arrangements that coordinate economic activities (cf. Hollingsworth and Boyer, 1997).

A first important differentiation has been made between markets and hierarchies. Market coordination involves autonomous actors that define the rules of exchange through contracts, while hierarchical coordination takes place within a single organization with a formal administrative and bureaucratic command system (Lindberg *et al.*, 1994, pp.19–22). Both coordination mechanisms thus differentiate primarily in view of the actors involved in economic exchanges. In view of these alternatives, transaction cost theory, for example, has argued that actors tend to coordinate their activities within a hierarchical structure, for example within a vertically integrated firm, if the costs of exchange through the market become prohibitive (Williamson, 1975, 1985). For the coordination of innovation processes, however, both institutional arrangements have their limits. Roughly speaking, markets and hierarchies provide for only two alternatives for the acquisition of an innovation. It is either purchased from an external provider or developed within the firm. Whereas the first alternative requires that characteristics and performance of an innovative product or process can be specified on a contractual basis, the latter case implies that the respective knowledge already exists within the organization.

Networks are a third coordination mechanism that has increased in recent years both in number and in variety. In contrast to hierarchies, actors involved in networks remain autonomous, while, compared to market coordination, there are more complex institutional settings that include decision-making processes at various levels (Hage and Alter 1997, p.96). In a sense, network arrangements combine the advantages of market and hierarchical coordination without incurring the disadvantages. Networks offer more flexibility than hierarchies as they guarantee permanent access to critical resources. There are, however, various kinds of networks that differ in size, purpose and governance mechanisms. Lindberg *et al.*, have differentiated between obligational networks that coordinate flows of resources among a limited number of actors in order to serve individual interests and promotional networks that are aimed at reducing excessive competition or facilitating cooperation throughout an industrial sector (1994, pp.18–26). The most common forms of networks that coordinate innovation activities are joint ventures and strategic alliances. Depending on their size, aim and their reach within an industrial sector, joint ventures and strategic alliances can be characterized as either obligational or promotional networks.

The state, as a fourth institutional arrangement, has a twofold impact on the coordination of economic activities. Firstly, primarily as a procurer of private sector goods and services, the state is directly involved in coordination processes with the industry. Secondly, through various public policies, the state sanctions and regulates the non-state coordinating mechanisms. These forms of direct and indirect coordination play an important role for innovations. Procurement policies, for example, can be designed in a way that demands certain technological developments, for example concerning environmental innovations. In the field of research and development, indirect coordination takes place especially through regulations that determine interactions with the public R&D infrastructure. This concerns financial incentives, such as availability of funds for collaborative research projects, infrastructural issues, for example mobility of personnel or existence of technology transfer offices, and the legal framework, especially in view of regulations on intellectual property rights.

A fifth mode of coordination is the interaction of actors within associations. In contrast to markets, corporate hierarchies and networks, associations comprised similar types of actors engaged in similar kinds of activities (Lindberg *et al.*, 1994, pp.26–8). Within associations, the coordination of actors takes place on the basis of formal agreements which define common goals and interests (cf. Streeck and Schmitter, 1985). The importance of associations for the coordination of economic activities varies significantly between economies and nation-states. In coordinated market economies, as they exist to a varying degree in most countries in continental Europe, associations have a strong role in determining industrial relations, whereas in liberal market economies, such as in Britain or the United States, the institutional capacity for collective action is considerably less developed (Soskice, 1999).

In view of innovation processes in science-based industries, these different coordination mechanisms have various consequences. Market coordination, for example, increases the pressure on universities and non-university research organizations to realign efforts from basic research towards short-term and applied research projects. As a consequence, the state has to ensure that publicly funded research organizations adapt to market needs (for example through the establishment of technology transfer or patent units), whereas the orientation towards applied research demands that public funds be increasingly delegated to basic research. Within firms, hierarchical coordination becomes less likely the more the required knowledge tends to be interdisciplinary. As firms increasingly require external knowledge, the innovative performance depends more and more on the organization's absorptive capacity, that is the ability to scan technological developments especially outside the firms' business activities (Cohen and Levinthal, 1989).

Inter-firm networks are an important coordination mechanism primarily for science-based industries. As Hagedoorn has shown, about 70 per cent of alliances that were established in the 1980s originated from only three technical fields: information technology, biotechnology and new materials

(1995, pp.207f). Public policies have a certain influence on the ways and means of network arrangements. They can support such networks through the provision of R&D funds for collaborative research while competition law or regulations on foreign investment may hinder network arrangements. As for the role of associations, it has been argued more generally that coordinated market economies tend to specialize in complex products as they develop innovation strategies that favour incremental technological advance in established fields (Soskice, 1999, p.114). Comparing Germany with the United States, Porter (1990) showed that Germany was significantly behind at the end of the 1980s in terms of the creation of internationally competitive industries in newer fields, such as electronics, biotechnology and new materials. However, more recently, Germany was able to catch up in these fields, primarily thanks to significant institutional reforms within the national innovation system (cf. Kaiser, 2003; Kaiser and Grande, 2002a, 2002b).

TECHNOLOGICAL PARADIGM SHIFTS IN TELECOMMUNICATIONS AND BIOTECHNOLOGY

Technological paradigms can be understood as strong prescriptions on the directions of technical change pursued or neglected by innovative organizations (cf. Dosi, 1982, p.152). Those paradigms comprehensively influence innovation processes as they concern not only theoretical approaches, but also methods and tools applied for technical change (Green *et al.*, 1999). For that reason, it is obvious that technological paradigm shifts occur quite rarely since innovative organizations tend to be locked into a particular paradigm and thus become resistant to change. However those paradigm shifts clearly have taken place in the two technical fields of telecommunications and biotechnology.

In telecommunications a paradigm shift has occurred since the late 1970s from the electromechanical to the digital–optical paradigm. The major technological developments, that is the digitalization of communications equipment, the increasing share of software in network technology and the convergence of formerly separated transmission technologies to a universal network technology, have reshaped the traditional phases of the R&D process. Basic research lost importance, since the most fundamental inventions for today's communication technologies had already been made in the 1960s and 1970s. The use of software required different knowledge and development processes, whereas product life cycles and thus product development phases have been considerably shortened. Additionally, corporate actors found themselves confronted by significant changes caused by market liberalization. The liberalization of the German telecommunications market, for example, not only led to the emergence of new actors in the manufacturing and network operating segment, it also altered the relations between the different groups of actors. As a reaction, Germany's telecommunication equipment producers have dramatically decreased their investments in basic research. They also have exposed their internal research and development departments to competition with external R&D providers, especially universities and specialized non-university research institutes. In turn, these external R&D organizations have placed more emphasis on marketing their knowledge by introducing organizational reforms, such as quality and project management procedures, in order to become better equipped for short-term contract research projects (Kaiser and Grande, 2002a).

In the pharmaceutical biotechnology sector, changes have not only occurred in respect of already existing organizations. The technological paradigm shift from chemistry-driven to genomics-based drug development has led to the creation of specialized small and medium-sized research companies that did not only become fully integrated into the innovation process of traditional pharmaceutical companies. Instead, under the technological paradigm of genomics-based drug development, new phases have been added at the beginning of the innovation process in modern pharmaceutics. These new phases have been described as functional genomics, a process in which potential targets for the development of modern drugs and therapies are identified and validated. Traditional pharmaceutical companies were reluctant to use functional genomics. For a long time they continued to rely on chemistry-driven drug development programmes. Later on, when functional genomics was recognized as the new technological paradigm, they preferred to outsource these functions because their lack of knowledge would have caused high entry costs. As a result, small and medium-sized biotech companies were able to step into and to monopolize these early phases of the innovation process. They are engaged in these phases in various ways.

A first group of companies develops and markets platform technologies for individual steps within these phases, such as high-throughput screening or bioinformatics. A second group provides large substance libraries which are used for the process of compound testing against targets. A third group of firms is engaged in the identification and validation of targets, either under contract for traditional pharmaceutical companies or in order to initiate their own fully in-house drug development programmes.

Regardless of whether a biotech company is engaged in drug discovery and development or whether it is focusing on platform technologies, partnerships and alliances, primarily with established pharmaceutical firms, are equally important. On the one hand, these partnerships are essential to generate revenues, to stabilize the internal cash flow, to create resources for in-house

R&D programmes and to reduce the dependency on external capital. On the other hand, being selected by a big-pharmaceutical company as a partner in drug development or as a supplier for certain services or technologies underlines that the biotech company has gained ground in competition with important national and international biotech firms. In that way, these alliances are an integral part of their business activity and strategy (Kaiser and Grande, 2002b).

THE MARKET AS THE DOMINANT MODE OF COORDINATION IN THE GERMAN TELECOMMUNICATION EQUIPMENT SECTOR

Market liberalization as well as rapid technological progress have changed the German innovation system in telecommunications primarily in two aspects. Firstly, the number of actors engaged in R&D increased considerably not only because of a growing number of corporate actors, but also because of the fact that publicly funded research organizations gained importance. Secondly, the corporate R&D base has been internationalized in several ways, partly by foreign companies which have built up R&D facilities in Germany, partly by foreign takeovers of national companies and partly by the globalization of R&D activities of domestic firms. Both developments contrast with two important features that characterized the system within the electromechanical era. In times of the public monopoly over telecommunication services the incumbent operator, the Deutsche Bundespost (DBP), relied on a small number of institutionalized suppliers, especially Siemens and Alcatel SEL, which developed equipment in accordance with standards defined by the DBP. In turn, the DBP allowed for refinancing of R&D investments through its procurement decisions. Under these conditions, international suppliers played hardly any role, while external knowledge providers, for example universities, were of limited importance in the electromechanical era since telecommunications was not a science-based industry.

However, under the new digital–optical paradigm, which occurred more or less in parallel with market liberalization, Germany's telecommunication equipment manufacturers were forced to reorganize their internal R&D organization and to make use of knowledge provided by external actors. Both developments subsequently led to the emergence of an R&D market within the sector. This R&D market comprises internal research and development departments of the private sector industry as well as universities and public research institutes. The most striking feature of this R&D market is that all these actors are increasingly integrated into the manufacturers' innovation processes (Kaiser and Grande, 2002a).

Organizational Reforms and Different and Expanding Science–Industry Relations in the German Telecommunications R&D Market

The reorganization of the manufacturers' R&D organization has been the major precondition for the emergence of the R&D market. All major telecommunication equipment manufacturers significantly decreased their investment in basic research and decentralized development activities which are now pursued primarily under the responsibility of the business units. Siemens, for example, conducts development activities in more than 30 countries. Research, however, is still concentrated at the telecommunications lead markets in the United States, Great Britain and, especially, in Germany. Siemens traditionally delegated the main responsibility for research, basic development and advanced production technologies to its Corporate Technology Department ('Zentralabteilung Technik'). Product-related development activities, however, fall into the competence of the business units (Kaiser and Grande, 2002a). As a result, the vast majority of R&D funds and personnel is located within the business units, especially since the company reduced considerably the number of R&D employees in the corporate research department from 2650 in 1988 to 1270 in 1995 (Reger, 1997, p.215).

Today the corporate research department's main tasks are the provision of technology and research-related services (such as assistance with patenting) to the business units as well as the identification of long-term market and technology trends. Additionally the corporate technology department is highly involved in the management of a large number of international R&D cooperations. Until the mid-1990s, Siemens was engaged in more than 170 European R&D projects with more than 700 different partners. The company has also established relations with more than 150 universities and non-university research centres (ibid., p.217).

In terms of financing, the corporate technology department lost most of its institutional funding and has thus become exposed to competition. In 1994, about 70 per cent of the total budget originated from central funds, 15 per cent from the business units, and 15 per cent from public R&D funds. Today the share of institutional funding of the corporate technology department is only 35 per cent (which is only 5 per cent of Siemens' total R&D expenditures). Consequently the research department is forced to acquire about 60 per cent of its annual budget from Siemens' corporate business units and 5 per cent from public R&D funds. In this respect, the business units enjoy the advantage of competition between internal and external research organizations, whereas the corporate technology department has become better integrated into the firm's businesses, since it has to offer R&D services which enhance the position of the business units in a competitive market environment (Kaiser and Grande, 2002a).

Foreign telecommunication equipment manufacturers have started their engagement in Germany, especially since the early 1990s, in order to profit from a dynamic liberalized telecommunication market as well as from highly qualified personnel and the technical know how provided by German universities.

The introduction of digital mobile communications in Germany provided Nokia with the opportunity to expand its activities in that country. As part of the so-called ECR-900 consortium, the Finnish telecommunication equipment manufacturer joined forces in 1987 with Alcatel (including Alcatel SEL), and AEG. The Nokia Networks GmbH was established in 1990 as one of 40 R&D centres worldwide. From a total of 4600 employees Nokia has in Germany, 1200 work for the telecommunications business division. Nokia Telecommunications has established procedures for the engagement in applied research which were previously introduced by the Finnish parent company and later became a globally applied model in the course of Nokia's internationalization strategy. In this model, the company grants research funding to individual partners within universities or public research institutions for the preparation of diploma or doctoral theses. The results of that research then have to be transferred to central research centres which exist in most of the countries in which Nokia conducts R&D. From there, the research results may be used in development projects conducted by development centres of the respective business division. Nokia has established such a research centre in Bochum and is engaged in close relations with the universities in Aachen, Bochum and Dortmund.

With the foundation of the Ericsson Eurolab GmbH, the Swedish telecommunications equipment manufacturer established research and development capacities in Germany in 1992. Today about 1200 employees are working at the three Eurolab locations in Aachen, Hildesheim and Nuremberg which have been chosen primarily because of the neighbouring universities. The German division of Ericsson Eurolab concentrates on a broad spectrum of developmental work, reaching from the analysis of customer needs over technical feasibility studies, technical solution studies, development and testing to worldwide support. Each of the three R&D sites specializes in a certain field of Ericsson's business in telecommunications.

Within the telecommunications R&D market, internal and external knowledge providers differentiate themselves in terms of their respective functions within the innovation process. Universities as well as the companies' research departments are still more occupied with longer-term, pre-competitive R&D which has a time span of three to five years (sometimes even ten years), whereas the companies' development facilities as well as public research organizations and specialist university departments operate within a time perspective of one to three years, sometimes even shorter (Kaiser and Grande, 2002a).

The Role of Universities and Non-university Research Organizations

Even more than in the electromechanical era, universities are today the most important actors in long-term telecommunications research, but simultaneously they have become more and more involved in applied research and – to a lesser extent – in product development. Since telecommunications research takes place at a large number of universities. Germany possesses a very decentralized and complex structure in this field. According to a survey by the German electrical and electronic manufacturers' association (ZVEI), at least 56 departments at 28 universities are engaged in the various fields of telecommunications research. Moreover universities are the main target group for public research funds for basic research. The German Research Council ('Deutsche Forschungsgemeinschaft', DFG) finances three priority programmes ('Schwerpunktprogramme') aimed at fundamental research for next generation communications networks and for security systems for communications. Universities offer not only R&D services, such as contract research, but also highly qualified personnel. For that reason, private sector industry is strongly engaged in cooperation with universities, chiefly by supporting diploma and doctoral theses. In many cases, students are able to work on similar projects within the industry after graduation.

Most equipment manufacturers prefer project cooperation with neighbouring universities or with highly specialized university departments. In the latter case, geographical distance is not an obstacle to cooperation. Siemens, for example, still relies on departments of the Technical University of Munich in view of strategically important network infrastructure technologies. In other areas, such as mobile communications, projects have also been conducted with other national or specialized foreign universities, such as the Carnegie Mellon University or the universities of Madrid and Barcelona. Alcatel SEL's research centre in Stuttgart is engaged in strategic partnerships with 40 universities and research organizations worldwide. In Germany, the center cooperates with 20 universities mostly by participating in projects financed by the national research ministry (Kaiser and Grande, 2002a).

Non-university research organizations have adjusted even more to the new market environment. They are today significantly more engaged in marketing their service portfolio as they have increased efforts to patent or license their R&D results. The Heinrich-Hertz-Institute (HHI), which is Germany's leading non-university research organization in telecommunications, implemented internal reforms that consist of three major elements. Firstly, the HHI established a central marketing division and also strengthened decentralized marketing efforts through bilateral contacts between its researchers and their colleagues from the private sector in order to be more involved in the industry's R&D projects. Secondly, the institute intensified its efforts to patent major research results. Today the institute aims at applying for at least 20 patents per year. Consequently patent applications have steadily increased, from 26 in 1994 to 106 in 1999 (HHI, 2000, p.12). And thirdly, the HHI implemented professional project and quality management procedures which are comparable to those in the private sector industry. The R&D activities of the HHI can be described as a mixture of basic research as well as applied research and contract research. However the focus is clearly on applied research. At present, 20 per cent of the personnel is engaged in basic research, 60 per cent work in applied research, and 20 per cent of the scientific workforce is concerned with contract research. Consequently the institute has today considerably more external funding at its disposal. R&D contracts from the private sector increased from € 0·7 million in 1990 to € 3·6 million in 1999 (HHI, 2000).

If the private sector industry engages in project cooperation with publicly funded research organizations, the problems of project funding and intellectual property rights ownership are the most important ones. Many equipment manufacturers, such as Siemens, Alcatel SEL, Nokia or Lucent Technologies, cooperate with university departments under the condition of exclusivity and full ownership of patents and licences. Siemens and Alcatel SEL only engage in projects which are financed equally by the firm and by public R&D funds. In terms of longer-term research, private sector industry also observes university activities and, in cases of interest for the firm, acquires university patents. Universities, in return, have established specialist departments for technology transfer in order better to market their research results (Kaiser and Grande, 2002a).

All in all, the analysis of authorship of scientific papers gives an indication of the extent to which companies cooperate in R&D and what partners they prefer. Having explored the number of collaborative research papers of large enterprises in the telecommunication equipment sector between 1993 and 1996, Tijssen and van Wijk (1999) showed that Ericsson, and, especially, Siemens, cooperated mostly with external domestic public research organizations (27 per cent and 46 per cent, respectively of the co-authored papers), whereas the majority of papers (29 per cent) which were written by Alcatel's employees had a co-author from within the company. All three companies share the commonality that collaborative research papers linked them mostly with public or private organizations within the EU; co-authored papers with institutions from outside Europe amounted to a maximum of 9 to 15 per cent (ibid., p.532).

MODES OF COORDINATION IN THE GERMAN PHARMACEUTICAL BIOTECHNOLOGY INDUSTRY: INTERNATIONAL ALLIANCES AND THE LOCAL INNOVATION MILIEU

In the second half of the 1990s, the German pharmaceutical biotech industry developed from a latecomer into the most dynamic sector of its kind in Europe. In terms of commercialization of scientific knowledge, Germany surpassed Great Britain, which still has Europe's largest biotechnology industry. In 1999, Germany's biotech start-ups attracted a total venture capital sum of 260 million, the highest amount of early-stage financing in Europe. With the establishment of 279 start-up companies in this sector between 1995 and 1999, Germany scored most formations of new biotech companies in EU member states, beating Britain, France, Sweden, the Netherlands and Finland (Deutscher Bundestag, 2000, Ernst & Young 2000, pp.14–17).

Germany was able to catch up in pharmaceutical biotechnology mainly as a result of significant changes which occurred both in the institutional environment in which the sector is embedded, especially in regulation, financing and public policies, and in the organizational set-up of the innovation process implemented as a consequence of the new technological paradigm of genomics-based drug development. The emergence of the German pharmaceutical biotechnology industry took place in three major phases.

The first phase lasted until the early 1990s and was characterized by the existence of only a few small and medium-sized companies which were active as specialist technology suppliers for pharmaceutical firms. If any research was done, capacities remained very limited. In view of drug development, pharmaceutical companies as well as universities still adhered to the traditional path of chemistry-driven pharmaceutical research (Marschall, 2000, pp.144 ff).

The second phase took until 1997/8. Thanks to regulatory changes of the German genetical engineering law as well as a new approach in federal biotech funding, the dynamic of commercialization of scientific knowledge in biotechnology increased considerably. Initially newly established small and medium-sized companies concentrated very much on contract research and the development of platform technologies for the big pharma industry, especially because technology development was considered to be the less risky business strategy with which revenues could be generated at a very early stage.

In recent years, however, the industry clearly entered a third phase in which more and more firms engage in drug development programmes both in cooperation with big pharma and other biotech companies and by implementing fully in-house R&D programmes. In the meantime this new strategy has also been supported by the major financiers of the sector, since venture capital providers have recognized that drug development promises considerably larger revenues even if the risk of failure is high during perennial drug development processes (Kaiser and Grande, 2002b).

Roughly speaking, there is a typical business model for most of the biotech companies that are active in the pharmaceutical branch of the sector. This business model can be described as the development of a firm from a technology supplier to a drug-developing company. Normally biotech start-ups enter the market as a spinoff from academic research commercializing first a certain platform technology or tool. Where a company decides to enter drug development, it will seek strategic alliances or joint ventures with big pharmaceutical companies in order to develop the drug candidate in cooperation and thus sharing the financial risks during the R&D phases. The ultimate goal, however, is to reach a position in which the firm can set up individual drug development programmes financed by internal cash flow which originates from licences or royalty payments out of cooperative drug development programmes.

The fact that more and more German biotech SMEs are today focused on drug development underlines that the industry has entered the third phase of its development. Firms which do not have such programmes and instead decided to specialize in a certain platform technology were able to gain ground even in competition with companies in the United States or Great Britain. This third development phase is also characterized by an increasing integration of German biotech companies into the global pharmaceutical R&D system. Since 1998, the number of strategic alliances in which German biotech SMEs are involved has been increasing considerably, by nearly 100 per cent between 1998 and 1999 alone. Moreover, between 1999 and 2001, five German biotech companies (Medigene and GPC Biotech as well as Qiagen, Evotec Biosystems and Lion Bioscience) acquired biotech companies in the USA and Great Britain and thus gained access to the industry's lead markets and obtained certain competences which were at that time scarcely available in Germany, for example in bioinformatics (Kaiser and Grande, 2002b).

The Role of Universities and Non-university Research Institutes in Biotechnology

For German biotech companies, cooperations and alliances have a strong international dimension, but also a regional and local one. The industry is highly decentralized and mainly clustered around the four leading locations in Berlin, Cologne, Heidelberg and Munich. Biotech firms obtain many of their resources from these clusters. This holds true especially for start-up companies which tend to settle in the immediate neighbourhood of the research organizations out of which they have been founded. In the Munich area, for example, about 30 of the total of 54 biotechnology start-ups originate from one of the three leading research organizations in the area: the Max-Planck-Institute for Biochemistry, the GSF Research Center, and the Gene Center of Munich University. Researchers from at least two of these institutions founded three of them. Many companies still have exclusive access to the technical infrastructure of publicly funded research organizations. Moreover a variety of supporting institutions have been established in the neighbourhood of the biotech cluster, such as technology transfer offices, patent lawyers, management consultancies, clinical consultancies and incubators (Kaiser and Grande, 2002b).

According to the nature of R&D in pharmaceutical biotechnology, which is to a considerable extent still basic research, Germany's universities and non-university research organizations differ enormously in their engagement in relations with biotech companies. Traditionally, universities are important actors in basic research in various academic disciplines. Since most of the universities, which have departments of biology, chemistry, medical sciences and so on are active in some field of biotechnology, it is hardly possible to determine the number of chairs or research groups and their specific research interests. However, according to the German Statistical Office, 450 university institutions were involved in biotechnological research in 1995 (European Commission, 2000, p.DE-24). About 48 universities offer academic programmes in biotechnology, of which 20 are more oriented towards technical aspects, the other 28 more towards studies in biology, microbiology or biochemistry. In addition 16 universities of applied sciences (polytechnics) initiated programmes in biotechnology in recent years.

The German Research Council ('Deutsche Forschungsgemeinschaft'), the major funding organization for academic research in Germany, has increased its budget for medical and biological research considerably. Since 1997, total expenditures in these areas have surged by more than 25 per cent to €431 million in the year 2000 (Deutsche Forschungsgemeinschaft, 2001, p.56). Of its 278 collaborative research centres ('Sonderforschungsbereiche') a total of 110 are engaged in the field of biotechnology.[2]

As regards biotechnological research, the most important non-university research organization in the field is the Max-Planck-Society (MPG). In January 2001, the MPG maintained 79 research institutes, which employed roughly 9500 scientists. In the wider area of biological and medical research, the MPG possesses 34 institutes or independent research groups which usually work outside the departmental structure of the respective institute. In recent years, the MPG has placed special emphasis on biological research and concentrated about a third of its total expenditures on this sector. In 1999, biological research was financed by a total of €325·9 million. Other research organizations, such as the Fraunhofer Society, the Helmholtz Society or the so-called 'Blue-List Institutes' are considerably less involved in biotechnological research, either because of their focus on applied research or because of their concentration on research areas, which require an extensive technical infrastructure (Kaiser and Grande, 2002b).

THE ROLE OF PUBLIC R&D POLICIES

Since the end of the 1970s, public R&D policies in Germany have been continuously expanded, from already implemented measures of science, research and technology funding to a more comprehensive innovation-oriented approach. In most recent years those instruments of innovation policy have focused on improving networking between science and industry either in less favoured regions or in view of certain science-based industries that tend to develop most dynamically within local clusters. Various measures have been initiated in order to facilitate cooperation between publicly funded research organizations and the private sector industry. These measures have aimed at reform of university patenting regulations, mobility of researchers and project-oriented instead of institutional funding (cf. OECD, 2002). Public R&D policies in Germany are organized along federal lines. Accordingly the infrastructure is highly decentralized whereas various vertical policy coordination arrangements exist especially in view of public R&D funding. Additionally, since the early 1980s, the European Union has emerged as an increasingly important actor in R&D policies and funding (Grande, 1999; Kaiser, 2003; Kaiser and Prange, 2001, 2002; Krull and Meyer-Krahmer, 1996; Kuhlmann, 2001; Peterson and Sharp, 1998).

Funding of science, research and development in Germany takes place both at the federal and the subnational level. The federal level provides R&D funds particularly as institutional (co-) funding of non-university research organizations and as project funds issued through various thematic R&D programmes. Within the last two decades, federal R&D funds have been primarily provided by the Federal Ministry of Education and Research (BMBF). Its share in federal funding remained relatively constant between 1981 (64.7 per cent) and 1996 (65.3 per cent). The federal states contribute to the R&D infrastructure primarily by financing the university system. Additionally they are cofinanciers of the various national research organizations. In 1999, the federal government spent €8·7 billion for R&D of which more than 50 per cent was delegated to non-university research organizations. The federal states' R&D expenditures amounted to €7·9 billion, of which €5·6 billion was directed to the higher education sector (BMBF, 2002). Apart from these general trends there are at least some specific measures that have been applied to the sectors of telecommunications and biotechnology.

Telecommunications

The national government started to provide public R&D subsidies to the German telecommunications industry in the late 197Cs, mainly as a response to the declining technological performance and international competitiveness of the German equipment industry. After a significant reduction of funding in the 1980s, the BMBF re-engaged in the promotion of R&D in telecommunications during the 1990s as part of its overall strategy aimed at encouraging the development and use of modern information and communications technologies for the information society. Within this context, the financial support was concentrated on basic communications technologies, that is mobile multi-media communications systems and optical communications networks. The BMBF further increased its funding for the period 1999–2000. The total budget amounts to about € 500 million per year especially owing to a disproportionate rise in federal funds in the areas of multi-media and informatics. Funding for basic communication technologies as well as micro technologies and production technologies remained relatively constant. However most funds (roughly a third of the total budget in information technologies) are still directed towards research and development in basic communication technologies.

At the subnational level, the German states support R&D in telecommunications through the institutional funding of universities and the co-funding of non-university research organization, but also with their own R&D programmes aimed at promoting use and development of information and communication technologies at the regional or local level. The states of Baden-Württemberg and Rhineland-Palatinate, for example, established a joint research programme in advanced media technologies in 1992 which promotes, among other things, the development of multi-media access networks. Between 1997 and 2001, both states provided about € 12 million, of which 70 per cent was given by Baden-Württemberg. Bavaria initiated two programmes, 'Offensive Zukunft Bayern' in 1994 and 'High-Tech Offensive Bayern' in 2000, which are aimed at investing more than € 4 billion from privatization of former state-owned companies in modern technologies. These programmes are focused on five technology areas: life sciences, communication technologies, material sciences, environmental technologies and mechatronics.

In the early 1980s, the European Union became active in the field of telecommunications. The establishment of a European telecommunications policy was motivated primarily by the belief that the development of the information and communications technology industry would be crucial for Europe's competitiveness. Since the first European programmes in communications technologies, ESPRIT and RACE, funding R&D in this field has increased steadily. In the fifth framework programme (1998–2002), the European Commission annexed its research funding in the area of information and communications technologies to the EU's overall strategy for the creation of the information society. Accordingly, the fifth framework programme provides €3·6 billion for a thematic programme called 'user-friendly information society' (IST). This programme promoted activities aimed at improving the usability, dependability, interoperability and affordability of technologies and applications for the information society. With more than 20 per cent of the total budget, the IST programme was by far the most important single action of the fifth framework programme (Kaiser and Grande, 2002a).

Biotechnology

Germany's position as a latecomer in the commercialization of biotechnology does not mean that public policy was not engaged early enough in this field. On the contrary, Germany was the first leading industrialized country that implemented a publicly funded research programme in biotechnology, in 1972. However early public investment in biotechnological R&D did not prevent a country known as the 'pharmacy of the world' losing ground in an emerging technology. During the 1980s, Germany fell significantly behind other industrialized nations in terms of the existence of small or medium-sized biotechnology companies. Whereas 245 such companies existed in the USA in 1984, and 157 in Japan, Germany had only 15. Even five years later the situation had not improved. The number of biotechnology SMEs in the USA had further increased to 388 in 1989, while only 17 were active in Germany.

One reason for this development was certainly the chemistry-driven research tradition of big pharmaceutical companies. This tradition was not only reflected by strategic decisions of corporate actors concerning their own R&D programmes, but also influenced public R&D policies, since the Research Ministry invited the leading industry association, the DECHEMA (German Society for Chemical Engineering), to define the policy goals. DECHEMA, along with its corporate members, proposed to support traditional second-generation bioprocessing, but not third-generation post-DNA recombination which was already on the research agenda in other countries (cf. Adelberger, 2000, pp.107f). The second reason was that public policies did support R&D efforts of the industry, but were not active in providing incentives for the commercialization of scientific knowledge, which consequently did not emerge from its traditional places, universities and non-university research organizations. Nevertheless the federal government did invest in the academic infrastructure and established four national centres for genetic research, in Berlin, Cologne, Heidelberg and Munich. The selection of these locations was not accidental, but aimed at strengthening those regions in which the scientific infrastructure (that is universities and Max-Planck-Institutes) was already strong (Kaiser and Grande, 2002b).

The situation changed significantly when the federal government initiated the BioRegio programme in 1995 and simultaneously proclaimed a pretty ambitious goal: to become the leading biotechnology nation in Europe by the year 2000. Indeed the BioRegio programme itself was an innovative policy tool, which had no model at that time, but was copied by many countries thereafter. The BioRegio programme was actually a contest aimed at stimulating the creation of biotechnology clusters, and thereby the commercialization of scientific knowledge. All in all, the BMBF supported 57 R&D projects within the four winning regions – Berlin, Cologne/Duesseldorf, Heidelberg and Munich – between 1996 and 2000 and invested a total of €72 million. In fact it was not primarily by the provision of funds that the BioRegio programme was able to initiate the commercialization of biotechnological research. The more important factor was clearly the establishment of a network structure in the different local clusters involving all relevant private and public actors.

The European Union has been increasingly engaged in the promotion of R&D in biotechnology since the 1990s. In contrast to the EU's actions in other technology fields, such as information technology, companies from the chemical and pharmaceutical sector were not overly interested in European programmes such as ESPRIT for the IT sector, because of their engagement in their own transnational research programmes, which were mostly concerned with competitive rather than pre-competitive research as proposed by the EU Commission. From the industry's perspective, the dialogue with the Commission was aimed at liberalizing national regulation, which the private sector considered to be too restrictive. As a result, within the context of the first three framework programmes (FP), the EU financed R&D in biotechnology with a relatively limited budget. This situation changed, however, with the fourth framework programme, which made it easier for the participants to cooperate with non-European research groups, especially in the USA and Japan. Moreover, from the fourth framework programme, the Commission began to consider biotechnology as one of the key technologies, along with information technology, material sciences and telecommunications.

The fifth framework programme (1998–2002) placed more emphasis on the efficient interaction between research organizations and industry. In this sense the EU explicitly encouraged applicants to cluster their projects involving core centres and associated laboratories in order to create a critical mass and with a view to promoting interaction between fundamental and applied research as well as between academic research and industry. Between 1998 and 2002, the EU financed the above-mentioned activities with a total of €483 million. Additionally the quality of life programme provided money for a key action called 'The cell factory' which was addressed to companies in the life sciences sector engaged either in health, environment or agriculture. This action was financed by about €400 million (Kaiser and Grande 2002b).[3]

CONCLUSIONS

This chapter has argued that new modes of coordination within the German telecommunication equipment and pharmaceutical biotechnology industries have emerged primarily as a result of technological paradigm shifts. Those changes have significantly altered relations between industry and universities as well as non-university research institutes. In the case of telecommunications, equipment manufacturers and publicly funded research institutes conducted organizational reforms that allowed universities and specialist non-university research organizations to become an integral part of the firms' R&D system. In biotechnology the technological paradigm shift created totally new phases at the beginning of the innovation process in which specialist small and medium-sized research companies play the dominant role. Public innovation policies at different territorial levels have reacted to and supported these changes.

In both industries knowledge environments are today certainly more integrated as interorganizational and intraorganizational borders have become blurred. Within the publicly funded research organizations as well as within large telecommunication equipment corporations creative people were forced to acquire management competences, as they have to market their knowledge to industry or decentralized business units. The same holds true for the biotechnology sector in which scientists opened up businesses often on the basis of a single invention or idea. Furthermore external knowledge gained importance in both industries, regardless of whether it exists within the national or international sphere. As a consequence, creative knowledge environments have become not only more integrated but also more internationalized. In both industries there are several indications that specialized knowledge (for example, internet protocol (IP) network technology in telecommunications or bioinformatics in biotechnology) is not similarly available at many place around the world. Therefore corporate R&D organizations and thus creative knowledge environments tend more and more to span different geographical locations.

The analysis further showed that science–industry interactions develop sector-specific characteristics. In telecommunications, publicly funded research organizations enhanced the innovative productivity of established manufacturers while internal research units were forced to orient themselves more towards customer needs. In biotechnology, the public R&D infrastructure was most important as the basis for commercialization in this technical field. Owing to the nature of biotechnological research, science–industry relations remained strong even though international alliances play a bigger role than they do in telecommunications. Both industries rely heavily on universities as the main providers of qualified personnel. This underlines the fact that science–industry relationships are equally important for optimizing the R&D process and for recruiting specialist employees. In order to guarantee access to these critical resources, firms in both technical fields engage in strategic partnerships with publicly funded research organizations.

Many of these changes are likely to occur also in other science-based industries, such as nanotechnology or new materials, as they take place on an international scale. The case of pharmaceutical biotechnology impressively shows that there are only relatively few clusters around the world in which small and medium-sized research companies compete for resources and market shares. They all have in common that they rely heavily on a critical mass of knowledge and service providers that are engaged in the broader field of medical research. Nonetheless Germany is also a special case as it is the only country which had a dominant position under the old technological paradigm and whose firms relied for too long on the knowledge and methods applied under it. In order to bridge the knowledge gap, Germany's traditional pharmaceutical companies invested heavily in R&D cooperation with US-based private and public knowledge providers. Only with the emergence of a biotechnology industry in Germany did they re-engage in partnerships with domestic organizations.

Finally, as regards of coordination mechanisms, the technological paradigm shifts in both science-based industries have forced established corporate actors to engage more in relations with specialist private or public R&D organizations. As much as external knowledge gained in importance, the role of hierarchical modes of coordination has decreased. Exchanges of knowledge between established corporate actors and specialist research institutes have increasingly become coordinated by market mechanisms; however, in view of critical resources, actors rely primarily on various forms of network relations. The case of the telecommunication equipment sector is a remarkable example of the consequences that may occur if firms do not manage to change their established modes of coordination. In continental Europe, the paradigm shift in telecommunications led to the disappearance of a traditional equipment industry in the Netherlands, where Philips stepped out of this market segment, whereas in Finland Nokia's engagement in digital communication resulted in the emergence of a new global player.

NOTES

1. The chapter grows out of research done within the project, 'National Systems of Innovation and Networks in the Idea–Innovation Chain in Science-based Industries', funded by the European Community under the TSER programme (contract no. SOEl-CT-98-1102). The German project team was directed by Professor Edgar Grande at the Technical University Munich.
2. Statistical data of collaborative research centres financed by the Deutche Forschungsgemeinschaft refer to the year 2002. Cf. 'DFG-Collaborative Research centres' (http://www.dfg.de/english/funding/sfb/sfb_english.html).
3. Outside the EU system, public R&D funds are also provided by the Europesn research initiative, EUREKA. In the year 2000, EUREKA financed biotechnologial research 327 million. In view of the total funding, biotechnological research was ranked third out of nine technology areas

REFERENCES

Adelberger, K.E. (2000), 'Semi-ssovereign leadership? The state's role in German biotechnology and venture capital growth', *German Politics* **9**, 103–22.

Benner, M. and U. Sandström (2000), 'Institutionalizing the triple helix: research funding and norms in the academic system', *Research Policy*, **29**, 291–301.

Braczyk, H.-J., P. Cooke and M. Heidenreich (eds) (1998), *Regional Innovation Systems. The Role of Governances in a Globalized World*, London: UCL Press.

Bundesministerium für Bildung und Forschung (2002), *Facts and Figures. Research 2002*, Bonn: BMBF.

Cohen, W.M. and D.A. Levinthal (1989), 'Innovation and learning: the two faces of R&D', *Economic Journal*, **99**, 569–96.

Cooke, P. (2001), 'Regional innovation systems, clusters, and the knowledge economy', *Industrial and Corporate Change,* **10**, 945–74.

Deutscher Bundestag (2000), 'Zur Situation der Biotechnologie in Deutschland, Antwort der Bundesregierung auf die Kleine Anfrage der Abgeordneten Annette Widmann-Mauz, Wolfgang Lohmann (Lüdenscheid), Dr. Wolf Bauer, weiterer Abgeordneter und der Fraktion der CDU/CSU', BT-Drs. 14/3969, 2 August.

Deutsche Forschungsgemeinschaft (2001), *Jahresbericht 2000. Aufgaben und Ergebnisse*, Bonn.

Dosi, G. (1982), 'Technical paradigms and technological trajectories – a suggested interpretation of the determinants and directions of technological change', *Research Policy*, **11**, 147–62.

Dosi, G., C. Freeman, R. Nelson, G.S. Yverberg and L. Soete (eds) (1988), *Technical Change and Economic Theory*, London: Pinter.

Edquist, C. (ed.) (1997), *Systems of Innovation. Technologies, Institutions and Organizations*, London and Washington: Pinter.

Ernst & Young (2000), *Gründerzeit. Zweiter Deutscher Biotechnologie-Report 2000*, Stuttgart.

Etzkowitz, H. and L. Leydesdorff (2000), 'The dynamics of innovation: from national systems and 'Mode 2' to a triple helix of university–industry–government relations', *Research Policy*, **29**, 109–123.

European Commission (2000), *Inventory of Public Biotechnology R&D Programmes in Europe*, vol. 2, National Reports, Luxembourg.

Freeman, C. (1987), *Technology Policy and Economic Performance: Lessons from Japan*, London: Pinter.

Freeman, C. (1995), 'The "National System of Innovation' in historical perspective', *Cambridge Journal of Economics*, **19**, 4–24.

Grande, E. (1999), 'Innovationspolitik im europäischen Mehrebenensystem: Zur neuen Architektur des Staatlichen', in K. Grimmer, S. Kuhlmann and F. Meyer-Krahmer (eds), *Innovationspolitik in Globalisierten Arenen*, Opladen: Leske+Budrich, pp.87–103.

Green, K., R. Hull, A. Mcmeekin and V. Walsh (1999), 'The construction of the techno-economic: networks vs. paradigms', *Research Policy*, **28**, 777–92.

Grupp, H. and U. Schmoch (1992), 'Perception of scientification as measured by referencing between patents and papers', in H. Grupp (ed.), *Dynamics of Science-based Innovation*, Berlin, Springer-Verlag, pp.73–128.

Hage, J. and C. Alter (1997), 'A typology of interorganzational relationships and networks', in J.R. Hollingsworth and R. Boyer (eds), *Contemporary Capitalism: the Embeddedness of Institutions*, Cambridge: Cambridge University Press, pp.94–126.

Hagedoorn, J. (1995), 'Strategic technology partnering during the 1980s: trends, networks and corporate patterns in non-core technologies', *Research Policy*, **24**, 207–31.

Heinrich-Hertz-Institute (2000), *Report 1999*, Berlin: HHI.

Hollingsworth, J.R. and R. Boyer (1997), 'Coordination of economic actors and social systems of production', in J.R. Hollingsworth and R. Boyer (eds), *Contemporary Capitalism: the Embeddedness of Institutions*, Cambridge, UK: Cambridge University Press, pp.1–47.

Kaiser, R. (2003), 'Innovation policy in a multi-level governance system: the changing institutional environment for the establishment of science-based industries', in J. Edler, Stefan Kuhlmann and Maria Behrens (eds), *Changing Governance of Research and Technology Policy: The European Research Area*, Cheltenham, UK and Northampton, MA, USA: Edward Elgar.

Kaiser, R. and E. Grande (2002a), 'From the electro-mechanical to the opto-digital paradigm: organizational change and the management of research in the German telecommunication sector', *Building Bridges Between Ideas and Markets*, Final Report to the European Commission of the TSER Project 'National Systems of Innovation and Networks in the Idea–Innovation Chain in Science based Industries' (SOE1-CT98-1102), Munich: Technische Universität München, pp.1–23.

Kaiser, R. and E. Grande (2002b), 'The emergence of the German pharmaceutical biotech industry and the role of the national innovation system', *Building Bridges Between Ideas and Markets*, Final Report to the European Commission of the TSER Project 'National Systems of Innovation and Networks in the Idea–Innovation Chain in Science based Industries (SOE1-CT98-1102), Munich: Technische Universität München, 184–202.

Kaiser, R. and H. Prange (2001), 'Die Ausdifferenzierung nationaler Innovations-systeme: Deutschland und Österreich im Vergleich', *Österreichische Zeitschrift für Politikwissenschaft*, **30** (3), 313–30.

Kaiser, R. and H. Prange (2002), 'A new concept of deepening European integration? The European Research Area and the emerging role of policy coordination in a

multi-level governance system', *European Integration online Papers*, **6** (18).
Krull, W. and F. Meyer-Krahmer (1996), 'Science, technology, and innovation in Germany – changes and challenges in the 1990s', in W. Krull and F. Meyer-Krahmer (eds), *Science and Technology in Germany*, new edn, London: Cartermill, pp.3–29.
Kuhlmann, S. (2001), 'Future governance of innovation policy in Europe – three scenarios', *Research Policy*, **30**, 953–76.
Leydesdorff, L. (2000), 'The triple helix: an evolutionary model of innovations', *Research Policy* **29**, 243–55.
Leydesdorff, L. and H. Etzkowitz (1996), 'Emergence of a triple-helix of university–industry–government relations', *Science and Public Policy*, **23**, 279–86.
Lindberg, L.N., J.L. Campbell and J.R. Hollingsworth (1994), 'Economic governance and the analysis of structural change in the American economy', in J.L. Campbell, J.R. Hollingsworth and L.N. Lindberg (eds), *Governance of the American Economy*, Cambridge: Cambridge University Press, pp.3–34.
Lundvall B-Å. (ed.) (1992), *National Systems of Innovation: Towards a Theory of Innovation and Interactive Learning*, London: Pinter.
Marschall, L. (2000), *Im Schatten der chemischen Synthese. Industrielle Biotechnologie in Deutschland (1900–1970)*, Frankfurt a.M. and New York: Campus.
Meyer-Krahmer, F. (1997), 'Science-based technologies and interdisciplinarity: challenges for firms and policy', in C. Edquist (ed.), *Systems of Innovation. Technologies, Institutions and Organizations*, London and Washington: Pinter, pp.298–317.
Meyer-Krahmer, F. and U. Schmoch (1998), 'Science-based technologies: university–industry interactions in four fields', *Research Policy*, **27**, 835–51.
Nelson, R.R. (1987), *Understanding Technical Change as an Evolutionary Process*, Amsterdam: North-Holland.
Nelson, R.R. (ed.) (1993), *National Systems of Innovation: A Comparative Analysis*, New York and Oxford: Oxford University Press.
OECD (1999a), *Managing National Innovation Systems*, Paris.
OECD (1999b), *Boosting Innovation. The Cluster Approach*, Paris.
OECD (2001), *Innovative Clusters. Drivers of National Innovation Systems*, Paris.
OECD (2002), *Benchmarking Industry–Science Relationships*, Paris.
Peterson, J. and M. Sharp (1998), *Technology Policy in the European Union*, Basingstoke: Macmillan.
Porter, M. (1990), *The Competitive Advantage of Nations*, London: Free Press.
Reger, G. (1997), *Koordination und strategisches Management internationaler Innovationsprozesse*, Heidelberg: Physica.
Soskice, D. (1999), 'Divergent production regimes: coordinated and uncoordinated market economies in the 1980s and 1990s', in H. Kitschelt, P. Lange, G. Marks and J. Stephens (eds), *Continuity and Change in Contemporary Capitalism*, Cambridge, Cambridge University Press, pp.101–34.
Streeck, W. and P.C. Schmitter (eds) (1985), *Private Interest Government: Beyond Market and State*, Beverly Hills: Sage.
Tijssen, R. and E. van Wijk (1999), 'In search of the European paradox: an international comparison of Europe's scientific performance and knowledge flows in information and communication technology research', *Research Policy*, **28**, 519–43.
Williamson, O.E. (1975), *Markets and Hierarchies – Analysis and Antitrust*

Implications: A Study in the Economics of Internal Organization, New York: Free Press.

Williamson, O.E. (1985), *The Economic Institutions of Capitalism: Firms, Markets, Relational Contracting*, New York and London: Free Press.

8. Scientific research collaboration in South America as reflected in the SCI®

Isabel Bortagaray[1]

INTRODUCTION

The production of knowledge is undergoing major changes. Some of these changes include higher societal expectations regarding the usefulness of knowledge, transformations in the scientific process itself and transformations in the different institutional arrangements and actors engaged in that process. Increasingly knowledge production is distributed across institutions, making them more permeable and less self-contained. As part of this trend, researchers tend to approach science in a more collective way, collaborating not only with colleagues from the same institution, but also with researchers from different institutions, sectors (university, government, industry) and countries.

Even though this process seems to be a global trend, there are some variations across countries. These variations are in part due to institutional settings, cultural patterns of the scientific community and its relation with society, as well as to resources dedicated to the scientific enterprise. South American countries, for instance, share many features of this process of transformation but with some differences, not only when compared to more industrialized countries, but also among themselves. A common pattern among them, however, is the leading role of the university in academic research, and low private commitment to research and development. Collaboration is therefore expected to occur more frequently among actors of the same nature, and more particularly between academic researchers because of the preponderant role of the university in the research enterprise.

This study attempts to contribute to this general discussion by describing the patterns of scientific collaboration in South American countries, using scientific articles indexed in the Science Citations Index® (SCI Expanded, ISI Web of Knowledge) published in 2001 in all scientific fields. Research collaboration is analysed through co-authorship, even though co-authorship is only a partial measure of collaboration. Different levels of collaboration are analysed: interpersonal (two authors or more), interinstitutional[2] (two institutions or more), intersectoral (two or more institutions of different nature) and international (authors with affiliation in two or more countries).[3] Within the cases of interpersonal collaboration, we specifically explore the different patterns of collaboration at each of these levels.

Research collaboration constitutes an important element in the emergence of creative knowledge environments. In the new mode of knowledge production, creativity is a collective phenomenon as research is embedded in networks and is driven by collaboration. Furthermore collaboration among researchers with different backgrounds, and of different institutional settings and countries, foster the emergence of creative knowledge environments as their diverse backgrounds and settings translate into different approaches to the research problem, different ways of representing and conceptualizing these problems, and different analytical tools used to understand them.

This chapter is organized as follows. First, I briefly review the literature related to research collaboration. Second, I characterize certain features of science in South America. Third, I address the methodological aspects of this study. Fourth, I present the major findings, and finally I discuss some implications and introduce some issues for future analysis.

REVIEW OF THE LITERATURE

The new mode of knowledge production, identified as 'Mode 2' (Gibbons *et al.*, 1994) concerns major changes in the context in which knowledge is being produced. The context of knowledge production is shifting from one that is hierarchically organized, and based on disciplines, to a more transdisciplinary, organizationally diverse and heterogeneous context (Gibbons *et al.*, 1994; Ziman, 1994). This transformation involves changes not only in the mechanisms and dynamics of knowledge production, but also in the structures and institutions related to the research endeavour. The new context of knowledge production is more diffuse because the loci of knowledge production are distributed across institutions, making them more permeable, less self-contained and more dependent on linkages and interactions (Gibbons *et al.*, 1994: Hicks and Katz, 1996).

Knowledge production is becoming a highly collective enterprise (Gibbons *et al.*, 1994; Ziman, 1994). Researchers cannot act in isolation given the increasing complexity of knowledge, and the need for transdisciplinary approaches, specialized skills and research projects that are more sophisticated and based on a larger scale, among other factors. This increasing complexity of knowledge requires multidimensional approaches, involving actors with different rationales, and embedded in different institutional settings.

Transdisciplinarity and collaboration between multiple institutions, sectors and countries become important resources to cope with the changing nature of knowledge. Creativity in 'Mode 2' is driven by collaboration and interaction among actors of diverse nature, and from different institutional settings. The interaction of multiple and diverse actors enhances creativity as they bring different rationales and cognitive approaches. The accumulation of knowledge takes place through flexible arrangements, and creativity and quality control are essentially becoming a group activity (Gibbons *et al.*, 1994).

The 'triple helix' approach (Leydesdorff and Etzkowitz, 1996) and previously the 'Sabato triangle' (Sábato and Botana, 1968) address the need to introduce new ways to examine the current dynamics surrounding the production of scientific knowledge. The novelty is based on the idea that, if we examine the individual units of the triangle, we will miss the characteristics that emerge in the actual dynamic, such as the exchanges and interactions between these three types of actors. In both cases, each actor (universities, industry and government) is located at a vertex, but the triangle only exists if the lines between the axes (that is, the collaborations between the actors) are there to connect them.

The increasing presence of collaborative efforts is not only reshaping the context of knowledge production but also demanding new institutional designs including policy mechanisms (Hicks and Katz, 1996). This shifting pattern in the production of knowledge is widespread internationally (Etzkowitz and Leydesdorff, 2000; Senker, 1999; Wagner, 1999), even though there is still significant international variation in the mechanisms and relationships between the production and consumption of knowledge, and in the overall institutional settings in which knowledge is produced (Arocena and Sutz, 2001). In the case of industrialized countries, there is a common path in the evolution of science, which comprises three phases: institutionalization, professionalization and industrialization (Salomon, 1994). This has not been the case of the evolution of modern science in less developed countries, where science is still going through the phases of institutionalization and professionalization (Gaillard, 1994; Salomon, 1994). Even though in the last two decades there has been a trend towards the industrialization of science, locally produced knowledge is still somewhat divorced from the economic system. In Latin American countries the private sector is definitely not committed to R&D, leaving the university as the main and somewhat isolated producer of knowledge (Arocena and Sutz, 2001, p.1222).

It is not only the evolution of science that differs between more and less developed countries. In less developed countries, science faces higher levels of adversity, mainly because of budget constraints reinforced by fewer sources of funding. Scientists have to cope with worse levels of underinvestment, and one way to cope with this is through the international scientific community and international resources. The international scientific community is not only a source of learning and exchange, but also provides external funds and opportunities. For scientists in a less developed country, to belong to the international community may make the difference between being able to pursue their research project or not. This strong dependence on international mechanisms entails some vicious circles. Publication in mainstream journals is functional and necessary if a scientist wants to belong to the international community. The need to publish in mainstream journals leads to a subtle tension between being part of the international scientific community, and therefore focusing on mainstream topics, and concentrating on domestic research agendas related to the social and economic needs of their countries (Arocena and Sutz, 2001; Gaillard, 1992; Sancho, 1992; Sutz, 1996).

Potential international variations are critical when designing policy mechanisms. It is often the case that international trends are thought to consist of similar processes, and so are approached with similar strategies, when in reality they are embedded in very distinct systems. As was indicated above, the South American research system presents some differences when compared to those in industrialized countries, and so do the relations between science and society. Policy mechanisms oriented to foster the production of knowledge have to take into account these differences. The international research system is becoming highly collaborative (Hicks and Katz, 1996), but are these patterns common to all countries? Are the incentives to engage in collaboration the same across countries and contexts? One of the reasons for scientists from less developed countries being involved in collaboration is the lack of resources dominating scientific production at home. Another reason is that articles with authors from developed countries are cited more often, and therefore have a greater impact (Gaillard, 1992; Garfield, 1983). Scientists who studied abroad are more likely to pursue collaborative strategies, particularly in the years following their programme of study (El Alami *et al.*, 1992; Gaillard, 1992), though this trend depends on the scientific field (El Alami *et al.*, 1992).

One way to observe empirically the extent of these trends and the extent to which increasing collaboration is characterizing the research system is by looking at bibliometric indicators, as a way to trace these changes and thus find out about possible directions for future science policy. Research collaboration in science has traditionally been measured through looking at multiple-authored and addressed articles, in spite of the fact that research collaboration and co-authorship are not identical concepts. Research collaboration exceeds co-authorship, while co-authorship does not always embody a collaborative process (Katz and Martin, 1997). However co-authorship is considered a proxy for measuring connections between researchers, disciplines, sectors, institutions and nations, as well as indicators of knowledge flows and knowledge transfer (Katz and Hicks, 1997a, 1997b; Narin *et al.*, 1991).

Co-authorship seems to affect the impact of research. On average the impact is related to the number of authors, institutions and countries involved (Katz and Hicks, 1997b, p.541), and papers with multiple institutions and foreign collaboration are more often cited (as much as twice as often) than domestic papers (Narin *et al.*, 1991). Some of the determinants of research collaboration are related to the nature of research (such as higher collaboration in experimental research than in theoretical), geographical proximity (for example, proximity facilitates collaboration via informal communication channels) and social distance (for example, peers are more likely to collaborate than unequally ranked researchers) (Katz and Martin, 1997).

Yet the decision to co-author an article might respond to social norms rather than reflecting a truly collaborative research process. Furthermore co-authorship only reflects those instances in which, for whatever reason, a group of authors decide to co-participate in responsibility for the publication. A co-authored article does not necessarily capture informal collaboration, nor does it reflect an equally shared collaborative effort since we cannot infer the extent to which the effort was truly collaborative, and the different levels of commitment of the authors.

SCIENCE IN SOUTH AMERICA

Bibliometric indicators are an output measure related to inputs such as gross expenditure on R&D (GERD), or human capital (number of researchers). Looking at South American publications indexed in the SCI in relation to input indicators, either expenditure on R&D or number of researchers, suggests an ambiguous and partial picture. As noted below, it is misleading to concentrate on the number of publications indexed in the SCI, because of its overall underrepresentation. This is an important factor to consider when reading the figures presented in Table 8.2. Small countries like Ecuador and Uruguay with very low levels of GERD (0.08 per cent, and 0.26 per cent GERD as a percentage of GDP, respectively) present a higher ratio of publications indexed in SCI related to GERD than a country like Brazil, which makes a significantly greater commitment to R&D. Tables 8.1 and 8.2 present some general features regarding bibliometric indicators from the SCI.

This study does not contribute to that finer discussion regarding how and why scientists from South American countries choose to collaborate. Even though this work is descriptive in nature and only attempts to identify a broad picture, it nevertheless provides some important insights into patterns that seem to be guiding mainstream science in South America.

Table 8.1   Gross expenditure on R&D (GERD) in selected South American countries, 1999 or last year available

Country	GERD % GDP	GERD (million US$)	GERD per inhabitant (US$)
Brazil	0.91	6 574	42
Chile	0.63	425	28
Argentina	0.47	1 321	36
Colombia	0.41	398	10
Bolivia	0.29	25	3
Uruguay	0.26	54	16
Ecuador	0.08	15	1
Peru	0.06	39	2
Latin America and the Caribbean	0.59	11	23

Source: RICYT (2000).

Table 8.2   Publications in SCI related to GERD (per million US$), selected South American countries, 1998 or last year available

Ecuador	6.9
Uruguay	6.6
Peru	4.2
Chile	4.1
Argentina	3.5
Bolivia	3.4
Brazil	1.1
Latin America and the Caribbean	2.2

Source: RICYT (2000).

METHOD

This work is based on articles published in 2001 and indexed by the SCI® Expanded from South American countries, including Argentina, Bolivia, Brazil, Chile, Colombia, Ecuador, Paraguay, Peru, Uruguay and Venezuela. The data source is the SCI® online (ISI Web of Knowledge), and the search was performed through the 'address' field, by looking for articles that included at least one of the ten South American countries. Only the authors' names, addresses, year of publication (2001), language and type of publication (articles) were considered for this study, while citations, scientific field and the source of publication were dismissed.

The use of scientific databases, such as the SCI, entails some problematic aspects. It could be very misleading to infer issues related to the scientific production of a less developed country exclusively through looking at an international database. It is problematic because international databases in general and the SCI in particular, are biased towards publications from English-speaking authors from industrialized countries, and they under-represent journals from less developed countries.[4] It is claimed that high-quality journals are included in the SCI. However a study conducted by CAPES in Brazil found more than three hundred journals of 'acceptable quality' in Brazil but only three of those journals were indexed in the SCI (Spagnolo, 2000). International databases are misleading if used to determine a total picture regarding the extent of scientific production in less developed countries: they can only provide a partial illustration of 'relative strengths of various countries in mainstream science' (Gaillard, 1992, p.70).

As Garfield (1983) notes, the ISI coverage 'represents the major channels of international scientific communication. It should be borne in mind that we are assessing the level and impact of Third World research in international scientific journals – it is not intended to provide an inventory of Third World scientific output in every journal from every country of the world' (pp.113–14). The problem is not only that the SCI is limited, but also that it is not known how limited it is because we are missing the attributes of the population frame of high-quality journals from which this biased sample is gathered. The problem is more serious because of the scarcity of formalized and standardized mechanisms to index domestic publications in less developed countries, which, if available, could enable comparative analyses and inform us about the size of the gap.[5]

This study does not consider indicators of quality, nor does it attempt to assess the scientific productivity of the South American countries, and therefore the limitations mentioned previously do not affect it directly. However, in the paragraphs below I discuss a different set of limitations which have constrained this study.

A first constraint is related to the criterion for gathering the data in this case, which is based on the 'address' field of the indexed article. This way of searching does not only retrieve articles from the country indicated in the address, it also collects articles in which that name is included in the address. For instance, when performing the search for articles from Paraguay for the year 2001, the SCI online retrieved a total of 82 articles. However, after they had been looked at carefully, only 24 of those articles had some of their affiliation in Paraguay, while the rest of the articles had Paraguay in the address because of a street named Paraguay in a different country. The problem is that there is no embedded mechanism in the search process that could prevent us from getting that type of result, which makes it impossible to know exactly the total number of national publications through searching by address in the online SCI Expanded.

A second constraint is related to access to the search results. The online platform of the SCI Expanded has a built-in mechanism that only displays 500 records. That is not a problem in the case of countries whose annual appearance in mainstream journals indexed by SCI is lower than 500 articles. However it does constitute a problem in the case of countries like Argentina, Brazil, Chile, Colombia and Venezuela in which the number of indexed articles per year exceeds that 500 limit. In these five countries I have only included the latest 500 articles published in 2001.[5] Finally, a third constraint is based on the absence of standardization in the way that the addresses are notated. An article with authors from the same institution can present different notations regarding the name of the institution, and the departments within it.

MAIN FINDINGS

Interpersonal collaboration is definitely the current trend in the South American science indexed in SCI. This pattern is aligned with what seems to be a global trend.[7] In all the countries studied, co-authored articles represent around 90 per cent of the cases, and the variation among countries is between 89 and 98 per cent (Table 8.3). Within the set of co-authored articles, the relative majority of them involve two or three authors (20 per cent in each category).

If we distinguish between individual and organizational collaboration, including in the latter not only interinstitutional but also intersectoral collaboration, it is the interinstitutional level at which most of the organizational collaboration takes place. That is, most co-authored articles are from different institutions, although they are institutions of a similar nature. As can be seen in Table 8.3, in all ten countries the majority of the articles entails interinstitutional collaboration. However the similarity of this pattern presents some finer distinctions when considering differences between countries. It is interesting to note that articles from larger countries have less interinstitutional collaboration than those from smaller countries.[8] In larger countries, collaboration at the interinstitutional level varies between 57 per cent and 70 per cent, while in smaller countries the corresponding figures are between 72 per cent and 93 per cent.[9] It is possible that, in contexts with fewer scientific resources, scientists must cross institutional boundaries to find complementarities and a wider variety of resources, while in larger countries

Table 8.3 South American research collaboration, as reflected in co-authorship

	Articles published in English (%)	Interpersonal collaboration (%)	Interinstitutional collaboration (%)	Intersectoral collaboration (%)	International collaboration (%)	Number of articles
Argentina	90.9 (452)	94.2 (468)	62.6 (311)	28.4 (141)	41.9 (208)	497
Bolivia	96.3 (77)	98.8 (79)	92.5 (74)	73.8 (59)	96.3 (77)	80
Brazil	96.6 (483)	91.2 (456)	57.4 (287)	25.2 (126)	33.5 (165)	500
Chile	88.6 (442)	93.0 (464)	70.3 (351)	42.7 (213)	54.5 (272)	499
Colombia	94.4 (472)	92.4 (462)	77.8 (389)	50.2 (251)	67.4 (337)	500
Ecuador	92.6 (88)	89.5 (85)	84.2 (80)	56.8 (54)	80.0 (76)	95
Paraguay	95.8 (23)	95.8 (23)	87.5 (21)	58.3 (14)	87.5 (21)	24
Peru	98.2 (218)	95.5 (212)	89.2 (198)	57.7 (128)	85.1 (189)	222
Uruguay	95.2 (297)	94.2 (294)	71.8 (224)	37.2 (116)	68.6 (214)	312
Venezuela	86.8 (433)	93.4 (466)	62.1 (310)	32.7 (162)	48.7 (243)	499

Source: The author's elaboration, based on data from SCI expanded.

scientists might have enough resources available within their own institutions and therefore do not experience the same incentives to engage in that type of collaboration. In this chapter, collaboration among departments within the same institution is not studied, but in the future analysis should be done on whether there is some type of substitution and/or complementarity between interinstitutional collaboration and intrainstitutional collaboration, that is collaboration among different departments but within same institutions.

Intersectoral collaboration involves numerous institutions but different in nature, such as universities, industry, non-profit organizations, government and others such as international organizations. It is expected that this type of collaboration would gain ground in a 'triple helix' mode of scientific production. According to the results of this study there are two main groups, one with scant collaboration among different sectors and the other with higher levels of intersectoral collaboration. The former is to some extent related to larger countries, and the latter to smaller countries. As Table 8.3 indicates, in five out of ten countries the majority of articles present intersectoral collaboration. That is, in Bolivia, Colombia, Ecuador, Paraguay and Peru, most articles do show collaboration among sectors.

However intersectoral collaboration first requires interinstitutional collaboration, thus interinstitutional collaboration antecedes intersectoral collaboration. Intersectoral collaboration entails interinstitutional collaboration, that is, collaboration between industry and university (intersectoral) implies interinstitutional collaboration as there are two institutions engaged. In other words, interinstitutional collaboration is a necessary condition for intersectoral collaboration since, if there are not two or more institutions collaborating, it is not possible to have collaboration between sectors. The results of intersectoral collaboration shown in Table 8.3 only illustrate the share of intersectoral collaboration versus its absence. Table 8.4 presents this distinction as we can examine the share of interinstitutional collaboration that involves different sectors, compared to the one that only involves institutions within the same sector.

So, when we look at the share of intersectoral collaboration only in the cases in which there is interinstitutional collaboration, the resulting picture is different. In this case, the group of countries from which the majority of articles present intersectoral collaboration includes not only the five countries mentioned above (from Table 8.3), but also Chile, Uruguay and Venezuela. The difference is that most articles from Chile, Uruguay and Venezuela do not involve intersectoral collaboration. But if, instead of looking at the total number of articles, we only consider those that have co-authors from different institutions, and then examine how many of them are affiliated to institutions from different sectors, we find that in these countries most interinstitutional

Table 8.4　Interinstitutional and intersectoral collaboration

		Intersectoral collaboration	
		No	Yes
Argentina	No	100 (182)	
Interinstitutional collaboration	Yes	54.8 (170)	45.4 (141)
Bolivia	No	100 (6)	
Interinstitutional collaboration	Yes	20.3 (15)	79.7 (59)
Brazil	No	100 (205)	
Interinstitutional collaboration	Yes	56.1 (161)	43.9 (126)
Chile	No	100 (148)	
Interinstitutional collaboration	Yes	39.3 (138)	60.7 (213)
Colombia	No	100 (111)	
Interinstitutional collaboration	Yes	35.5 (138)	64.5 (251)
Ecuador	No	100 (15)	
Interinstitutional collaboration	Yes	32.5 (26)	67.5 (54)
Paraguay	No	100 (7)	
Interinstitutional collaboration	Yes	33.3 (7)	66.7 (14)
Peru	No	100 (23)	
Interinstitutional collaboration	Yes	35.4 (70)	64.6 (128)
Uruguay	No	100 (88)	
Interinstitutional collaboration	Yes	48.2 (108)	51.8 (116)
Venezuela	No	100 (189)	
Interinstitutional collaboration	Yes	47.7 (148)	52.3 (162)

Source:　The author's elaboration, based on data from SCI Expanded.

collaboration does involve institutions from different sectors. Yet in the case of Argentina and Brazil the picture remains the same in both cases (Table 8.3 and 8.4), indicating that the collaborating institutions collaborate within the same sectors.

It is argued that international collaboration is one symptom of the globalization phenomenon. But the phenomenon of globalization is not evenly distributed, and some countries may be more attractive than others. It is plausible to think that scientists in less developed countries are more likely to collaborate with colleagues in developed countries than with colleagues in peripheral ones. There could be many reasons for these types of incentives. The Latin American scientific community has been fragmented and uncoordinated at both levels, within countries and across them (Velho, 1987).

One key question is related to international networks and the extent to which South American scientists engage in collaboration with neighbours, or whether geographical proximity and even topic are important factors in determining the interconnections.

On the question of international collaboration, as with interinstitutional collaboration, there is a variation in terms of indexed publications according to the size of the country. Small countries are more engaged in international collaboration than larger ones. While the range of variation among countries with international collaboration is, for larger countries, between 33 per cent (Brazil) and 54 per cent (Chile), in small countries it varies between 69 per cent (Uruguay) and 96 per cent (Bolivia). Collaboration at the international level is very similar to collaboration at the interinstitutional level.

International collaboration was divided between bilateral and multilateral. As indicated in Table 8.5, in all countries most international collaboration is bilateral rather than multilateral. In all countries, the majority of the bilateral collaboration takes place outside the region (see Table 8.6). Only Bolivia has most of its bilateral collaboration with another Latin American country (37.5 per cent), even though it is almost similar to its involvement with a Western European country (35.7 per cent). The rest of the countries have most of their bilateral collaboration with a Western European country. This is the case of Argentina, Chile, Colombia, Ecuador, Paraguay and Uruguay. But in the case of Brazil, Peru and Venezuela their bilateral collaboration is more oriented to North America.

When the focus is on bilateral collaboration with a Latin American country, the differences between smaller and larger countries remain, even though these two groups are not as sharply distinct as before (see Table 8.6). In general small countries are more oriented towards their neighbours than larger countries. But in all countries, with the only exception of Bolivia, most of their bilateral collaboration is with countries from outside the region. Small countries' collaboration with another Latin American country varies between 20 per cent in Ecuador to 37.5 per cent in Bolivia, including Paraguay with 26.6 per cent and Uruguay with 36.4 per cent. Large countries' bilateral engagement with other Latin American countries is smaller than in the case of small countries. Colombia is an exception in this group: in Colombia the share of articles with bilateral collaboration with a Latin American country is 25.7 per cent, while in the other four large countries it ranges between 4.6 per cent in Brazil, and 18.8 per cent in Chile, including Argentina with 17.9 per cent and Venezuela with 12.1 per cent.

These differences between smaller and larger countries might also be related to the fewer resources in smaller countries. The benefits of geographical proximity might be a powerful advantage for countries with

Table 8.5 *International collaboration*

	No international collaboration[a] (%)	International collaboration[b]		
		Total (%)	Bilateral (%)	Multilateral (%)
Argentina	58.1 (289)	41.9 (208)	77.9 (162)	22.1 (46)
Bolivia	3.8 (3)	96.3 (77)	72.7 (56)	27.3 (21)
Brazil	67 (335)	33.5 (165)	78.8 (130)	21.2 (35)
Chile	45.5 (227)	54.5 (272)	70.6 (192)	29.4 (80)
Colombia	32.6 (163)	67.4 (337)	73.9 (249)	26.1 (88)
Ecuador	20 (19)	80 (76)	52.6 (40)	47.4 (36)
Paraguay	12.5 (3)	87.5 (21)	71.4 (15)	28.6 (6)
Peru	15 (33)	85.1 (189)	59.8 (113)	40.2 (76)
Uruguay	31.4 (98)	68.6 (214)	80.8 (173)	19.2 (41)
Venezuela	51.3 (256)	48.7 (243)	78.2 (190)	21.8 (53)

Notes:
a   Percentages are estimated based on the total of articles included in this study.
b   Percentages are estimated based on total international collaboration, that is the sum of bilateral and multilateral collaboration.

Source: The author's elaboration based on data from SCI Expanded.

Table 8.6 Bilateral collaboration: regions with which South American countries collaborate (percentages and numbers)

	With a Latin American country	With a North American country	With a West European country	With an East European country	With an Asian country	With an African country
Argentina	17.9 (29)	27.8 (45)	47.5 (77)	1.2 (2)	5.5 (9)	–
Bolivia	37.5 (21)	19.6 (11)	35.7 (20)	–	7.1 (4)	–
Brazil	4.6 (6)	43.1 (56)	40.0 (52)	3.8 (5)	6.9 (9)	1.5 (2)
Chile	18.8 (36)	25.0 (48)	48.4 (93)	4.2 (8)	3.6 (7)	–
Colombia	25.7 (64)	27.3 (68)	44.6 (111)	1.6 (4)	0.4 (1)	0.4 (1)
Ecuador	20.0 (8)	20.0 (8)	57.5 (23)	–	2.5 (1)	–
Paraguay	26.6 (4)	20.0 (3)	53.3 (8)	–	–	–
Peru	21.2 (24)	51.3 (58)	23.0 (26)	–	3.5 (4)	0.9 (1)
Uruguay	36.4 (63)	19.1 (33)	41.6 (72)	0.6 (1)	2.3 (4)	–
Venezuela	12.1 (23)	41.6 (79)	38.9 (74)	2.6 (5)	4.2 (8)	0.5 (1)

Note: In this table percentages are estimated, based on the total of bilateral collaboration.

Source: The author's elaboration, based on data from SCI Expanded.

187

lower capabilities, while in the case of larger countries the leverage may be driven by collaborating with countries from outside the region, with different expertise, improved resources and technological capabilities.

FINAL CONSIDERATIONS

With respect to the broader question of whether the trend towards highly collaborative research is a continuing phenomenon among South American scientists, the results discussed above show high levels of interpersonal and interinstitutional collaboration. Once again, from this study it is not possible to infer the extent to which this pattern is embedded in all science produced in those countries, or whether it is a feature of science published in mainstream science. Studies from other less developed countries indicate a similar research system with high levels of collaboration.[10]

Smaller countries show higher levels of interinstitutional collaboration than larger countries. Interpersonal and interinstitutional collaboration are common practice in all South American countries. The cross-country differences are relatively small, but, even more importantly, in all of them the majority of the articles show collaboration at the interpersonal and at the interinstitutional level. Nevertheless the picture is rather different when we look at patterns of international collaboration. In this case the gap among countries gets larger: smaller countries are more oriented to international collaboration than larger ones. This result is coincident with Luukkonen's (1992) finding, in which '[scientific] size seems to be inversely related to the rate of international coauthorships' (p.104). This stronger orientation to international collaboration on the part of smaller countries can be partly explained by necessity. The need to expand their scarce local resources and critical mass drives smaller countries to engage in international collaboration as a means to overcome those domestic constraints (Luukkonen, 1992). Also one of the benefits of collaboration, as was stated above, is its relation with research impact, since co-authored papers that involve international collaboration are cited more often.[11]

Not only do smaller countries have higher levels of international collaboration, but also their bilateral collaboration is more reliant on countries in the region as compared to larger countries, even though in almost all countries, with the sole exception of Bolivia, most bilateral collaboration involves a country outside the region. Overall most bilateral collaboration at the international level takes place with a Western European country. Collaboration with multiple countries represents a considerable part of international collaboration, even though the main share of international collaboration takes place in bilateral relationships.

These findings could suggest that one type of organizational collaboration (interinstitutional, intersectoral or international) might displace other types. Collaboration involves both benefits and costs. It may be the case that engaging in one type of collaboration tends to rule out another type, as a trade-off between costs and benefits. For instance, international collaboration might generate high costs which make intersectoral collaboration less attractive. Collaboration between different sectors, such as industry and university, is complex, particularly given their different organizational cultures and rationales. Indeed, in Latin America, the private sector does not have a tradition of commitment to research and development, which leaves the universities as the main locus of knowledge production (Arocena and Sutz, 2001). It seems fundamental to inform this analysis and discussion with in-depth interviews, so as to understand better the incentives that lead scientists from less developed countries to engage in research collaboration. It would be particularly useful to analyse in more depth the dynamics between these different types of collaboration.

ISSUES FOR FURTHER ANALYSIS

I note here some of the elements I consider it critical to include in a further stage. First, I would include a longitudinal dimension to the analysis. A significant weakness of this work is its one-year snapshot, since bibliometric analysis should be longitudinal to illustrate general trends. However time constraints made that task impossible at this stage.

Secondly, scientific field should be taken into consideration in an attempt to account for possible differences in collaboration according to the nature of research. One should assess whether experimentalists are more likely to engage in collaboration than theorists, as suggested by Hagstrom (1965), or if more basic research is more open to international collaboration, as suggested by Frame and Carpenter (1979, reviewed in Katz and Martin, 1997).

Thirdly, it would be important to pursue a more in-depth analysis to study the type of collaborations among researchers, and observe whether the collaboration ties reflect established networks concentrated around some set of closed ties with high levels of reciprocity, or more open and dispersed collaborative ties.[12] Fourthly, it seems critical to investigate the costs and benefits involved in collaboration practices through case studies.

Finally, in a further stage it would be interesting to include articles indexed by a domestic or regional database in South America, to compare the extent of the collaborative patterns and establish the variations between them and international mainstream databases.

NOTES

1. I would like to thank, for generous comments, Carl Martin Allwood, Sven Hemlin and Ben Martin, who coordinated the 'Creative Knowledge Environments' track of the Triple Helix Conference, Copenhagen 2003. However the findings, interpretations and conclusions presented here are the entire responsibility of the author. Finally I would like to thank Susan E. Cozzens, whose mentorship allowed me to participate in the conference, and the School of Public Policy at the Georgia Institute of Technology where I am pursuing my PhD studies.
2. In this chapter the term 'institutions' refers to organizations.
3. Since these different combinations are not mutually exclusive, it is possible to find different combinations of these categories operating at different levels.
4. For more details see Narvaez-Bertheemot *et al.* (1992), Sancho (1992) and Velho (1986, 1987).
5. There is wide variation within less developed countries. In South America, for instance, countries such as Brazil, Venezuela and Colombia have pursued systematic efforts and are concerned with science and technology issues.
6. The online interface from ISI offers different alternatives for sorting those articles, including by latest date, by times cited, by relevance, by first author or by title of the source. I considered that the least harmful alternative would be to have them sorted by latest date.
7. See Gibbons *et al.* (1994), Hicks and Katz (1996), Ziman (1994).
8. The reference to large and small countries is based on number of publications indexed in the SCI Expanded in the year 2001. The larger countries are those that exceed 500 articles: Argentina, Brazil, Chile, Colombia and Venezuela.
9. Among the larger countries, Brazil has the lowest percentage of interinstitutional collaboration, with 57 per cent, and Chile has the highest with 70 per cent. Within the set of smaller countries Uruguay has interinstitutional collaboration in 72 per cent of them, while Bolivia has the highest percentage, with 93 per cent.
10. For more details, see El Alami *et al.* (1992).
11. Highly cited papers are seen as high-impact papers, and by some authors as high-quality papers. Cozzens (1989, p.440) points out that citations are claimed to be made between two systems: the rhetorical, which entails the claims of authorship that scholars pursue when publishing and is related to citations seen as a measure of impact, and the reward system, which is related to the credit that authors get by publishing and is linked to citations as a measure of quality.
12. For an interesting approach to the topic, see Peters and van Raan (1991) and Pradvic and Oluic-Vokovic (1986).

REFERENCES

Arocena, R. and J.Sutz (2001), 'Changing knowledge production and Latin American Universities', *Research Policy*, **30**(8), 1221–34.

Cozzens, S. (1989), 'What do citations count? The rhetoric-first model', *Scientometrics*, **15** (5–6), 437–47.

El Alami, J., J.C.Dore and J.F. Miquel (1992), 'International scientific collaboration in Arab countries', *Scientometrics*, **23**(1), 249–63.

Eztkowitz, H. and L. Leydesdorff (2000), 'The dynamics of innovation: from National Systems and "Mode 2" to a Triple Helix of university–industry–government relation', *Research Policy*, **29**, 109–23.

Frame, J.D. and M.P. Carpenter (1979), 'International Research Collaboration', *Social Studies of Science*, **9**, 481–87.

Gaillard, J. (1992), 'Use of publication lists to study scientific production and strategies of scientists in developing countries', *Scientometrics*, **23**(1), 57–73.

Gaillard, J. (1994), 'The behavior of scientists and scientific communities', in J.J. Salomon, F. Sagasti and C. Sachs-Jeantet (eds), *The Uncertain Quest: Science, Technology, and Development*, Tokyo: The United Nations University.

Garfield, E. (1983), 'Mapping science in the Third World', *Science and Public Policy* **10**(3), 112–27.

Gibbons, M., C. Limoges, H. Nowotny, S. Schwartzman, P. Scott and M. Trow (1994), *The New Production of Knowledge*, London: Sage.

Hagstrom, W.O. (1965), *The Scientific Community*, New York: Basic Books.

Hicks, D. and J.S. Katz (1996), 'Science policy for a highly collaborative science system', *Science and Public Policy*, **23**(1), 39–44.

Katz, J.S. and D. Hicks (1997a), 'Bibliometric Indicators for National Systems of Innovation', SPRU, University of Sussex.

Katz, J.S. and D.Hicks (1997b), 'How much is collaboration worth? A calibrated bibliometric model', *Scientometrics*, **40**(3), 541–54.

Katz J.S. and B.R. Martin (1997), 'What is research collaboration?', *Research Policy* **26**(1), 1–18.

Leydesdorff, L. and H.Etzkowitz (1996), 'Emergence of a Triple Helix of university–industry–government relations', *Science and Public Policy*, **23**(5), 279–86.

Luukkonen, T. (1992), 'Understanding patterns of international scientific collaboration', *Science, Technology & Human Values*, **17**(1), 101–26.

Narin, F., K. Stevens and E. Withlow (1991), 'Scientific co-operation in Europe and the citation of multinationally authored papers', *Scientometrics*, **21**(2), 313–23.

Narvaez-Bertheemot, N.P. Frigoletto and J.F. Miquel (1992), 'International scientific collaboration in Latin America', *Scientometrics*, **24**(3), 373–92.

Peters, H.P.F. and A.F.J.van Raan (1991), 'Structuring scientific activities by co-author analysis', *Scientometrics*, **20**(1), 235–55.

Pradvic, N. and V. Oluic-Vokovic (1986), 'Dual approach to multiple authorship in the study of collaboration/scientific output relationship', *Scientometrics*, **10**(5–6), 259–80.

RICYT (2000), *El Estado de la Ciencia* (The State of Science), Buenos Aires: RICYT–CYTED–OAS.

Sábato, J. and N.Botana (1968), 'La Ciencia y la Tecnología en el desarrollo futuro de América Latina', paper presented to 'The World Order Models' Conference, Bellagio, available online at the Tecla project, (http://www.cecae.usp.br/tecla/html/index_br.html), São Paulo.

Salomon, J.J (1994), 'Modern science and technology', in J.J. Salomon, F. Sagasti and C. Sachs-Jeantet (eds), *The Uncertain Quest: Science, Technology and Development*, Tokyo: The United Nations University.

Sancho, R. (1992), 'Misjudgments and shortcomings in the measurement of scientific activities in less developed countries', *Scientometrics*, **23**(1), 221–33.

Senker, J.(1999), 'University Research Funding', a report prepared for the OECD, SPRU, University of Sussex.

Spagnolo, F. (2000), 'Brazilian scientists' publication and mainstream science: some policy implications', *Scientometrics*, **18** (3–4), 205–18.

Sutz, J. (1996), *Universidad, producción, gobierno: encuentros y desencuentros*, Montevideo: CIESU-TRILCE.

Velho, L. (1986), 'The meaning of citation in the context of a scientifically peripheral country', *Scientometrics*, **9**(1–2),71–89.

Velho, L. (1987), 'The author and the beholder', *Scientometrics*, **11**(1–2), 59–70.

Wagner, C.S. (1999), 'International alliances and technology transfer: challenging national foresight?', reprinted in *Forward Thinking Proceedings Report*, Washington, DC: RAND.

Ziman, J.M. (1994), *Prometheus Bound: Science in a Dynamic Steady State*, Cambridge: Cambridge University Press.

9. Conclusions: how to stimulate creative knowledge environments

Ben R. Martin, Carl Martin Allwood and Sven Hemlin

INTRODUCTION

There are at least two related but somewhat distinct reasons why creative knowledge environments (CKEs) are of interest to study. The first is that they represent an obvious focus if one is interested in understanding the process of knowledge generation. The second is related to the shift to a more knowledge-intensive economy or the 'knowledge society' (Stehr, 1994). In this there is an increasing premium on creativity and innovation in order to respond successfully to growing competitive pressures. If one wants to improve creativity and other aspects of knowledge production, one needs to analyse and understand what constitutes a 'creative knowledge environment' and how this might best be stimulated or improved. The first reason might be said to involve primarily a descriptive and analytical approach, while the second involves not only a descriptive but also a normative approach to the study of human knowledge generation.

Different types of CKEs differ with respect to the way they produce knowledge and therefore may give rise to knowledge that differs in its properties; for example, the physical sciences, life sciences, social sciences and humanities all differ quite appreciably with respect to what aspects of reality they are concerned with and on what types of arguments and evidence they are based. In this context, the normative perspective on CKEs is important since it creates an opportunity for policy makers, administrators and others to take a stance with respect to the type of knowledge they deem it desirable to produce.

The approach in the various chapters in this book has mostly been descriptive and analytical rather than normative. An important goal for research on CKEs that integrates the descriptive/analytical and normative perspectives is to establish more clearly what conditions (for example, with respect to the physical, cognitive, social and motivational aspects) can provide individuals, groups and organizations with a CKE that promotes their creativity not only in the short term but in the long term as well.

In this chapter we first elaborate on the discussion of the nature of CKEs that has taken place in previous chapters. Secondly, we summarize the main lessons we have learnt about CKEs from the studies reported in this book. Thirdly, we identify and analyse what circumstances and conditions promote creativity in organizations and which ones hinder it. We also identify some of the main policy implications of our findings. We end by pointing to issues on which further research is needed.

As we observed in Chapter 1, creativity involves interactions between individuals and their environments. The latter include other individuals as well as the organization and its relationship with other institutions and with the wider regional or national system of innovation or knowledge generation. Likewise micro-level CKEs are nested within meso-level CKEs (groups, organizations and so on) that, in turn, are nested within the macro-level CKE (national, international or global). Thus the different scale-levels – micro, meso and macro (see the discussion in Chapter 1) – can perhaps best be seen as three analytical perspectives, since there is a general interdependence between the different scale levels. Across these environmental layers, knowledge production is also influenced by the prevailing scientific discipline and its associated culture.

Our emphasis on the interaction between individuals and their environments in order to understand scientific creativity is in contrast to the view of creativity as the property of particular, gifted individuals. According to what is sometimes referred to as 'the sacred spark' theory (for example, Cole and Cole, 1973), creativity emanates from a few outstanding performers who are highly motivated and hard working. Their primary drive is inner motivation. However, the question of what type of motivation promotes creativity deserves more attention and research. In line with other research by, for example, Amabile (1999), which stresses the importance of internal motivation, Spangenberg *et al.* (1990) concluded that external factors such as financial reward can actually be a negative influence. In contrast, other research discussed by Unsworth and Parker (2003) suggests that, depending on its administration and the context, external reward can be beneficial to innovative activities.

In addition, certain factors other than motivation, factors that still relate to the individual but which are of a more context-sensitive kind, have been put forward as influences on creativity. One example is the suggestion by Klahr and Simon (1999) that creative problem solving might have to rely more on 'weak methods' as opposed to 'powerful domain-specific search heuristics' (ibid., p.540).[1] Weak methods can be defined as general, context-independent methods that bring about advances towards the problem solution only in relatively small steps. The reason for using weak methods stems from the fact that problems requiring a creative solution often tend to be less well structured than other problems. Thus researchers who are more adept at using weak methods than strong methods might be better placed to produce creative knowledge. The use and development of weak methods might be encouraged by special training and also by researchers occasionally changing research fields.

Let us now turn to consider what lessons emerge from the analyses reported in earlier chapters of this book.

SYNTHESIS OF MAIN CONCLUSIONS FROM PREVIOUS CHAPTERS

We first deal with features of creative knowledge environments at the micro level. We then discuss the features and interactions between micro-, meso- and macro-level CKEs.

Micro-level CKEs

The characteristics of micro-level CKEs are analysed in some detail in the chapters by Gulbrandsen and Nieminen. From these and other authors there appears to be consensus that a very wide variety of organizational factors are relevant to creativity. These include autonomy, close cooperation within the group and strong group cohesiveness, a common vision, good project management (including supportive leadership offering encouragement, enough time to try out new ideas and adequate resources), good internal and external communication and knowledge transfer (Graversen *et al.*, 2002), effective collaboration with other groups, inter- or multi-disciplinarity (Hollingsworth, 2000), trust, liveliness, good social interactions (characterized, for example, by humour and after-work interactions) and an open, tolerant culture where innovation is the norm and individuals are free to try out 'crazy' ideas (Pelz and Andrews, 1966; Mohamed and Rickards, 1996; see also Gulbrandsen, Chapter 2, this volume, Nieminen, Chapter 3, this volume).

There is also widespread agreement on what are the main constraints on CKEs: lack of funding, limited time, too few other researchers (or too narrow a range of expertise or disciplinary perspectives) in the group, difficulties in combining knowledge generation with other tasks (for example teaching and administration), excessive evaluation and other accountability pressures (which signal distrust and may divert attention from creativity to meeting external evaluation criteria) (Chapters 2 and 3, this volume; also Ziman,

1987). Another constraint is a lack of core funding and a consequent heavy dependency on external project funding which may lead to researchers feeling that they are on a 'treadmill', especially if there is weak or little leadership (see Chapter 3). 'Bureaucracy' in particular is seen as perhaps the principal 'enemy' of creativity, along with poor leadership (whether too weak, authoritarian, conservative or unpredictable).

From these various factors that may influence CKEs, it is clear that there may be contradictions or tensions between positive and negative factors. Furthermore even a single factor can, if taken beyond a certain point, change from exerting a positive influence to imposing a negative one. Let us consider some of these factors in turn.

The importance of autonomy in ensuring creativity has been stressed by many researchers. The concept of 'autonomy' has several different aspects, including the freedom to choose and formulate the research problem, to select the best approach or theoretical framework, to implement the research plan and carry out the research and to publish the results. However it is important to recognize that autonomy on its own, or to too great an extent, may actually be a negative influence on a CKE. In particular, if there is little coordination between members of the research team, or if there is no clear strategy, or if the staff have a high level of security so that there is little to challenge them, or if the goal of activities is unclear or ambiguous, the research group may be ineffective and uncreative: the knowledge environment, while safeguarding autonomy, will not promote creativity.

Similarly collaboration with other groups is usually a strong positive contribution to CKEs, yet collaboration takes time and effort to develop and manage (Katz and Martin, 1997). If conducted with little clear sense of strategy, or if carried too far, it will leave insufficient time for creativity and knowledge generation. One reason for this is that creativity might be helped if, in addition to group interaction, time is also allowed for individual reflection. Evidence supporting this suggestion comes from research by Diehl and Stroebe and others (reviewed by Wilke and Kaplan, 2001) who show that one explanation for the lower productivity commonly found when using the technique of 'brainstorming', as compared to nominal groups consisting of individuals working independently of one another, is that listening to others may cause group members to forget their own ideas or hinder individuals' own reflections (see also Paulus and Yang, 2000).

Likewise interaction with other disciplines, that is, inter-, multi- or trans-disciplinary approaches, can often be very fruitful for creativity. Again, however, this takes time and effort to organize and manage, for example because of differences in 'culture' across disciplines or because of administrative boundaries separating the collaborating organizations (see, for instance, Allwood and Bärmark, 1999). Consequently any benefits may be exceeded by the 'costs'. Even having researchers with high levels of personal creativity may result in the generation of wild ideas that are of little use or relevance to others or to the goal of creating knowledge or innovations. If the ideas generated are too original, they may become detached from scholarly research or the world of innovation. Thus, there is a fine line between the genius and the 'mad man' (Gulbrandsen). As was noted in Chapter 1, originality on its own, in contrast to originality that serves some useful purpose and is of good quality, is not sufficient for the product to be deemed to be 'creative' in the context of CKE research.

Similarly apparently negative influences on CKEs can have a positive side. Auditing and evaluation, besides diverting attention from knowledge generation to meet external assessment criteria, may nevertheless result in better ways of doing things (see Chapter 3). Reduction or removal of core funding and a shift to a reliance on external project funds may mean less autonomy and less creativity, but they can also facilitate links to new research networks and different perspectives, and hence in some cases stimulate new ideas and creativity (also see Ziman, 1987). Time pressures may leave little opportunity to be creative, or they may encourage new approaches or ways of thinking. Likewise, competition with others to be first to make an original contribution to knowledge can be either negative or positive in its influence on CKEs (Amabile, 1988). High ambitions and expectations may also be both a source of inspiration and a source of stress (see Chapter 2).

Some analysts go further and argue that creativity involves an intrinsic process of discord as well as accord, that CKEs are beset by tensions that cannot and indeed should not be removed because they are fundamental stimuli to the creative act. This is in contrast to the more traditional assumption that creativity is facilitated by maximizing the degree of accord in the work environment, by giving scientists autonomy and subjecting them to little interference, by providing them with good facilities and adequate resources, by adopting a very 'light' style of management and imposing a minimum of bureaucracy, by encouraging them to collaborate with one other, and so on. This conventional view is consistent with much management and organization theory, which is aimed at removing constraints and tensions. As Åkerman (1998) has pointed out, this paradigm can be seen as part of the 'modern rationality project', which is based on the assumption that removing obstacles like tensions and friction will generate efficiency and perhaps ultimately even perfection.

The view emerging here, by contrast, is that tensions should not be removed but rather be maintained and balanced in order to enhance creativity. According to this view, a CKE should combine not only positive characteristics and processes aimed at achieving accord, but also certain 'negative' characteristics and processes that create some level of discord if it is to be truly creative. Jacobsen (cited in Gulbrandsen) has noted that a 'nice' place to work may not be creative. Similarly Amabile (1988) concludes that a balanced amount of pressure or tension is appropriate to creativity, Tardif and Sternberg (1988) note that creativity always involves some tension and Foss Hansen (1995) argues that tensions release energy and keep organizations alive. Mohamed and Rickards (1996) list the presence of tensions as one of the key 'dimensions' of a CKE. In this book, Gulbrandsen points to tensions in all organizations between the need for efficiency, control and effective action, on the one hand, and learning, individuality and creativity, on the other.

Different authors have identified various types of creative tension. Pelz and Andrews (1966) identify seven types: basic science v. application, independence v. interaction, specialization v. breadth, autonomy v. meeting external demands, influencing others v. being controlled by others, intellectual harmony v. debate and conflict, and young researchers v. old. A somewhat different list of four main types of creative tension has been drawn up by Dougherty (1996), these being internal v. external, old v. new, top-down v. bottom-up, and responsibility v. freedom. Gulbrandsen (in Chapter 2) produces a further list of tensions, including autonomy v. structure and control, social support v. critical feedback, non-interfering v. creative leadership, similar v. diverse range of colleagues, and larger v. smaller research units. However, none of these lists or typologies is exhaustive. Other possible creative tensions include, for example, ambition v. stress, autonomy v. mutual dependence and 'weak methods' v. 'strong methods'.

Another possible source of creativity is the tension between divergent and convergent thinking. Already in the 1950s, Kuhn (1959) was pointing to the essential tension between divergent and convergent thinking in promoting creativity in research. Moreover, in contrast to many subsequent analysts, Kuhn argued that the researcher, in order to be usefully creative, should be well acquainted with, and should make use of, assumptions in the established paradigm. Hence, in contrast to Klahr and Simon (1999) above, Kuhn appears to be emphasizing the importance of 'strong methods' over weak ones.

It would seem that the tensions identified in the research literature are of rather different kinds. In the case of some tensions, the terms making up the tension are contradictory (for instance, intellectual harmony v. debate and conflict, or similar v. diverse range of colleagues). In such cases it is unclear how both features can be present at the same time. Rather the tension relates to the fact that there are positive and negative effects of the situations depicted by both terms. In other tensions, the terms making up the tension focus our attention on different aspects of the same or similar phenomena (for example, non-interfering v. creative leadership – a creative leadership might well be a non-interfering leadership and vice versa). These observations suggest that the term 'tension' is used in different and sometimes unclear ways in the literature. Future research might profitably attempt to analyse in more detail the processes associated with different types of situations denoted by the various terms making up the respective tensions.

The analysis is further complicated by the fact that what constitutes an optimum balance in relation to such 'creative tensions' may vary considerably among individuals and CKEs. In other words, one particular balance of tensions may suit some researchers but not others. For example, some may prefer a more stable working environment than others (see Chapter 2 of the present volume; see also Chapter 6, on the differences between CKEs in British and French firms).

Finally, it is worth noting that not all tensions may be good for creativity. For example, the tension between the career interests of researchers (particularly young ones) and the interests of a research group as a whole (Jacob and Hellström, 2000) may not be productive.

Interaction between Micro-, Meso- and Macro-level CKEs

In Chapter 1, we put forward the notion of 'nested layers' of CKEs and their components: starting at the micro level, with the individual within a group, working within an institution, in turn situated within a sector (for example university, industry) but also within a region and perhaps also within a network (for example a supply chain), located within a nation, and perhaps also within a multinational (for example EU) or global (for example WTO) environment. Several of the chapters in this book analyse different aspects of the interactions between CKEs at different micro, meso and macro levels.

One key component of CKEs comprises the qualified scientists and engineers (QSEs) employed by the organization (see Chapters 5 and 6 in this book). In their study, Wallgren and Hägglund focus on those QSEs who possess a PhD and they examine how these are trained. As part of the shift to a knowledge society characterized by the growing importance of knowledge for competitiveness, many countries are now witnessing the emergence of doctoral training programmes that are specifically geared to the production of PhDs for careers in industry. As Wallgren and Hägglund note, this represents an attempt to combine the Mode 1 and Mode 2 forms of knowledge production within one CKE (Gibbons *et al.*, 1994).

Wallgren and Hägglund focus on CKEs in the companies in which the doctoral students carry out their training. Their analysis shows that those CKEs can be clustered into three main types: research-intensive, engineering and consultant CKEs. In 'research-intensive CKEs', the focus is on original research and advanced development. There are good opportunities to write scientific papers and in addition there are other staff with PhDs to provide the doctoral student with knowledge and help. In other words, the CKE may not be greatly different from that found in a university. One possible drawback, however, is that the PhD student may feel somewhat isolated and perhaps gain little stimulation from the business operations of the company.

In an 'engineering CKE', there is closer contact with business operations and the PhD project is generally linked to product development. The students are likely to participate in several projects, which widens their experience but which may result in competing interests. The production process tends to have a high impact on their work, but the emphasis on product development may interfere with the time scale of their PhD. The larger impact of market forces is normally associated with a shorter time perspective and may mean that usefulness becomes one of the criteria for judging the success of the PhD. There are also fewer experienced researchers around to help the PhD student.

In a 'consultant CKE', the focus is on services offered by the company rather than production, and the PhD student may have no fixed place of work. The company is likely to view the student as a source of competence to use in marketing their services. There are few staff around who know what a PhD education involves, so there will be little dialogue about the PhD research. Empirical results will tend to come almost entirely from clients, thus creating a dependency on the client. Time perspectives will generally be very short and the connection between the company and the university may be rather weak. In such an environment, it is difficult to 'anchor' a PhD student.

In all three types of CKE, creative tensions are likely to be present to a greater or lesser extent. For example, there tends to be a clash between the time perspectives of a PhD and of the company, especially in the engineering and consultant environments. There will be tensions as to what constitutes a successful PhD project and the criteria for judging this. In principle, there may be tensions over the company's need to keep certain parts of its knowledge secret and the imperative of the PhD student to make his or her results public (although it is interesting that none of the students surveyed in this study experienced major problems with respect to publication of their results). As other authors in this volume have shown, a successful CKE involves managing and balancing such creative tensions.

Wallgren and Hägglund conclude that industrial doctoral students play important roles as intermediaries and change agents in CKEs, building bridges between the two separate 'worlds' of academia and industry with their different values and culture. Such students may therefore promote creativity and innovation in industry. Similarly the establishment and development of the industrial doctoral programme forms part of the (creative) process of renewal in the university and in research education. Lastly, the results support the thesis of Gibbons *et al.* (1994) that knowledge production is increasingly taking place in a variety of new 'hybrid' sites.

Another key aspect of CKEs is that creativity and innovativeness depend greatly on the ways in which QSEs are deployed. As we have seen above, vital to the success of a CKE is its openness to external knowledge sources. A successful CKE depends on research interactions and collaborations, and these in turn are influenced by the staff that are recruited and the contacts and networks that they bring with them. Mason *et al.* (in Chapter 6) set out to test various hypotheses as to how differences in labour markets, mobility, careers and education for QSEs are likely to result in different types of CKEs in British and French companies (in the optoelectronics sector), especially with regard to different patterns of external links, networks and knowledge transfer. French QSEs generally spend five years at university (equivalent to a postgraduate MSc degree in the UK) during which they may have a placement at a company (which may subsequently recruit them when they graduate). French companies prefer to recruit QSEs straight from university and to train those recruits further in-house. Those QSEs then tend to stay with the same company during their career. In contrast, the QSEs recruited by UK companies mostly have a BSc level (three-year) degree qualification only. There is much greater mobility between UK firms; the companies prefer to recruit experienced people who bring in new ideas and new ways of thinking (apart from large defence companies, which are more similar in outlook to French companies). Those experienced QSEs also bring with them new networks of contacts and help maintain the momentum of relationship building between companies. In France, the large companies in particular tend to have long-established relationships with each other and with SMEs (small and medium-sized enterprises), which results in more structured supply-chain partnerships than in the UK. The process of relationship building and maintenance is less 'risky' than in the UK, where more interactions and relationships are entered into on an ad hoc and opportunistic basis. (The exception is again the large defence-based electronics companies in UK.)

The analysis in Chapter 6 highlights a central 'creative tension' in CKEs: how to balance, on the one hand, stability in personnel, perspectives and relationships with other 'actors' in national systems of innovation (relationships with other companies, universities, institutes and so on) with, on the other, flexibility and continuous change in these relationships. Another creative tension is the dilemma faced by each company regarding the need to exchange knowledge with other companies without at the same time giving away 'too much'. This is an example of a creative tension in micro- and meso-level CKEs.

Mason *et al.* conclude from their interviews that there are significant national differences, with a faster rate of building new relationships in the UK because of the greater flow of QSEs between companies. This widens the range of external knowledge sources and helps to create new collaborations. In France, the external research relationships and knowledge-sourcing patterns are more stable. This saves time, effort and resources needed to develop innovation networks (it can take considerable time, for example, to build up the requisite trust between partners in a network or collaborative project). In a sector characterized by rapid changes in technology, companies and other actors need to be open to new sources of knowledge and ideas. In this respect, UK companies may be at an advantage with the greater efforts they devote to enhancing creativity and innovation potential. However, this is not fully evaluated in Chapter 6. One implication of these conclusions is that different countries may need different public policies. In France, incentives are perhaps needed to encourage companies to seek new partners, whereas the UK may need incentives to develop and strengthen relationships of a more strategic nature.

Another key issue in relation to CKEs at the meso level is their relationship to the regional system of innovation and to clusters. How can one set about stimulating creativity and innovation at the regional level? One mechanism is through the establishment of science parks, incubators and other similar organizational entities. These represent a key 'crucible' for the formation of CKEs at the meso level. Since they involve interactions between academic institutions, firms and regional or local government, they also offer an opportunity for observing the evolving 'Triple Helix' relationships (see Bengtsson and Lind, Chapter 4 in this book; also Leydesdorff and Etzkowitz, 1996; Etzkowitz and Leydesdorff, 1998; Etzkowitz *et al.*, 2000).

Bengtsson and Lind report a case study of the development of the first Swedish science park, along with a comparison with similar parks in Cambridge and Grenoble. They show that the creation and development of a science park depends heavily on the local actors, resources and conditions. Their study highlights the importance of 'relational entrepreneurs' in developing links between different actors in the regional system of innovation. In the particular case they describe, the extensive network of contacts of one of the central actors proved to be of great importance. By virtue of that individual's network of social contacts, there was a unique possibility to coordinate representatives of the three parts of the 'Triple Helix' and consequently he played a crucial role in the creation of the science park. In the early stages of a science park, the links between companies and academic institutions are often few in number and relatively weak. It takes time to develop the necessary 'critical mass' and in particular for the formation of specialist companies offering specific services (such as venture capital, and patenting and licensing expertise). Once these are established, however, these entities in turn foster further links, resulting in more effective CKEs and in a stronger, more effective and more creative regional system of innovation.

The chapter by Kaiser (Chapter 7) focuses on science–industry relations and on the interaction between different types of CKEs and wider national systems of innovation. His study also sheds light on changes in the relationships between the three principal actors in the 'Triple Helix': industry, government and academia. Kaiser analyses two sectors, telecommunications and pharmaceutical biotechnology. Both have been characterized by recent major shifts in technological paradigm; telecommunications has shifted from an electromechanical to a digital–optical paradigm, and pharmaceutical biotechnology from a chemistry-driven paradigm to genomic-based drug development.

Kaiser shows that the combined effects of these paradigm shifts and of various other macro environment changes has been the emergence of new 'modes of coordination'. (The two traditional 'modes of coordination' are markets and hierarchies, but in recent years attention has focused on a number of other modes of coordination including networks, the state and associations.) Different modes of coordination have different consequences for research and knowledge production. For example, under market coordination, there will often be increasing pressures on universities towards short-term and more applied research. Hence the emergence of new modes of coordination within and between organizations will generally have an impact on CKEs.

Kaiser analyses how different events at the macro level affect conditions for CKEs at the meso level. In the case of the telecommunications industry, market liberalization of the sector in Germany resulted in a considerable reduction in the amount of in-house R&D by companies. Coupled with the changing technological paradigm and the provision of government funding for basic technologies (such as multimedia and informatics), this resulted in the 'outsourcing' of much research from companies to universities and research institutes. Universities and institutes have consequently become an integral part of the industrial R&D system in the sector.

In the pharmaceutical sector, under the old paradigm, chemistry-driven R&D was primarily carried out by large pharmaceutical companies. At that time there was little incentive in Germany for the commercialization of academic research. The changed technological paradigm has resulted in the creation of new phases at the beginning of the innovation process, in particular the emergence of 'functional genomics'. Combined with various changes in the macro environment – in particular, changes in policy (for example, to stimulate networks and collaboration and the mobility of researchers), in finance (for example through the 'BioRegio' competition to stimulate biotechnology clusters and commercialization) and in regulations (for example university patenting regulations) – this has resulted in the emergence of SMEs to carry out contract research and to develop platform technologies. Indeed, those SMEs now virtually monopolize the early phases of the innovation process.

In short, Kaiser shows how technological paradigm shifts have resulted in new modes of coordination in these two sectors, thereby altering the relations between industry, universities and institutes and the more macro-level environment for knowledge generation. In both sectors, knowledge environments have become more integrated and interorganisational boundaries more blurred – in line with the changes outlined by Gibbons *et al.* (1994) in their analysis of 'Mode 2' knowledge production. Those changes have been stimulated in part by government policies. The CKEs in question have become not only more integrated but also more internationalized as they have developed closer links with specialist sources of knowledge. Kaiser's other main conclusion is that science–industry relations and CKEs are sector-specific (in biotechnology, for example, links between industry and universities or institutes are more important). This has important implications for public policy.

In Nieminen's study (Chapter 3), there are two aspects relating to the interaction between different levels of CKEs that should be highlighted here. First, there is an emphasis on research policy implementation and its effects on university research groups in Finland. In other words, he considers the macro-level influences on micro-level CKEs, an important component of any analysis aimed at understanding CKEs. Secondly, Nieminen focuses on changes in CKEs at the micro level when research policies at the national level are altered. He identifies some of the positive and negative effects on research groups and their CKEs experienced in Finland during the period after major policy changes during the 1990s. One important finding is that the stronger reliance on external research funding did not apparently have a detrimental effect on the quality of their research output during the period assessed. Indeed academic researchers who were put under pressure to develop collaborations with non-academic partners often found that this could be stimulating from the point of view of creativity because it extended their networks of contacts and presented them with new research challenges. However some of the researchers interviewed did express concerns about the effects in the longer term.

Collaboration among researchers is, as we noted earlier, a crucial component for enhancing creativity in knowledge environments. The ability to draw on different cognitive and organizational backgrounds in networks of collaborating researchers is often critical in promoting creativity. In her bibliometric analysis of co-authorships among Latin American scientists, Bortagaray shows how much research is dependent on collaboration. This analysis, which focuses on the meso and macro level of CKEs, involves the use of bibliometric indicators based on co-authored publications. These offer a suitable tool for analyses at this level, although, as Bortagary notes, there are various shortcomings in the databases used in such analyses which one needs to take into consideration (for instance individual, institutional and even country names can be misspelt, confused or ambiguous).

Her results show that both interpersonal and interinstitutional collaboration is relatively common among researchers in Latin American countries (as elsewhere nowadays). Her analysis of bilateral and international collaboration patterns reveals that, for most Latin American countries, a majority of the collaborations are with a Western European country. In the more restricted CKEs found in smaller countries, there is a higher degree of collaboration among institutions. The incentive to expand one's CKE is apparently greater in small nations; their researchers tend to collaborate more internationally than those in larger countries in Latin America (cf. Luukkonen, 1992), although their partnerships tend to be somewhat more oriented to neighbouring states than is the case for larger nations (which may have more leverage when choosing their research partners).

The fact that interaction with researchers from different backgrounds is likely to promote creativity is one reason for collaborating. However, as Bortagary notes, another important reason may be a lack of economic resources for research, as experienced by many of the smaller Latin American countries. This illustrates how the macro-level situation with respect to economic resources creates conditions with far-reaching consequences for CKEs. A further reason noted by Bortagaray for researchers from developing countries to engage in collaboration with researchers from developed countries is that it can reap rewards in terms of the number of citations (and hence the impact) that co-authored articles with established researchers from developed countries will often generate. In such collaborations it is important to consider the respective roles in the research played by those from developed and developing countries. Researchers from less developed countries may be relegated to a secondary role with less influence on the overall direction of the so-called 'collaborative' project and may therefore have a secondary status.[2] From these observations it is evident that CKEs in developed and developing countries differ in a number of respects. Future research is needed in order to improve our understanding of the conditions of different types of CKEs in developing countries.

STIMULATING CREATIVE KNOWLEDGE ENVIRONMENTS

From the studies reported in the chapters of this book and from the wider literature that we have reviewed, it would seem to be possible to shape, at least to some degree, and to stimulate CKEs[3] and their development with a view to achieving sustainable creativity and innovation. Such an influence could be exerted in a number of ways, as is apparent from the descriptions of CKEs in previous chapters. Let us outline a number of possibilities for achieving this.

First, CKEs can be stimulated at the micro, meso and macro levels.

Obviously there are different types of stimuli that might be applied at a micro level in comparison with the macro level. At the micro level, it is possible in principle to arrange suitable conditions for individuals and smaller work groups that should stimulate creative ideas and actions. By focusing on the various components of knowledge environments depicted in Table 1.1: task characteristics, discipline or field, individual characteristics, group characteristics, the general work situation for individuals, the physical environment, organization, and the extraorganizational environment, we may be able to obtain some ideas how to make knowledge environments more creative and innovative (and on what is likely to hinder this) with respect to the physical, social and cognitive aspects. Let us discuss each component to see what might be achieved.

Task Characteristics

To begin with, the task characteristics (that is, whether the work is short-term or long-term, simple or complex, routine or novel, modularized or integrated and so on) evidently have implications for what form of CKE will be most effective. Some tasks are apparently more difficult to approach in a creative way than others. For instance, it is probable that simple and routine tasks have a negative effect on creativity. One way of avoiding this may be to give such tasks to specialist staff not directly involved in research or knowledge creation. For example, in research laboratories it is common to employ personnel who are responsible for constructing or maintaining the equipment or for looking after the animals, or who carry out routine testing, who are not formal members of the research groups (at least in the sense that they are not authors of the resulting scientific articles). Of course, it is also vital for the research group to be alert to any relevant observations made by these specialist staff. In addition the selection of appropriate staff members is crucial; it is important to have staff suited to the task characteristics and able to deal with the specific tasks involved. For example, integrated tasks (as opposed to modularized ones) are likely to be better handled by individuals or groups having a broader knowledge base than a specialist or group of specialists in one field. (This is consistent with the heterogeneity thesis discussed in the section on group characteristics below.)

Discipline/Field

Another important aspect of CKEs is the type of knowledge (and skills) created in that environment. In an academic environment much knowledge production is still relatively strongly bound to disciplines and fields or specialities within disciplines. In other settings, for instance in industry or the public sector, there is often a more problem-driven approach to knowledge creation that is not linked directly to the internally generated problems in a discipline. However, during the last decade or so, we have seen even in academia the development of more inter-, multi- or trans-disciplinary research and of research that is focused on 'problem solving' rather than aimed primarily at generating new knowledge. (This is obviously also linked to the 'Mode 2' and 'Triple Helix' models referred to above.) Creativity is not, as we see it, directly related to specialization or to inter- or trans-disciplinarity; instead, such general factors as the ability to identify fruitful problems (Allwood, 1997) and to carry out both deep and broad analyses of such problems may be more important. Nevertheless it is of interest to note that different types of disciplines (for example those more or less characterized by 'normal science' constraints in Kuhn's sense) may demand different types of properties in the creative researcher. More restricted associations may be demanded in disciplines operating in a normal science mode (Simonton, 2003).

However, wherever it is located, knowledge creation is dependent on being able to draw upon previous knowledge from various sources, with academic knowledge often being a primary source. This means that the promotion of good access to disciplinary as well as non-disciplinary knowledge is crucial to creativity and innovation. For micro-level knowledge environments, the selection of appropriate staff will obviously depend on the nature of the discipline or field concerned. For example, in fields with an established paradigm, there is often a formal division of labour between theorists, experimentalists, equipment builders, modellers and so on. Clearly a group working in such an area will need to have the full range of such capabilities if it is to be creative. Likewise, in a multidisciplinary field, members of the team need to have a range of disciplinary backgrounds. The employing organization then needs to ensure that the system of incentives and rewards is appropriate for stimulating the creative efforts of such a diverse team. At the meso level, attention needs to be paid to the organizational structure.[4] For example, if the organizational structure is based on traditional disciplines (as in many universities), it may adversely affect the organization's ability to carry out creative multidisciplinary or interdisciplinary research.

Likewise, at the macro level, care needs to be given to ensuring that government policies do not result in pressures that will constrain interdisciplinary research. In the UK, for example, over the last ten years the government has encouraged publicly funded researchers in universities and elsewhere to relate their research more closely to the needs of 'users' in industry and elsewhere. Since the problems of users tend not to be located within a single scientific discipline, this often stimulates research of a multidisciplinary or interdisciplinary nature. Yet, over the same period, the government has subjected universities every four or five years to a 'Research Assessment Exercise' to identify those departments or units that have been most successful. This exercise is carried out by discipline-based panels. These panels have difficulty in assessing the performance of groups engaged in multidisciplinary research, and such groups have often felt that the ranking they have been given is lower than if they had been working in the disciplinary mainstream. Consequently the Research Assessment Exercise is viewed by some as constraining the willingness of academics to become involved in research of a multidisciplinary nature. Governments need to give some thought to ensuring that their policies do not contain internal contradictions of this type if creativity is to flourish in research and innovation.

Individuals

Individuals are perhaps the main components of CKEs. Without them no knowledge would be produced and creativity would not exist (although some would perhaps argue that artificial intelligence may come to represent a substitute). We suggest that creativity is enhanced in environments where individual autonomy is stimulated (but only up to a certain degree and often when linked to a collective goal), where communication with other individuals flows easily and an individual feels secure to express any view, where individuals have expert knowledge at least in one domain, where individuals are left alone to fulfil tasks that are not done better in a group (for instance, brainstorming is enhanced by letting individuals prepare ideas alone before meeting to brainstorm in comparison to letting groups of individuals meet directly to brainstorm together; see Paulus and Yang, 2000).

There are a number of studies that have attempted to identify the crucial personal characteristics of the successful and creative researcher. Reviews of these can be found in Hemlin (1996) and in Simonton (2003). This includes a study by Hirschberg and Itkin (1978), who showed that PhD students who produce research publications (this being taken as a measure of success) are more bright, achieving, enduring, committed to the field and skilled in research than other PhD students who do not publish. Similarly a study by Rushton *et al.* (1982), focusing on university professors, concluded that the creative professor is ambitious, energetic and enduring, looks for clarity, is dominant, shows leadership, exhibits independence and is aggressive but not meek or particularly supportive of others.

In addition it has been found that Type A behaviour (strong and persistent aggressive behaviour to achieve more in a shorter time and under pressure) is related to prestigious research in the case of male researchers (Matthews *et al.*, 1980). Earlier, McClelland (1963) had argued that successful researchers as well as successful industry leaders have a high achievement motivation that makes them take moderate calculated risks where their fate is dependent on their own efforts.[5] This was supported by Rushton *et al.* (1982), who found that motivation, ambition and achievement are important factors in predicting who will be a successful and creative researcher. Such a result leads us to the conclusion that the selection of individuals with those personal characteristics might be conducive to creativity. Also the personal characteristics found to be associated with creativity may be fostered by the environments in which the individuals act. For example, at least some of these characteristics, such as the tendency to work hard, could be enhanced by providing the members of knowledge-intensive groups with appropriate reward structures.

On closer inspection, however, the results reviewed, about which individuals could be successful researchers, are somewhat contradictory. For example, some balance between work and free time might be more conducive to creativity in the long run, even though peaks of intensive work might help creativity. Moreover Kasperson (1978) found that personal characteristics do not explain success among academic and industrial researchers. Instead he concluded that creativity on the part of researchers (as assessed by peer evaluation) is linked to patterns of information use (which may again be linked, if not to personality, at least to the researcher's cognitive style). Creative researchers expose themselves (in comparison to their less creative counterparts) to a greater variety of information sources, including those outside their specialities. On a more general level, much research has found that creative people show a greater openness to experience and a higher tolerance for ambiguity 'and even thrive on high degrees of ambiguity and ... inconsistency' (Stoycheva and Lubart, 2001, p.28). Simonton (2003) relates these features to creative individuals having flatter hierarchies of associations, in contrast to less creative persons who have steeper hierarchies of associations. Such personality traits might possibly be developed through the educational system. However, Simonton also notes that creative people can sometimes show signs of psychopathology (for example by scoring higher on scales measuring psychoticism).

In conclusion, it would appear that there is a sophisticated interplay between able individuals, their colleagues and the environmental characteristics (for example, good access to information and knowledge) that should be taken into account when planning for CKEs.

Group Characteristics

Group characteristics such as the size of the group, whether it is integrated or loosely coupled, or inward or outward-looking, the leadership style, the degree of tension or harmony, the group's structure with respect to the presence of majorities and minorities, and the heterogeneity or homogeneity of group members are all potential influences on creativity. To take the last of these, we know that the heterogeneity of group members in terms of a number of cognitive and social parameters in groups is generally beneficial. In particular, a variety of expertise is often necessary to ensure creativity. However, a harmonious social atmosphere does not, as is often imagined, necessarily lead to greater creativity. Instead different creative cognitive styles that may cause some (but not too much) 'irritation' should be tolerated and indeed encouraged in the light of earlier comments about the beneficial effects of 'creative tensions'. However, a more fundamental difference in beliefs or underlying assumptions among group members is probably not beneficial if this leads to entrenched positions with respect to the way to approach a problem or, even worse, what problems to pursue. Moreover, a tight time frame for the task might make such a situation more tense and more difficult to handle.

The leadership of research groups has often been found to be a crucial factor in relation to performance including creativity. To enrol leaders who have a long experience and wide-ranging competence in the field and who express clear goals and grant autonomy to team members is likely to promote creative performance in research. Regarding the size and structure of work groups, studies indicate that the form of the task and the stage of the work process appear to be more important than group characteristics per se. It may also be that some group members make better contributions when it comes to problem finding and other group members when the focus is on problem solving. Thus, it may be beneficial for the group's performance if changes are made in the composition of the group at different stages in the problem-solving process (although not to such an extent that this benefit is offset by effects of the resulting loss of continuity, collective memory and so on).

General Work Situation for Individuals

The evidence seems to indicate that a creative knowledge environment is one where individuals are confronted with a number of tasks or projects and where experiences from one domain can exert a positive influence on another. However, such a view presupposes that there is enough time for researchers to devote to each of the tasks or projects, since severe time constraints are generally not beneficial to creativity. Furthermore, information communication technology (ICT), databases, libraries and so on are likely to be conducive to creativity if they support access to relevant and reliable information in the domains required for the tasks. (However there are concerns emerging that the 'information explosion' made possible by the Internet and Worldwide Web may at times be more of a hindrance and a distraction in relation to creativity because of the dangers of unreliable information and the constant interruptions imposed by e-mails.) For example, more direct retrieval of information that is needed for a specific purpose is often very helpful, while more casual browsing (without a very specific purpose) may also result in eliciting new information, which in turn might contribute to the production of creative knowledge products (although there are again dangers that this may turn into a distraction if taken too far).

One of the important issues dealt with in the literature on 'knowledge management' (see, for instance, Fuller, 2002; Hedelin and Allwood, 2002; Von Krogh *et al.*, 2000) is whether ICT could be advantageous to companies in organizing routines for handling knowledge creatively in the innovation process.[6] Some software gives direct support for creative idea generation (for examples of such software in the context of computer aided design (CAD), see Allwood and Kalén, 1994).[7] The knowledge management literature is rather less fruitful in terms of suggesting new ideas and new ways of individuals, groups and organizations handling knowledge. Such studies simply rely to a great extent on what was previously found in cognitive and social psychology about creativity and communication (as reported in Chapter 1, and earlier in the present chapter).

Physical Environment

The physical environment almost certainly has some bearing on the creativity of individuals and groups, but probably less directly and less strongly than some of the other factors discussed here. In particular, facilities that make it easier for individuals to contact one another when needed are likely to be beneficial to creativity. In addition, individuals need facilities that offer solitude, where creative thoughts and ideas can be nurtured and where reflections on other people's ideas can be arrived at. These two functions of providing both places for meeting other people and individual spaces for reflection are probably basic to any human creative act. Such places should be created (through a suitable combination of architecture, climate, furniture, decorations and so on) in such a way that the wishes of the individuals working there are met as far as is possible.

Organization

Organizations frequently assert that they are creative: that they have a creative culture or creative climate. One basic aspect of organizations' creativity is capital and other resources, and the provision of adequate funding for research or innovation is likely to be important for creativity. Another important related aspect is organizational structures; these are often claimed to be 'flat' in order to promote knowledge management and innovation in business companies as well as in academic research departments and research groups. This links up with the work discussed earlier by Dougherty (1996) who has analysed organizational creativity in terms of four dichotomies or tensions (internal v. external, old v. new, top-down v. bottom-up, and responsibility v. freedom) that need to be balanced in the organization if it is to be creative. According to Dougherty, the most difficult is the last of these, which traditionally is addressed by careful and systematic staff selection and by the establishment of an organizational culture stressing creativity. We believe that this is very much a leadership task, something which we discuss further below.

External rewards are generally given lesser emphasis in the literature on creativity than personal or intrinsic motivation. Yet, as noted earlier, this does not mean that they are unimportant for creativity. A supportive (but intellectually demanding) atmosphere or climate where individuals including managers express their appreciation to others for their creative efforts is likely to be beneficial for creativity (see the review by Mumford and Gustafson, 1988).

The leadership of organizations is responsible for providing frames and rules (and a wider 'culture') that support the relative freedom for individuals and groups to behave in a creative way. If the management is successful in promoting a feeling of trust in the organization, this may stimulate creativity, for example with less time being spent worrying about the possibility of losing one's income. Hence a certain degree of security of employment is probably good for creativity. However, if this is taken too far, staff may not be 'stretched' to exert themselves. Conversely researchers who have only fixed-term contracts may be driven by the sense of insecurity to aspire to greater efforts in pursuit of creativity. However, if the sense of insecurity is too pervasive, this might have a demotivating effect on morale and creativity.

Extraorganizational Environment

An organization's creative potential is inevitably linked to external events and structures at various levels or scales. We have seen above how, for example, researchers in developing countries, because of a lack of economic or other resources, may be forced to some extent to depend on the creative efforts of those in developed nations. As a consequence they may be either stimulated or hindered in the development of their own creative potential. Apart from the extent of a nation's economic development, the evidence would suggest that a general 'openness' in society and the free exchange of information are beneficial to creativity. Linked to this is the greater range of job opportunities and voluntary mobility of personnel to be found in more open societies, factors which again are likely to enhance creativity. In the world of private companies, markets clearly play a vital role for innovations. Chapter 6 of this volume shows how differences in labour markets between countries can have a significant impact on the way firms organize their innovative activities, as can other national or cultural specificities.

SOME POLICY IMPLICATIONS

In the light of the above conclusions about the factors likely to enhance (or constrain) creative knowledge environments, what are some of the policy implications we can draw?

First, at a micro level, from the above analysis of the elements required for creative knowledge production, it would seem that at least some of them are capable of being taught. Higher education and research policies need to ensure that those embarking on a career in knowledge production are furnished with the requisite skills for creativity. For example, we have seen how creativity relies perhaps more on 'weak methods' than on discipline or domain-specific knowledge. Yet, in many science departments, the desire to bring students close to the ever-advancing 'frontier' for that field may result in a temptation to cram in as much discipline-specific knowledge as possible, leaving little time for developing broader creative skills. This temptation needs to be resisted. Other creativity-enhancing properties and abilities that should be more systematically trained are openness to experience, tolerance of ambiguity and clear and understandable oral and written communication.

Secondly, we have seen the crucial importance of leadership in stimulating creativity, whether at the group, department or institutional level. In particular leadership is essential in creating a 'climate' of trust and open communication for organizational members to express creative ideas. Again higher education and research policies should ensure that future researchers receive a training in the aspects of leadership vital to a creative knowledge environment. Research leaders have to be able to deal with the many complex 'dimensions' of a CKE. In particular they must be able to identify and maintain a healthy balance with regard to the various creative tensions that characterize a CKE.

Thirdly, if we accept the claims of the proponents of Mode 2 that a growing proportion of knowledge production is trans-disciplinary in nature (reflecting the efforts of researchers to meet the needs of 'users' and to produce knowledge 'in the context of application'), then a number of policy implications follow:

- institutions engaged in the production of knowledge must have an appropriate organizational structure, in particular one that is not overly constrained by traditional scientific and engineering disciplines and the 'boundaries' between them;
- organizational recruitment policies need to ensure that research teams

recruit staff with the necessary range of disciplinary backgrounds to provide a suitably heterogeneous mix of skills, perspectives and professional contacts;
- staff development policies must enable researchers from a given discipline to develop the skills required to communicate effectively with those from other disciplines, and provide them with an incentive and reward structure that encourages this.

Fourthly, if knowledge production increasingly involves cross-institutional and cross-sectoral collaboration, policies are needed to provide suitable incentives and rewards at the individual and interorganizational levels, and to encourage the mobility of researchers during the course of their careers. Particularly important are policies to encourage the emergence of 'relational entrepreneurs' who are so crucial in building bridges between different organizations and sectors. Such individuals play an essential role in the 'wiring up' of regional and national systems of innovation (cf. Martin and Johnston, 1999), thereby enabling those systems to function more effectively and creatively.

Fifthly, the trend towards a more managerial approach to knowledge generation in pursuit of increased 'efficiency' and with greater emphasis on auditing and accountability may well result in less 'free' time. Yet free time is so often the source of the most creative contributions. In other words, policies that result in an overemphasis on 'efficiency' may well be detrimental to truly creative knowledge production.

Sixthly, polices based on the premise that 'one size fits all' are likely to prove too crude. Instead macro-level policies should reflect the fact that the needs of different scientific fields, technologies and industrial sectors may differ significantly (for example between biotechnology and information technology). They should also take account of the specific form and structure of the country's (or region's) innovation system. However, there is perhaps one common feature for all government level systems: the need to ensure the openness that is basic to all successful macro-level CKEs, permitting and indeed stimulating the free flow of information and knowledge.

Finally, policy makers should recognize that policies are dealing with a complex, interconnected, multi-level system, that policies aimed at one component or aspect of the national (or regional) innovation system or knowledge production system will almost certainly have repercussions for other components. Likewise, policies aimed at one level (for instance the macro level) will have implications at other levels. This points to the need for careful policy analysis to ensure the development of 'joined up' policies that minimize the risk of the effects of two (or more) policies being in conflict.

A FUTURE RESEARCH AGENDA

Research on creative knowledge environments is at a comparatively early stage. The various chapters in this book point to the desirability of further research in the area of CKEs. For example, although previous studies have improved our understanding of the way the conditions for CKEs are shaped in different contexts, there is a need for research that more specifically and systematically attempts to evaluate the effects on the creativity of the knowledge produced under different specific constellations of the factors making up CKEs. This is no easy task. One reason is that it is not clear when, and with respect to what criteria, the creativity of a knowledge product is to be evaluated. For example, should creativity be evaluated with respect to the potential creativity of research ideas or research problems, or at the end of the knowledge-generation process, or after the wider social world has had an opportunity to react to the knowledge product, for example after the knowledge product has been implemented in the form of a research article or an innovative product from industry? Likewise should the judgments of an ad hoc expert panel, for example, or the number of citations in research journals, or the sales figures of a resulting industrial innovation, or estimates of the social impact of the knowledge product be used as evaluation criteria? One interesting version of research along these lines is longitudinal studies of the 'same' CKE over time in order to analyse how the creativity of the knowledge outputs of a CKE changes in response to other changes in the CKE.

Secondly, more research on different types of CKEs needs to be carried out. In addition to the three main forms of CKE identified in the Triple Helix literature (academia, industry and government, although the properties of different forms of government CKE are currently less well researched), other important categories of CKEs should be identified. One example is the distinction between CKEs in developed and developing countries discussed above, where we particularly need to improve our understanding of the characteristics of different types of CKEs in developing countries. Another example is further work on the differences between CKEs in different cultures (see, for example, the work comparing social psychology in individualistic and collectivist cultures by Triandis, 1994, and Oyserman *et al.*, 2002). Obviously the distinction between CKEs in developed and developing countries and that between CKEs in different types of cultures will entail the identification of further subcategories. Other forms of CKEs may be identified on the basis of typologies of industrial sectors or organizations (or of key features of organizations). For example, the typology of organizational decision-making contexts outlined by Koopman and Pool (1991) might represent one potential starting point. This typology includes such entries as the rational model, the information model, the bureaucratic model, the 'garbage can' model the political or arena model and the participation model. Some of these might prove fruitful for identifying potentially interesting types of CKEs.

A third area of research approaches the question of what promotes creativity in a more circumscribed manner. It would be interesting to establish more specifically the effectiveness of particular means and measures for promoting creativity. Some examples of this type of research issue are the following. To what extent, and in what circumstances, do shorter or longer visits to other research centres promote creativity? To what extent does participating in different types of research conferences promote creativity, and how close or distant to one's own speciality should the conference be in order best to enhance creativity? What is the optimum balance between group interaction and individual reflection in order to promote creativity? Do the answers to such questions differ according to the phase one is focusing on in the knowledge production process, or to the type of research task or the type of CKE? One relatively topical issue concerns the question of how best to stimulate individuals and smaller groups of individuals into creative action. This would consider the extent to which various personality characteristics are compatible in a particular type of CKE, how to select the best individuals for a specific CKE, how to enhance creativity in groups, and so on.

A fourth suggestion for further research relates to the topic of 'creative tensions'. Earlier we pointed out that this concept suffers from a certain vagueness or ambiguity. It would be desirable for future work to attempt to bring more clarity to our understanding of this potentially valuable concept, and to analyse in more detail the processes associated with different types of situations denoted by the various terms making up the respective tensions. In addition the contribution of creative tensions in different types of CKEs and at different stages of the knowledge-production process needs to be better understood.

Fifthly, another issue to be considered in future research is what forms of CKEs bring about different types of creative tasks that could lead to various creative behaviours (for instance, the four types of expected creativity, responsive creativity, proactive creativity and contributory creativity in Unsworth's typology described in Chapter 1). It is possible that CKEs are differently 'shaped' for different types of creativity. For instance, one might expect proactive creativity to be associated with curiosity-driven research environments characterized by a great deal of autonomy, while more applied research and development activities may be shaped rather differently by their environments. Such questions deserve attention and further research.

Lastly, we would suggest that there is much potentially fruitful research to be carried out following up our notion of different levels of CKEs being nested within one another. How do different types of CKEs at one level (say, the meso level) interact with each another? And how do knowledge environments at the different levels (micro, meso and macro) interact with one another? In particular, work is needed on what government policies are likely to be most effective in stimulating creative knowledge environments at the meso and micro level, and for ensuring that they are properly integrated to ensure a well functioning national (or regional) innovation system.

In conclusion, this book has explored the concept of 'creative knowledge environments'. We have demonstrated why these are likely to prove of increasing importance as we move towards a more knowledge-intensive society. The studies brought together in earlier chapters give some indication of the potential power of this concept in obtaining a better understanding of creativity in relation to knowledge and innovation, and of the factors that are likely to stimulate this. However, as this final section makes clear, much more research is needed before we are in a position reliably to construct management strategies and government policies that will bring about a significant improvement in our creative endeavours.

NOTES

1. For a discussion of the concept of 'strong methods' that is related to the notion of 'powerful domain-specific search heuristics', see Rogoff and Lave (1984).
2. For an example in the field of psychology, see Kim (1995). For a more general description of the conditions for research in developing countries, see Adair (1995). However researchers from smaller or less-developed countries are not always confined to playing a secondary role, as Thorsteinsdottir (1998) has shown in relation to the research collaborations in which Icelandic scientists have become involved.
3. Conversely, misguided attempts to influence CKEs may militate against creativity rather than enhancing it.
4. This links up with the discussion below in the subsection on 'group characteristics'.
5. However, for research on cultural variability with respect to the prevalence and forms of achievement motivation, see Marcus and Kitayama (1991).
6. A prime example of a somewhat 'mechanical' approach to knowledge management is given by Peters (1993), who describes three different ICT systems used by the consultancy firm, McKinsey, to improve knowledge management. First, they used a 'Firm Practice Information System' to store 'accessible ideas', project approaches and plans made up by project leaders. Secondly, the 'Practice Development Network' organised around McKinsey's 31 'Practice Centers' in the US was used for storing lessons from practice and field work on consultancy activities. In order to avoid the problems associated with information being stored for ever, there was an annual clearing of outdated material from this database. Finally, McKinsey used a 'Knowledge Resource Directory' which contained a guide to 'who knows what' (among consultancy colleagues and experts) and to core documents (located in the previously mentioned databases) about consultancy work in the company.
7. At a more general level, there may be potential lessons from the active research area on Computer Supported Cooperative Work (CSCW) (see, for example, articles in the journal of the same name).

REFERENCES

Adair, J.G. (1995), 'The research environment in developing countries: contributions to the national development of the discipline', *International Journal of Psychology*, **30**, 643–62.

Åkerman, N. (1998), 'A free-falling society? Six introductory notes', in N. Åkerman (ed.), *The Necessity of Friction*, Boulder, CO: Westview Press, pp.3–27.

Allwood, C.M. (1997), 'The function and handling of research problems in the social sciences', *Science Studies*, **10**, 50–73.

Allwood, C.M. and J. Bärmark (1999), 'The role of research problems in the process of research', *Social Epistemology*, **13**, 59–83.

Allwood, C.M. and T. Kalén (1994), 'Usability in CAD – a psychological perspective', *The International Journal of Human Factors in Manufacturing*, **4**, 145–65.

Amabile, T.M. (1988), 'A model of creativity and innovation in organizations', *Research in Organizational Behavior*, **10**, 123–67.

Amabile, T.M. (1999), 'How to kill creativity', *Harvard Business Review on Breakthrough Thinking*, Boston: Harvard Business School Press, pp.1–28.

Cole, J.R. and S. Cole (1973), *Social Stratification in Science*, Chicago: University of Chicago Press.

Dougherty, D. (1996), 'Organizing for innovation', in S.R. Clegg, C. Hardy and W.R. Nord (eds), *Handbook of Organization Studies*, London: Sage Publications, pp.424–39.

Etzkowitz, H. and L. Leydesdorff (1998), 'The endless transition: a "Triple Helix" of university–industry–government relations', *Minerva*, **36**, 203–8.

Etzkowitz, H., E. Schuler and M. Gulbrandsen (2000), 'The evolution of the entrepreneurial university', in M. Jacob and T. Hellström (eds), *The Future of Knowledge Production in the Academy*, Buckingham, UK: The Society for Research into Higher Education and Open University Press, pp.40–60.

Foss Hansen, H. (1995), 'Organizing for quality – a discussion of different evaluation methods as a means for improving quality in research', *Science Studies*, **8**, 36–43.

Fuller, S. (2002), *Knowledge Management Foundations*, Boston: Butterworth-Heinemann.

Gibbons, M., C. Limoges, H. Nowotny, S. Schwartzman, P. Scott and M. Trow (1994), *The New Production of Knowledge: The Dynamics of Science and Research in Contemporary Societies*, London: Sage Publications.

Graversen, E.K., E.K. Schmidt, K. Langberg and P.S. Lauridsen (2002), 'Dynamism and innovation at Danish universities and sector research institutions. An analysis of common characteristics in dynamic and innovative research environments', summary of Report 2002/1 from the Danish Institute for Studies in Research and Research Policy.

Hedelin, L. and C.M. Allwood (2002), 'IT and strategic decision-making', *Industrial Management & Data Systems*, **102**, 125–39.

Hemlin, S. (1996), 'Research on research evaluation', *Social Epistemology*, **10**, 209–50.

Hirschberg, N. and S. Itkin (1978), 'Graduate student success in psychology', *American Psychologist*, **33**, 1083–93.

Hollingsworth, R. (2000), 'Why do some research organizations make multiple breakthroughs in the development of new knowledge but most make none?', lecture at the seminar 'Research Programme on the Finnish Innovation System' organized by SITRA, Helsinki, 13 January.

Jacob, M. and T. Hellström (2000), 'Introduction', in M. Jacob and T. Hellström (eds), *The Future of Knowledge Production in the Academy*, Buckingham, UK: The Society for Research into Higher Education and Open University Press.

Kasperson, C.J. (1978), 'An analysis of the relationship between information sources and creativity in scientists and engineers', *Human Communication Research*, 4(2), 111–19.

Katz, S. and B.R. Martin, 1997, 'What is research collaboration?', *Research Policy*, 26, 1–18.

Kim, U. (1995), 'Psychology, science, and culture: cross-cultural analysis of national psychologies', *International Journal of Psychology*, 30, 663–79.

Klahr, D. and H.A. Simon (1999), 'Studies of scientific discovery: complementary approaches and convergent findings', *Psychological Bulletin*, 125, 524–43.

Koopman, P. and J. Pool (1991), 'Organizational decision making: models, contingencies and strategies', in J. Rasmussen, B. Brehmmer and J. Leplat (eds), *Distributed Decision Making: Cognitive Models for Cooperative Work*, New York: John Wiley & Sons, pp.19–46.

Kuhn, T.S. (1959), 'The essential tension: tradition and innovation in scientific research', in C.W. Taylor (ed.) (1959), *The Third (1959) University of Utah Research Conference on the Identification of Scientific Talent*, Salt Lake City: University of Utah Press, pp.162–74 and in T.S. Kuhn (1977), *The Essential Tension: Selected Studies in Scientific Tradition and Change*, Chicago: University of Chicago Press, pp.225–39).

Leydesdorff, L. and H. Etzkowitz (1996), 'Emergence of a triple helix of university–industry–government relations', *Science and Public Policy*, 23, 279–86.

Luukkonen, T. (1992), 'Understanding patterns of international scientific collaboration', *Science, Technology & Human Values*, 17, 101–26.

Marcus, H.R. and S. Kitayama (1991), 'Culture and self: implications for cognition motivation and motivation', *Psychological Review*, 98, 224–53.

Martin, B.R. and R. Johnston (1999), 'Technology foresight for wiring up the national innovation system: experiences in Britain, Australia and New Zealand', *Technological Forecasting and Social Change*, 60, 37–54.

Matthews, K.A., R.L. Helmreich, W.E. Beane and G.W. Lucker (1980), 'Pattern A, achievement striving, and scientific merit: does Pattern A help or hinder?', *Journal of Personality and Social Psychology*, 39(5), 962–7.

McClelland, D.C. (1963), 'The calculated risk: an aspect of scientific performance', in C.W. Taylor and F. Barron (eds), *Scientific Creativity: Its Recognition and Development*, New York, London and Sydney: John Wiley & Sons, pp.184–92.

Mohamed, M.Z. and T. Rickards (1996), 'Assessing and comparing the innovativeness and creative climate of firms', *Scandinavian Journal of Management*, 12(2), 109–21.

Mumford, M.D. and S.B. Gustafson (1988), 'Creativity syndrome: integration, application, and innovation', *Psychological Bulletin*, 103(1), 27–43.

Oyserman, D., H.M. Coon and M. Kemmelmeier (2002), 'Rethinking individualism and collectivism: evaluation of theoretical assumptions and meta-analyses', *Psychological Bulletin*, 128, 3–72.

Paulus, P.B. and H.-C. Yang (2000), 'Idea generation in groups: a basis for creativity in organisations', *Organisational Behavior and Human Decision Processes*, 82(1), 76–87.

Pelz, D.C. and F.M. Andrews (eds) (1966), *Scientists in Organizations: Productive Climates for Research and Development*, New York: John Wiley and Sons.

Peters, T. (1993), *Liberation Management*, London: Pan Books.
Rogoff, B. and J. Lave (eds) (1984), *Everyday Cognition*, Cambridge, MA: Harvard University Press.
Rushton, J.P., H.G. Murray and S.V. Paunonen (1982), 'Personality, research creativity, and teaching effectiveness in university professors', *Scientometrics*, **5**(2), 93–116.
Simonton, D.K. (2003), 'Scientific creativity as constrained stochastic behaviour: the integration of product, person, and process perspectives', *Psychological Bulletin*, **129**, 475–94.
Spangenberg, J.F.A., R. Starmans, Y.W. Bally, B. Breemhaar, F.J.N. Nijhuis and C.A.F. van Dorp (1990), 'Prediction of scientific performance in clinical medicine', *Research Policy*, **19**, 239–55.
Stehr, N. (1994), *Knowledge Societies*, London: Sage.
Stoycheva, K.G. and T.I. Lubart (2001), 'The nature of creative decision making', in C.M. Allwood and M. Selart (eds), *Decision Making: Creative and Social Dimensions*, Dordrecht: Kluwer Academic Publishers, pp.15–33.
Tardif, T.Z. and R.J. Sternberg (1988), 'What do we know about creativity?', in R.J. Sternberg (ed.), *The Nature of Creativity: Contemporary Psychological Perspectives*, Cambridge: Cambridge University Press, pp.429–40.
Thorsteinsdottir, O.H. (1998), 'Islands reaching out? External research collaboration in Iceland and Newfoundland', DPhil thesis, SPRU, Brighton: University of Sussex.
Triandis, H.C. (1994), 'Major cultural syndromes and emotion', in S. Kitayama and H.R. Marcus (eds), *Emotion and Culture. Empirical Studies of Mutual Influence*, Washington, DC: American Psychological Association.
Unsworth, K.L. and S.K. Parker (2003), 'Promoting a pro-active and innovative workforce for the new workplace', in D. Holman, T.D. Wall, C.W. Clegg, P. Sparrow and A. Howard (eds), *The New Workplace: A Guide to the Human Impact of Modern Working Practices*, Chichester: Wiley.
Von Krogh, G., K. Ichijo and I. Nonaka, (2000), *Enabling Knowledge Creation. How to Unlock the Mystery of Tacit Knowledge and Release the Power of Innovation*, Oxford: Oxford University Press.
Wilke, H. and M. Kaplan (2001), 'Task creativity and social creativity in decision-making groups', in C.M. Allwood and M. Selart (eds), *Decision Making: Social and Creative Dimensions*, Dordrecht: Kluwer Academic Publishers, pp.35–51.
Ziman, J.M. (1987), *Knowing Everything about Nothing: Specialization and Change in Scientific Careers*, Cambridge: Cambridge University Press.

Index